W9-CCW-456

Working with Groups

Working with Groups

Group Process and Individual Growth

Walter M. Lifton

Coordinator of Pupil Personnel Services
City School District
Rochester, New York

Second Edition

34296

John Wiley & Sons Inc., New York · London · Sydney

Library of Congress Catalog Card Number: 66-14138
Printed in the United States of America

Preface

Writing a revision of a book, especially if one uses it as a vehicle to express a personal value system, is a traumatic experience. In some ways it is similar to rediscovering one's high-school yearbook. The faces are similar to their adult counterparts, yet the experiences of the intervening years have left their mark.

When I first wrote this book in 1958, I was a college professor. My experiences in that role convinced me that beyond using the help available through counseling, educators could function more effectively if they had available materials which could help them structure their teaching roles and which might also provide them with support if their background or anxiety level did not permit them to operate in situations with broad limits. Moreover, I became convinced that the helping agencies in our society were on a treadmill, trying to produce more and more professionals to provide therapy for the many unhappy people in our society when they should be placing their major emphasis on the prevention of problems. Accordingly, I left university life and spent the years 1959–1963 in educational publishing, trying to develop materials which, starting in the primary grades, could establish a base on which successive layers of positive experiences, designed to produce a stable, mature citizen, could be built.

The experiences obtained during these years are reflected in many ways in the current revision. The reader will find an increased emphasis on the role of groups in the educational setting. Having become aware of the way educational technology now makes feasible a wide variety of devices for information retrieval, I have also emphasized the serious lag that exists between the roles now being lived by members of the helping professions and the roles they may have in the not too distant future. These emerging roles will demand an emphasis on prevention rather than remediation, work with

v

groups more often than with individuals, and an acceptance of a more broadly conceived professional role where psychologists, social workers, counselors, educators, and human relations specialists will join together in a re-evaluation of each discipline's contribution to the cause of mental health.

The role of the mental health worker as a source of information will be dramatically affected by the new educational media. That part of group guidance designed as a means for mass dissemination of information may soon be accomplished through a variety of nonhuman devices. Increasingly, society will search for means to facilitate the incorporation of the mass of information being spewed forth. Society will be faced with the challenge of being either master of or slave to the technology developed to cope with new problems.

The growing skill evidenced by practitioners using systems of rewards and punishments to effect behavior change makes it imperative that society monitor the change agents and insure that gadgets or techniques are selected to achieve goals desired by society.

At the time of this revision I am employed as the Coordinator of Pupil Personnel Services for the Rochester School System. A recent experience had a major impact on my ideas about group process. For six months, starting in December 1964, I was drafted from my school position to serve as the Interim Director of Action for a Better Community, Incorporated, the Community Action Agency for Rochester and Monroe County, funded under the Economic Opportunity Act of 1964. In this role I found myself working with an executive board composed of twenty-one members reflecting almost every significant group or institution in the community. I also worked with a Citizens Advisory Group composed of the clients to be served. On a daily basis I had to find ways to keep open the channels of communication between people with vastly different value systems and with different concepts about the way people can and should be helped. This experience indelibly reinforced the importance of facilitating the expression of feelings among group members before group action becomes possible. It drove home the democratic imperative that the purpose of an institution is to serve its clients, not to meet the needs of its staff.

At the time of this writing I am experiencing the growing pains of helping a large city school system to evaluate its Pupil Personnel Services and to try different approaches on an experimental basis. Between 1965 and 1966, five elementary schools will have added to their staff a full-time pupil personnel worker with the title Elementary School Counselor. The first five people to fill these slots will come from three different disciplines, psychology, social work, and guidance. This year (1965–1966) will provide a pragmatic test of the areas where all three disciplines work comfortably. It will also demonstrate the kinds of training that will be most helpful for the hybrid role envisioned.

I am now also serving as Interim Director of a new Center for Cooperative Action in Urban Education. This Center serves as a catalytic agent, combining the resources of the school, university, and industry. Only through combined effort involving the total community is there any hope for solving problems of urban education.

This rather detailed chronology is included purposefully. This is a personal book. It represents one man's point of view and way of functioning. The reader, to be benefited, needs to evaluate critically the author's bias and to determine the way in which each idea fits the reader's skills, values, and philosophical orientation.

As the material will reveal, it is virtually impossible to recognize the people who have been involved in developing this book. Every student I taught, every teacher with whom I studied, and each life experience made a contribution.

I am grateful to the editors of the *Review of Educational Research, Human Relations, Progressive Education, Educational Administration and Supervision, The Vocational Guidance Quarterly, Audio-Visual Communication Review, Exceptional Children, The School Library,* and *Counselor Education and Supervision* for their permission to quote from their journals. The following publishers have also helped by permitting quotations from books they produced: Houghton Mifflin Company, Science Research Associates, Inc., and John Wiley & Sons, Inc.

As every author knows, there is a long way between original notes and final typed manuscript. I am grateful for the help given to me by my secretary, Esther Gargano, who could decipher the unreadable and produce a typed page which looked the way I always hoped it would.

To my wife and children I owe a special debt. They are the ones who always provide love and support when I need it most. Hazel and Robert, as teen-agers, served the invaluable function of forcing me to examine my ideas, as they challenge the status quo and seek to improve the world they inherited from their elders.

WALTER M. LIFTON

Rochester, New York
December 1965

Contents

Working with Groups

1

Group Process and Individual Growth

One of the easiest ways to pick a fight in our society is to imply that the larger group takes precedence over the individual. As a nation dedicated to the right of each person to find happiness in his own way, we tend to look with suspicion on any organization where the individual becomes submerged and the group becomes more important. This strong preoccupation with the individual has been equally present in the field of mental health. Convinced that the road to a healthy society depends on treating people in a one-to-one relationship, many professions have predicted the need for additional personnel, based upon their estimates of how many people each professional can treat.

This numbers game leads to some ludicrous results. The Office of Education states that approximately 25,000 full-time counselors will be needed by 1967 to staff the seventh to twelfth grades in our public schools. This represents an increase of almost 85% over the number currently employed. Similarly, the Council of Social Work Education indicates that 10,000 vacancies in social work went unfilled in 1963. They estimate they will need more than 15,000 workers trained each year during the rest of the decade. On and on it goes. The incidence of people needing help grows larger, and the gap in available professional workers grows. Even if by some miracle suitable people could be located, trained, and employed, the dimension of the problem suggests that other approaches must be explored.[1] There can be no doubt that we must reassess ways in which people can be helped. It is also time for us to question the validity of the belief

1

that using group processes necessarily robs people of their individuality.

Let's face it. The values we cherish in our society are apparently contradictory. On the one hand, we value our heritage of rugged individualism; on the other, we are proud of the picture of ourselves as the champions of democracy.

Contradictions provoke controversies. We need but to glance at some major controversies in our society—labor-management-government interrelations, integration-segregation problems, national defense needs, the role of government in health, education, welfare, and science—and we see that they stem from this common contradiction of values.

Is this apparent contradiction of values real? Is the point at which the rights of the individual end and society's rights begin a Never Never Land of inevitable conflict? It seems unlikely. A major premise of this book is that there is no necessary contradiction between individual growth and societal, or group, process. And it follows that as the speed of communication increases and the complexity of our problems increases, so also it becomes increasingly imperative that we find a way to communicate how group action can be a source and a means of freeing the individual rather than enslaving him.[2]

The role of the group in politics represents a major present concern. The freedom of the mob to express their hostility under the cover of lost identity, the right of a property owner to decide who his neighbors will be, the use of laws and government to change behavior, even when they cannot affect feelings—all these represent examples of why the day-to-day experiences of the average man have left him with a mistrust of groups. Few people have experienced truly democratic groups. Until they do, it will be hard for them to realize that along with the rights granted to people in a democracy there is also responsibility—responsibility not only for oneself but also for one's neighbor.

Although the earlier edition of this book focused on using the group to help members look at themselves, this revision includes the idea that societal values in times of rapid social change cannot be ignored. Although each individual needs to clarify his own beliefs, these beliefs cannot be considered in a vacuum. The salvation of the democratic way of life depends basically on our skill in teaching people how to use the group process as a means to preserve an environment not only where all may live, but also where individual difference is valued and where each person's happiness is truly believed to be the vital concern of all. This teaching process needs to be felt in all aspects of our lives; it cannot be limited to the school setting. Church groups, social agencies, industrial organizations, all contribute to the flavor and operating philosophy of a society. Value systems do not develop in people at a specific age but grow and change from infancy on. Hence this book directs itself to group experiences found in the entire spectrum of society, regardless of age or setting.

One of the major purposes of a group has been the dissemination of information. The growth of the many new media of instruction and the new technologies of information storage and retrieval raises provocative questions about their effect on instruction and group orientation procedures. As machines facilitate some phases of individual instruction, and as computers become a ready and accurate resource, some of the traditional roles found in learning groups may disappear.

Group guidance will soon involve a variety of nonhuman devices. Increasingly, society will search for places where the mass of information being spewed forth can be incorporated. Increasingly, society will be faced with the challenge of being either master of or slave to industrialization.

Concern over the effects of our rapidly growing technology and its effects on man was concisely stated by Rollo May[3] in a speech entitled "Freedom and Responsibility Reexamined":

> . . . if we accept the proposal sometimes made in psychological conferences that our computers can set our goals and our technicians determine our policies, we are in my judgment making the most serious error of all. For we are abdicating in the face of our lack of goals and values. The one thing our computers cannot tell us is what our goals ought to be. In this day when we and all sensitive contemporary people are so confused and anxious, it is not surprising we tend to abdicate in favor of the machine. We then tend more and more to ask only the questions the machine can answer, we teach more and more only the things the machine can teach, and limit our research to the quantitative work the machine can do. There then is bound to emerge a real and inexorable tendency to make our image of man over into the image of the very machine by which we study and control him.

Many of our major concerns today seem to be wrapped up in the term "Manpower Utilization." Regardless of the reasons for this concern, society finds itself seeking means of motivating people to make optimal use of their educational and occupational potentials. The underachiever, whether his behavior stems from cultural or from psychological factors, needs to be helped to gain the higher rewards that are available and are given in our society to productive citizens. Much of our concern, unfortunately, has not come from our interest in the specific individual. Rather, looking at the aggregate of our potential, we seek security in a world of conflicting political ideologies by stressing material productivity. This concern with things rather than with people has led to some panaceas which may well cure the symptom but kill the patient.

Recently a book on counseling[4] raised the basic issue as to whether we should not learn from the communists and employ their techniques of brainwashing. We, of course, would use it to propagandize for democracy. This approach, at the opposite end of the continuum from Freud, rejects self knowledge or insight as the main source of change. Learning theory and the development of systems of rewards and punishments to control behavior have particular appeal to a technologically oriented society.[5] This may account for their recent rapid growth. Apparently, however, we have not yet learned that the means determine the end. We also seem to be confused over ways of developing intrinsic rather than extrinsic rewards for behavior.

For democracy to achieve the efficiency we seek, we obviously must develop skills in having our society's goals reflect the concensus of the needs of individuals. We must also help each individual to clarify his personal goals and to relate them to the objectives of the community. This "I-We" dialogue develops best when the individual can test his ideas against those of his peers.

Even at age levels where we have long recognized the importance of the group to the individual, we have been extremely slow in using sociological and psychiatric insights which employ the group as a vehicle for therapeutic change.

Social workers and sociologists have had much to tell us about gangs, juvenile delinquency, peer-group pressures, and group-work process. Psychiatrists looking at the developmental stages of man have stressed the need for children to belong to clubs and peer groups as part of their search for identity. Within the last ten years the message seems to be getting through. There is a ground swell of demand for people trained to work in group settings. One example may help illustrate the point. Some time ago, the College of Education of the University of Illinois wished to assess the effectiveness and appropriateness of its counselor training program. Administrators from all over the state were invited to the campus. During the day they were presented with a detailed description of the kinds of skills and abilities being developed in students who were in training to be counselors. At the end of the day, the administrators were asked to comment on their impressions and to provide suggestions for revision in the program.

Almost to a man, the group placed major priority on group work and group therapy skills. Recognizing that they could not hire enough counselors to work with all students individually, they wanted the counselors to work with groups of teachers. In groups, they felt, counselors would provide teachers with skills and insights which might enable teachers to help some of the youngsters now being referred to the counselors. The administrators also wanted the counselors to help students in their group activities, whether it might be the student council or such groups as those organized to help failing students. And, recognizing the importance of parent understanding, they sought help from the counselors in working with P.T.A.'s and child study groups. Over and over again the cry was for people trained to work in group settings—people with the skills to transform group settings into effective learning experiences.

This demand for group work skills did not stem purely from a desire for economy of effort or a desire to relieve staff shortages. The demand also stemmed from a growing awareness—an awareness that there are some peculiar growth experiences available to individuals in groups that are not present in a one-to-one relationship.

The need for group workers is clear and present. How, then, do we go about training in group work skills? One cannot train people to help others with just a book. The process is too complicated. A counselor not only has to try to understand one person, but, as is more vital in a group, he must also be aware of the interplay between several people. Obviously the demands on the counselor are for an extremely high level of skill and sensitivity.

But every day, whether anyone likes it or not, laymen and professionals alike find themselves thrust into group environments. And they have to do the best job they can under the circumstances. Increasingly, they call for help in understanding the problems involved in group process. They want also a clear statement of appropriate techniques to employ. Therefore, this book is intended both to provide some immediate help for the beginner and to help potential group workers to recognize their need for formal professional training.

Why This Book Was Written

Every teacher experiences the day when he is asked by his students "How did you do that?" or "Why did you do it that way?" Although he may be successful in presenting a rationale for his behavior, the day will arrive when the student says, "Teach me how to do it."

When the subject to be taught involves human relationships, it soon becomes obvious that what helps one person just does not work with the next person. The initial limitation of this book, if the book is to be useful, is that it can present some ideas and ways of relating that have proved useful to at least one person—the author.

To avoid the cookbook concept of teaching, this book will be organized in the following way. First there is a summary of issues involved in group process, which is followed by definitions of some of the terms to be employed in the text. Chapters 4, 5, 6, and 7 offer descriptions of several group situations that are instructional. Each of these situations is presented as completely as possible to allow the reader to come to his own conclusions. And further to stimulate the reader in the development of his individual philosophy, each chapter concludes with a résumé of writings by people who would interpret differently than I would the concepts being explored. In this way the lay reader may find concepts presented that are within his present experience, whereas the professionally trained person can go beyond this text to the controversial interpretations that are always present in such a young and multidisciplined area. Chapters 8 and 9 are designed to help the reader evaluate himself and the groups with which he works.

Roles Need to Be Defined*

Teachers and counselors are human beings. To be effective they must be secure. They must have a clear idea not only of their own values but also of the skills and abilities they possess which will enable them to do the jobs that are important to them. These facts we all recognize, but we apparently fail to see that it is equally important to understand clearly the job itself. The threats or rewards offered by society have a very real effect upon the productiveness and originality that a person exhibits. This is especially true when what society really wants is in question.

Years ago people used to say that every teacher did guidance—indeed, that education *was* guidance.[6] This saying probably meant that no matter what the teacher did, his actions affected and influenced the behavior of the people with whom he worked. Today, when we conceive of the teacher's role in its therapeutic aspects, we tend to say that the teacher helps people learn through doing. We now im-

---

* A restatement of excerpts from W. Lifton, "The Teacher's Role in Mental Hygiene, Therapy, and Social Reconstruction," *Progressive Education*, May 1955, pp. 65–67.

ply, correctly, that students are more sensitive to our actions than to the things we say.

The educator's role and the learning process are at heart psychological problems. For the educator to function adequately, it is important for him to know the philosophy of the agency within which he works, the limits of behavior which will be tolerated by the community, his own ability to tolerate differences with his own value system, and probably most crucial of all, the kind of behavior he exhibits as contrasted with the things he would like to be doing. Therefore, we need to look to the field of psychology and draw from it a better understanding of the job. In industrial psychology we learned a long time ago that the efficiency of an organization is vastly increased when the jobs for each individual within the organization are clearly defined. Then each individual not only knows what he is responsible for, but also clearly perceives the authority he has and the freedom that he possesses to act within the job limits that have been described.

But society's policies, limits, and definitions are not as clear as a corporation's. Whereas a corporation employee can know what ideas he should try because he knows the purposes, attitudes, and values of his organization, a teacher or group leader cannot. Differing concepts in society about the nature of man and differing criteria to employ in determining appropriate life goals make the job more difficult.

If man is perceived as having needs which are basically evil or as not having needs he ought to have, we cannot then comfortably develop an educational setting which will permit the needs of the individual to become an instrumental part of the learning process. Feeling the necessity for being our brother's keeper, we must develop every idea and technique within our power which will keep man from hurting himself. By every known device we must institute situations which will require behavior that will provide a more effective way of living.

For some, man is seen as initially rather neuter in quality. Through experiences and learned reactions he develops gradually a repertoire of typical responses. People most comfortable with this concept of man still cannot avoid value judgments in deciding what responses ought to be reinforced or led to extinction.

An opposite viewpoint of those presented has its philosophical root in the idea that man is basically good and that he is striving constantly toward a more effective kind of life. It also assumes that he has within him the desire, which is ever growing, to achieve a more satisfactory way of life. Those who hold this point of view make every effort to provide the individual with opportunities to recognize his needs and to test ways in which he can achieve satisfaction. This viewpoint holds that as the individual searches for a more satisfying life, he will, of his own volition, seek information about how others before him have solved his problem. Implicit is the idea that if the eternal truths are really eternal and vital to living, there need be no fear that the individual will discover them for himself. It is only when we are not sure that our answer is best that we fear having a person seek his own best solution.

One of the problems associated with this self-actualizing concept of man is the fear that the individual will develop into an antisocial, anarchistic kind of being. Initially the individual may start out with a selfish, egocentric point of view. He quickly discovers, as he tests out his needs in a group, that he can get from others the things he wants only when he has developed a relationship with them which will cause them to want to give to him what he seeks. When you help an individual face the world in which he finds himself, you also help him discover how his needs must be modified in order for him to get from society the security and rewards he desires.

The nature of the group atmosphere is basic to how people develop their security patterns. If we assume a democratic framework, an individual learns that his ability to gratify his needs can come only through developing in the group itself a climate and a relationship with others which will cause them to feel responsible to and dependent upon him to secure the kind of life they desire together.

It should become quickly apparent that I have accepted as my concept of man a philosophy based upon man's positive growth potential. With this point of view, it is possible to start with the society we now have, including its many faults, and to try to help the individual perceive realistically what he can get from his environment. But of greater importance for social change, this point of view helps the counselor assist the individual in developing the security that he needs when he begins to investigate the ways in which he can modify his own environment. Under a democratic educational setting, youngsters learn to be responsible for their own behavior. As they grow to be more responsible, however, they also begin to recognize the ways in which the society which their parents have developed does not necessarily represent their own needs and goals. Probably the greatest failure of this democratic framework is that, in it, teachers have not helped people learn a new kind of security that will go along with the changing environment which is now being created. A rather interesting illustration of this might be seen in the furor over the new methods of teaching reading or mathematics. Parents generally want to be seen by their children as wise and helpful. When a system is introduced that makes them unable to help their children because of their own ignorance of the procedure, parents resent being put in that position. Teachers who have discussed with parents the reasons for changes in teaching methods prior to their introduction have helped the parents prepare themselves for a new role before their security is threatened. In such schools, new methods are rarely the focus of public hostility.

George Sharp, in his book, *Curriculum Development as Reeducation of the Teacher*, Teachers College Bureau of Publications, 1951,[7] stated rather well the ethical and social problems within this point of view. On page 38 he writes, ". . . he must realize that he is embarking on a program aimed at the deliberate change of society and individuals, and as he has no sanction to do either, he must work to develop the insights of others instead of imposing his own views. He must have a working knowledge of the dynamics of behavioral change not only in terms of theory but in terms of human behavior. Finally, he must understand the ethical and psychological requirements of the role he is to play and be able to control his own behavior in accordance with these requirements."

This chapter has tried to demonstrate that the teacher's or group leader's role is deeply rooted in philosophical and ethical concepts. Because as a nation we have prided ourselves on our heterogeneity, we have not always been willing to face the need to homogenize our views when we define the teacher's or educator's job. In Chapter 2 these differing value systems will be related to theories of personality and terms commonly used in group settings.

Discussion

In subsequent chapters frequent reference is made to the thinking of different psychological schools as it applies to group situations. To prepare for this material, the following readings are suggested.

Good summaries of the positions of the Freudians can be found in Samuel Slavson's *The Practice of Group Therapy*,[8] and in Saul Scheidlinger's *Psychoanalysis and Group Behavior: A Study in Freudian Group Psychology.*[9]

Rudolph Dreikurs has described "Group Psychotherapy from the Viewpoint of Adlerian Psychology" in the *International Journal of Group Psychotherapy.*[10]

The nondirective point of view is clearly presented by Thomas Gordon in *Group-Centered Leadership.*[11]

Many of the other philosophical orientations to group process are covered in an anthology by Max Rosenbaum and Milton Berger, *Group Psychotherapy and Group Function.*[12]

Those readers seeking to relate psychological theory to classroom practice will find *Guidance and Counseling in Groups* by Margaret Bennett,[13] *Group Guidance* by Jane Warters,[14] and *Groups in Guidance* by Edward C Glanz[15] helpful.

A good definition of the activities of the social group worker is presented in the 1954 and 1960 Social Work Yearbooks.[16,17] Also helpful is Trecker's *Social Group Work.*[18]

BIBLIOGRAPHY

1. Hollister, William G. "Current Trends in Mental Health Programming in the Classroom." *The Journal of Social Issues,* **15,** No. 1, 51–52, 1959.
2. DeHuzar, George B. *Practical Applications of Democracy.* New York: Harper, 1945.
3. May, Rollo. "Freedom and Responsibility Reexamined." Speech given at the 1962 Convention of the American Personnel and Guidance Association.
4. Fullmer, Daniel, and Bernard, Harold. *Counseling Content and Process.* Chicago: Science Research Associates, 1964.
5. Haley, Jay. *Strategies of Psychotherapy.* New York: Grune and Stratton, 1963.
6. Association for Supervision and Curriculum Development, 1955 Yearbook. *Guidance in the Curriculum.* Washington, D. C.: ASCD, 1955.
7. Sharp, George. *Curriculum Development as Re-education of the Teacher.* New York: Teachers College Bureau of Publications, 1951.
8. Slavson, Samuel. *The Practice of Group Therapy.* New York: International Press, 1951.
9. Scheidlinger, Saul. *Psychoanalysis and Group Behavior: A Study in Freudian Group Psychology.* New York: Norton, 1952.
10. Dreikurs, Rudolph. "Group Psychotherapy from the Viewpoint of the Adlerian Psychology." *International Journal of Group Psychotherapy,* **VII,** No. 4, 363–375, October 1957.
11. Gordon, Thomas. *Group-Centered Leadership.* Boston: Houghton Mifflin, 1955.
12. Rosenbaum, Max, and Berger, Milton (Editors). *Group Psychotherapy and Group Function.* New York: Basic Books, 1963.
13. Bennett, Margaret. *Guidance and Counseling in Groups.* New York: McGraw-Hill, 1955.
14. Warters, Jane. *Group Guidance.* New York: McGraw-Hill, 1960.
15. Glanz, Edward C. *Groups in Guidance.* Boston: Allyn and Bacon, 1962.
16. Coyle, Grace. "Social Group Work." *Social Work Yearbook, 1954,* pp. 480–486. New York: Stratford Press.
17. Cogan, Juanita M. Luck. "Social Group Work." *Social Work Yearbook,* 1960, pp. 540–549. New York: National Association of Social Workers.
18. Trecker, Harleigh. *Social Group Work.* New York: Whiteside, 1955.

2

Theories, Professional Jargon, and Definitions

Words and labels are very important to people. For the practitioner who desires to help others grow in a group, it is vital that he think through his concept of the way personality develops, and subsequently, what is necessary to effect change. Because the theories of personality are based on such varied assumptions, the same terms have come to have different meanings in different psychological systems.

Hall and Lindsay,[1] in the beginning of their book exploring various theories of personality, set forth the attributes that serve to differentiate one theory of personality from the next. Included are the following:

1. Is man purposeful in his life or are his actions just mechanical reactions based upon learned patterns acquired early in life?

2. Is man's behavior determined by conscious or unconscious motives? Or, as a third possibility, is normality really a function of the degree to which man is aware of his needs and motives?

3. To what degree is man's behavior a function of seeking rewards? A corollary of this question is the concept that the only responses that will be learned are those accompanied by a reward or reinforcement.

4. Does the theory focus on the outcomes of learning rather than on the learning process itself?

5. How critical are the effects of early childhood experiences? Is personality an ever changing thing or is it jelled early in life?

6. Is there an objective reality that we all can perceive or is a person's perception a unique subjective experience?

11

There are many theories about what personality is. They involve an infinite combination of the factors listed previously, along with many others. Because any extensive discussion of this problem would detract from the major purpose of this text, the material which follows admittedly represents an oversimplification of the relationship of theory to the professional labels commonly employed.

Probably the most popular concept of personality structure is that personality has a basic core that is developed early in life. Personality is affected by specific major experiences, and to be changed it requires a reliving of these critical experiences. Such terms as "Oedipal situation," describing the child's experiences in coping with his parents, and "exploration of libidinal development," referring to the child's learning to express sex drives, are common to this point of view. With this concept also comes the idea of *depth* in effecting personality change. *Psychotherapy* is the term reserved for helping relationships that will require dealing with these basic experiences to help the person. The term *psychotherapy* refers only to those processes directed by a skilled, professional individual toward improvement of a client who needs help to remedy a defined pathological condition. The treatment is specifically focused toward this situation, and the therapist is concerned with the client's "basic" or "core" personality.[2,3] Some groups separate psychotherapy from counseling on two major counts: (*a*) the degree of pathology and (*b*) the focus of the therapist toward personality change instead solely of attitude change. Problems dealing with attitudes or situational factors are considered amenable to counseling. Because the situational factors are more superficial, different techniques may be employed to provide help. Commonly the Freudian philosophy and its descendents operate within this framework.

Another major group of theories does not differentiate between psychotherapy and counseling. Advocates of this point of view perceive as therapeutic any relationship which enables the individual more clearly to perceive his needs and to modify his behavior. Although all past experiences affect present behavior, any present experience can cause the past to have new meaning. Since it then becomes possible to help a person by dealing with his present perceptions, the concept of depth becomes meaningless. Counseling and psychotherapy become interchangeable terms. No special experiences become the focus of attention, since any problem of relationship or of needs which has persisted can be found and expressed in present behavior.

Treatment is oriented toward enabling the client to clarify his self-concept and to practice new methods of adjustment in a protected setting. Any change in the client's attitude toward himself is considered a change in the client's total personality. Rogers, Rank, Taft, and the Gestaltists fall within this frame of reference.

As described in Chapter 1, there are at least two other groups of importance. In both cases their concern is focused on changing current behavior. Although they differ in their ultimate concern about the importance of helping people eventually to develop insight into their emotional needs, they agree that the leader or therapist has the right to manipulate the environment so that only certain behaviors are permitted. Because these new behaviors cause others to act differently toward the client, the client learns the rewards he will receive if his changed behavior persists.

I have titled the book in general terms to avoid the confusion that exists over the meaning of such words as group guidance, group therapy, group dynamics, and group work. Many authors have differentiated these terms by alluding either to the primary purpose of the group or to the way in which different groups approach their goal.

It is interesting to note that although some nine years have passed since the earlier edition of this text was written, confusion and disagreement over the meaning of terms still exist. In an earlier article,[4] I tried to develop definitions that would reflect the varied concepts and the meanings of terms commonly used to describe group process.

In this article reviewing research on "Group Therapy in Educational Institutions"[*] I said that any review of research pertaining to group therapy in educational institutions is predicated on the belief that this area represents a defined body of common knowledge. It also assumes that the term "group therapy" is commonly understood and interpreted by the profession. Unfortunately, the limits of the field and an understanding of what can properly be called group therapy are interpreted in markedly different fashions by members of the profession. It is, for example, a clear commentary on the confusion of the profession—or more correctly, the lack of agreement as to the acceptable limits for purposes of definition—that in Combs' attempt[5] to define psychotherapy for legislative purposes, he found it impos-

---

[*] Excerpts in this chapter are quoted from W. Lifton, "Group Therapy in Educational Institutions." *Review of Educational Research*, **XXIV**, 156–158, April 1954.

sible to differentiate definitively what might be termed "counseling" from "psychotherapy," or "group therapy" from "education."

To quote further a section of my article which states the basic assumptions also made in this book—the school involves working with essentially normal people. It has also been assumed that the focus of the therapeutic situation in educational institutions arises through the relationship of a client's problem to his educational adjustment. Finally, to differentiate the term "group guidance" from "group therapy," group therapy in an educational setting is here considered to be operating in any group where the *emphasis* is upon providing group members with opportunities to explore their own feelings and attitudes, rather than upon imparting information.

A rather simplified way of making the differentiation between guidance and therapy might be in terms of the difference between a content-centered as contrasted to a pupil-centered type of classroom situation. However, the differentiation between guidance and therapy is not quite as clear-cut as that; for the student-centered classroom, in order to be therapeutic, needs to incorporate certain other characteristics beyond providing students with opportunities to meet their own needs. For therapy to exist, students must not only feel secure within the situation but must also experience some anxiety about a problem which they wish to resolve. The view taken here is that for *group therapy* to function in a classroom, there must be a sharing of these concerns.

It is not, however, the purpose of this book to discuss the nature of the classroom and the factors within a class which would militate against the security necessary for a therapeutic experience. Suffice it to say that where the teacher's role represents that of an evaluative authority figure, and where the individual will lose status within the group or within the community by exploring negative feelings or ideas, it is impossible for therapeutic growth to take place.[6-8] Wieder, for example,[9] has supplied evidence which suggests that this difference is a genuine one. He compared a classroom group led according to nondirective group-therapy procedures with another group taught according to traditional lecture methods. His results indicated that the "therapy group" measurably modified attitudes associated with racial, religious, and ethnic prejudice; the group taught according to traditional methods did not significantly modify these same attitudes.

Therapy and Counseling: Further Distinctions. Defining these boundaries helps clarify the area for discussion, but it does not heal the basic rift between two major opposing conceptions of the nature of psychotherapy and counseling.

The following selected fragments from letters received will point up, in terms of current practices in the field, the alternative conceptions of psychotherapy and counseling. The first two quotations are representative of the group which regards psychotherapy as dealing with basic personality change; the third quotation represents the philosophy of those who do not distinguish between psychotherapy and counseling.

Group therapy is a therapist working with more than one client having difficulties in areas with much communality. Prerequisite to operations, there must be individual assessment (diagnosis). Individual therapy is usually necessary either in the same time-span, or following group therapy. "They say" (and I believe) that group interaction speeds anxiety reduction but does not eliminate the need for individual attention. . . . Personally, I much prefer to think of "group preparation for counseling therapy" since, in my experience, good therapy tends to come ultimately from the one-to-one relationship.

. . . interested in the group-therapy approach to work with emotional problems of college students. He feels that it is a particularly suitable form of therapy for students in the educational setting since it sets limits on the identification with the individual therapist on the part of the patients. This makes the break at summers and vacation times much easier. . . . He finds that new students are more readily fitted into the group-therapy situation who would in the individual situation, find identification with the therapist difficult. Many students give up their physical symptoms very quickly in this setting. The patients are clients of the clinic for whom group therapy is prescribed by the psychiatrist in charge.

Certainly there is evidence year after year of increased self-insights and altered behavior. . . . At times I am confused as to the relative importance of the two directions—content, and exploration of feelings—as well as with my own ability to handle the latter experience. . . . I am hesitant even to use the word "therapy" in relation to any group experience. Perhaps "education" is more accurate for what I am describing, but it is education of feelings and emotions rather than an amassing of knowledge and concepts.

Education and Therapy. Symonds[10] makes the distinction between education and therapy in the following way:

Education is concerned with helping an individual to adjust to his environment and to form the habits and skills which enable him to do so most effectively. Therapy, on the other hand, is concerned with helping an individual to work out for himself a personal reorganization, and to achieve new points of view, new attitudes, new courage and self-assurance, so that he may find it possible to become educated, that is, to adjust to the situation with which he is faced.

This definition of education seems to hinge on the role of information and skill development. To a degree it suggests dichotomy between mind and body. Perception and behavior are seen as discrete.

Although it is certainly true that the individual who is preoccupied with his own difficulties finds it very hard to consider new ideas, it is equally true that learning appears to take place when the individual is aware of how an idea or skill meets his needs and is relevant to his goals and aims in life.[11-14] The conditions necessary for a good learning situation appear to be similar for both education and therapy. Both require that the student or client:

1. See a need to achieve something beyond his present status. (Unless a person has some discomfort with his present situation he has no motivation for change.)

2. Be secure enough in the situation to feel able to look at ideas or feelings which are threatening him. (Like the man who feels inadequate, the youngster who cannot spell cannot explore his inadequacy in a setting where to admit weakness is to make himself vulnerable.)

3. Select a setting which provides a basis for him to check the reality of his perception of himself. (Do others see me as I really am, and if they do, what do they think of me? Also, if others see me differently, whose estimate of me is correct?)

4. Receive help in discovering (information) new ways of acting, based upon a perceived need for new skills in relating or performing.

5. Have an opportunity to rehearse and practice these new skills or ideas until he feels equally competent in their use compared to the ones he had before. This practice must be in a setting which is protected so that his mistakes will not hurt him. (The boy who is learning to dance starts with his sister who may tease him, but who he basically knows is interested in helping him. He then moves on to his sister's girl friend. Only after he feels he has passed the grade here is he ready to consider asking *the* girl for a dance.)

Content versus Feelings

The dichotomy between emphasis on content versus feeling is reflected in the writings of many contemporary authors. Mahler and Caldwell[15] make a plea for "research on how much teaching for emotional understanding can be accomplished in a classroom, how much self-understanding can be acquired in group counseling sessions, and how much more self-understanding can be gained only in group therapy." In the meantime, however, they have attemped as shown in Table I to set up guidelines for school settings which reflect a concern for both the size of the group and its primary purpose.

Mahler and Caldwell realize that, regardless of the setting, the group will find itself dealing with areas of concern to group members.

TABLE I
Differences in Group Methods of Working with Youth

Unit	Number of Students Participating	Kinds of Groups
Class	100	Since all students will be taking these classes, the concern is with the topics and methods of instruction relating to the topics.
Large group	80–98	Vocational interest groups High-ability groups Retarded students School leaders Groups with difficulties in school subjects Speaking Math English Physical education
Small group	10–20	Classroom discipline groups Socially unskilled Overaggressive Underachievers Groups with difficulties in school subjects: Speaking Math English Physical education
Therapy group	5–10	Delinquents or predelinquents Truants Emotionally upset Very timid or shy

From Clarence Mahler and Edson Caldwell, *Group Counseling in the Secondary Schools*, Chicago: Science Research Associates, Inc., 1961, p. 27.

Using the common area of family relationships as an example, they have illustrated in Table II how the relative emphasis on content versus feelings affects methods employed by groups of varying size.

Group Dynamics

The term "group dynamics" actually covers all studies of group process and group roles.[16] There have been, however, a series of individuals who have developed techniques which they feel provide optimum group control for efficient problem solving. These techniques have been popularly labeled as the group-dynamics approach. Much of the theory and specific methodology arose through the activities of the National Training Laboratory, which has its roots in Bethel, Maine.

Because these pioneers have been so successful in setting forth their ideas and because the present position of the National Training Laboratory has shifted so dramatically from its earlier preoccupation on group member roles and group efficiency, it is helpful to review the changes that have occurred and the reasons for change in emphasis.

In earlier years, representatives of the group-dynamics movement objected to classifying every attempt to change attitudes in an educational setting as "group therapy." The point was made in numerous studies[17-20] that it is important to differentiate therapy groups from "problem-solving" and "action" groups. The significance of this distinction was registered in the observations of researchers in those studies, which focused toward therapy and which used the group-dynamics devices of process-observer and the like. They found that the presence of a nonparticipating, judgmental person limits the security that individuals need in a therapeutic situation before they can afford to face the threat within them.

Many of the early works focused primarily on how to help groups become more effective in achieving their goals.[21] This pragmatic orientation partially reflects the feeling that for democracy to prove its worth it must do so by demonstrating the results of group effort. For many, the yardstick becomes the speed with which a group achieves a goal external to the group. An illustration of this kind of concern can be seen in the writings of such people as Benne and Sheats.[22] Table III is an adaptation of the concept of group roles developed by them.

A survey of these labels quickly illustrates that the needs and personalities of the group members are judged by the way they facilitate

FAMILY RELATIONSHIPS

Unit	Size	Frequency of Meetings	Approach	Goals	Methods
Class	30	Extended homeroom program unit for one, two, or three weeks.	Unit outline prepared as part of course.	Understand roles of various family members, sibling relationships, parent-child relationships.	Text Outside readings Class discussion Individual projects Films on family life Speakers Role playing Group projects Attitude surveys
Large group	10–20	Usually a period a week for a semester. Frequency varies considerably depending on goals.	Topic chosen by group as an area of concern.	Understand oneself in context of family relationships.	No text Outside readings Personal logs or autobiographical writings Group discussion Attitude surveys
Small group	2–10	One or two hours a week for semester or school year.	Topic comes up only if a student brings it up. Group may or may not work on it for whole period.	Understand oneself in context of family relationships.	Primarily group discussion Role playing Sociodrama

TABLE III
MEMBER ROLES IN GROUPS ATTEMPTING TO IDENTIFY,
SELECT, AND SOLVE COMMON PROBLEMS

A. Group Task Roles.   Facilitation and coordination of group problem solving activities.

1. *Initiator contributor.*   Offers new ideas or changed ways of regarding group problem or goal. Suggests solutions. How to handle group difficulty. New procedure for group. New organization for group.
2. *Information seeker.*   Seeks clarification of suggestions in terms of factual adequacy and/or authoritative information and pertinent facts.
3. *Opinion seeker.*   Seeks clarification of values pertinent to what group is undertaking or values involved in suggestions made.
4. *Information giver.*   Offers facts or generalizations which are "authoritative" or relates own experience *pertinently* to group problem.
5. *Opinion giver.*   States belief or opinion pertinently to suggestions. Emphasis on his proposal of what should become group's views of pertinent values.
6. *Elaborator.*   Gives examples or develops meanings, offers rationale for suggestions made before, and tries to deduce how ideas might work out.
7. *Coordinator.*   Clarifies relationships among ideas and suggestions, pulls ideas and suggestions together, or tries to coordinate activities of members of subgroups.
8. *Orienter.*   Defines position of group with respect to goals. Summarizes. Shows departures from agreed directions or goals. Questions direction of discussion.
9. *Evaluator.*   Subjects accomplishment of group to "standards" of group functioning. May evaluate or question "practicability," "logic," "facts," or "procedure" of a suggestion or of some unit of group discussion.
10. *Energizer.*   Prods group to action or decision. Tries to stimulate group to "greater" or "higher quality" activity.
11. *Procedural technician.*   Performs routine tasks (distributes materials, etc.) or manipulates objects for group (rearranging chairs, etc.)
12. *Recorder.*   Writes down suggestions, group decision, or products of discussion. "Group memory."

B. Group Growing and Vitalizing Roles.   Building group-centered attitudes and orientation.

13. *Encourager.*   Praises, agrees with, and accepts others' ideas. Indicates warmth and solidarity in his attitude toward members.

14. *Harmonizer.* Mediates intragroup scraps. Relieves tensions.
15. *Compromiser.* Operates from within a conflict in which his idea or position is involved. May yield status, admit error, discipline himself, "come halfway."
16. *Gatekeeper and expediter.* Encourages and facilitates participation of others. Let's hear. . . . Why not limit length of contributions so all can react to problem?
17. *Standard setter or ego ideal.* Expresses standards for group to attempt to achieve in its functioning or applies standards in evaluating the quality of group processes.
18. *Group observer and commentator.* Keeps records of group processes and contributes these data with proposed interpretations into group's evaluation of its own procedures.
19. *Follower.* Goes along somewhat passively. Is friendly audience.

C. Antigroup Roles. Tries to meet felt individual needs at expense of group health rather than through cooperation with group.

20. *Aggressor.* Deflates status of others. Expresses disapproval of values, acts, or feelings of others. Attacks group or problem. Jokes aggressively, shows envy by trying to take credit for other's idea.
21. *Blocker.* Negativistic. Stubbornly and unreasoningly resistant. Tries to bring back issue group intentionally rejected or bypassed.
22. *Recognition-seeker.* Tries to call attention to himself. May boast, report on personal achievements, and in unusual ways, struggle to prevent being placed in "inferior" position, etc.
23. *Self-confessor.* Uses group to express personal, non-group oriented, "feeling," "insight," "ideology," etc.
24. *Playboy.* Displays lack of involvement in group's work. Actions may take form of cynicism, nonchalance, horseplay, or other more or less studied out of "field behavior."
25. *Dominator.* Tries to assert authority in manipulating group or some individuals in group. May be flattery, assertion of superior status or right to attention, giving of directions authoritatively, interrupting contributions of others, etc.
26. *Help-seeker.* Tries to get "sympathy" response from others through expressions of insecurity, personal confusion or depreciation of himself beyond "reason."
27. *Special interest pleader.* Verbally for "small business man," "grass roots" community, "housewife," "labor," etc. Actually cloaking own prejudices or biases on stereotype which best fits his individual need.

the rapid movement of the group toward the predetermined goal. Let us see how this type of group might function.

The newspapers announce that there will be a meeting of all citizens interested in helping promote the local bond issue. Mrs. Smith decides that this is just the kind of volunteer work she would like to do. She is tired of being cooped up in the house and aches for someone to talk to. At the meeting that night, Mrs. Smith pitches in with enthusiasm. She has found that to understand an idea she must put it in her own words. Since she is not very clear about the issue, and since she likes to talk, she unwittingly monopolizes the meeting. At the end of the session, the group process-observer points up the way in which her behavior slowed down the group. Since Mrs. Smith really wants friends, and since she is concerned about the group goal, she sits quietly through the next couple of meetings.

How can we evaluate what has happened? The group has exercised control over its members to insure maximum movement. Mrs. Smith has learned what not to do, but no longer knows how to participate, since her normal method of functioning brings group disapproval. The group has achieved conformity at the expense of a member's individual growth.

The early concern (1947) in the Basic Skills Training Group of the National Training Laboratory has shifted from a major preoccupation with skills development to a deeper and more sensitive concern with the problems confronting people who recognize the need to change. This awareness that the re-educative task has deeper therapeutic dimensions has led to the foundation of what is called the "T" Group.

As in an earlier day, the range of opinions and techniques encompassed by the National Training Laboratory is great. In the book entitled *T-Group Theory and Laboratory Method*[23] several statements define the relationship of the current concept of the "T" group to therapy and education.

> Each individual may learn also about groups in the processes of helping to build one. He may develop skills of membership and skills for changing and improving his social environment as well as himself. The staff who work with T Groups do not see any necessary opposition between participation in groups and autonomous individual functioning, though they are well aware that opposition does occur in many associations of our lives and that group forces may be used to inhibit personal development. In the T Group, on the contrary, the objective is to mobilize group forces to support the growth of members as unique individuals simultaneously with their growth as collaborators. Influences among peers are paramount in this learning process. In the T Group, members develop their own skills in giving and receiving help. They learn to

they more aptly could be called a crowd or a mass. They do not become a group until there is an awareness of their dependence on each other to accomplish a goal and an acceptance of their responsibility to each other in the process. An educative or therapeutic group demands that there is continual awareness of each person's behavior in the group and the acceptance by each person of responsibility for his own actions. Fundamental in a democracy to the use of any group technique is a concern over the rights and needs of the individual.

There can be little question that group processes such as those employed in the concentration camps can modify behavior and attitudes. When, however, the pressures for achievement need to arise from within each individual, it becomes very relevant that these motivating needs reflect the intrinsic values of each group member as he shares in developing group goals. Within this context, each term describing group techniques has to be considered as it relates to the way it facilitates or hinders individual growth. Within such a context, for example, group guidance is evaluated in terms of the conditions under which people develop the need for information and the environment which best facilitates the incorporation of the desired information.

The Common Denominators

Common in most groups is the feeling that basic to the development of any meaningful decisions or changes in behavior is the awareness and acceptance by group members of the needs or feelings which motivate their actions. Although groups may differ in the techniques they employ to facilitate self-understanding, all would accept the following concepts.

1. People need security in the group before they can afford to look at the underlying bases for their actions.
2. Topics form the basis for the group to pull together, but they are a vehicle rather than an end in itself. Therefore "digressions" are not seen as such, but rather an attempt is made to see what need the new topic is representing, and how it relates to the one it followed.
3. The group strives to put across the feeling which indicates a continued acceptance of the individual despite possible rejection of his behavior or idea. This concept reflects the epitome of the successful group. When group members can feel the continued interest and

concern in them as people and not feel rejected when others disagree with their idea, the group has achieved the kind of security which maximizes spontaneity and puts the premium on individual difference. Jung[33] has stated the basic concept here in clear terms:

> I fully approve of the integration of the individual into society. However, I want to defend the inalienable rights of the individual; for individuality alone is the bearer of life and is, in these times, gravely threatened by degradation. Even in the smallest group the individual is acceptable only if he appears acceptable to the majority. He has to be content with toleration. But mere toleration does not improve the individual; on the contrary, toleration causes a sense of insecurity, by which the lonely individual who has something to champion may be seriously hindered. Without intrinsic value social relations have no importance.

4. The group is a place to test the reality of an idea and it is the role of the leader or other members to react honestly.

5. Group members will present their feelings not only through the words they use but also by physical behavior.

6. The more a member participates in a group the more he gets out of it.

7. The group is strengthened by recognizing individual differences rather than merely focusing on the bases of similarity or consensus.

8. People react in terms of their present perception of a situation. This perception, however, is based on past experiences. To the degree that present perceptions can be related to the past, it is possible for the person to determine if he wishes to continue in the same direction for the future.

These are but a few of the common denominators to be found among groups that see the major reason for group life as being the means for most effectively recognizing and gratifying the needs of the individual. Like it or not, none of us lives in a vacuum. The ultimate lesson we have to learn is that we can find ourselves only as we relate to others.

Restatement of the Philosophy Expressed in the Text

Throughout this chapter there has been a recurrent theme indicating the conflict between the needs of the person and the needs of society. We also saw that in addition to this conflict there is conflict within a person whenever the thought of change from the status quo occurs. Being unsure of the effectiveness of any new approach, he has a real need, under stress, to return to the tried and true techniques of coping with society.

How then do we get change? Tillich[34] tells us that man cares enough for himself to act in behalf of himself even when such actions challenge his self-esteem and self-integration. May[35] feels that man becomes truly human at the moment of decision. Allport[36,37] states that much of our behavior involves seeking of challenges and tensions. And Frenkel-Brunswick[38] has shown that the antidemocratic author-itarian personality, when faced with anxiety, tends to avoid activities involving self-exploration or introspection. For the "authoritarian personality," consideration of his relationship with peers, friends, or family is threatening.

Our society includes both democratic and antidemocratic elements. Both elements seek help, and in both cases they need help from the leader they select. The basic responsibility of the initial group leader is to be responsive to the real goals of the group, including those not as yet articulated. Since the security of group members depends upon clearly defined limits, he defines the initial purpose of the group. Because under stress people tend to be unable to communicate, it is the leader's role to help the group develop and use their resources to provide support to group members.

One of the major differences in the role of the leader in a demo-cratic society from other types is that he derives his authority from the group. At any point where his perception of group goals deviates beyond the limits of group acceptance, he is no longer able to function. It is, therefore, the group's responsibility to give the leader the help he needs to shoulder the roles needed by the group. It is also their responsibility constantly to share their ideas and feelings so that the hidden agenda can come to light.

How do we help man transcend himself? My answer is both hu-manistic and existential. Since society cannot depend on answers coming from all people in every situation, leadership must be dele-gated. One of the most difficult roles of this leadership is to set limits which reflect society's wish for change, even when readiness is not re-flected by the sounds of the loudest voices.

A concrete example may clarify the point I am trying to make. Two school systems faced the inequities existing in their systems in the education of Negroes. In both systems the Board of Education knew that changes needed to be made. In one it was decided that in order to help teachers face the threat of change, changes would be made only when the teachers were ready. Time passed, but no one felt ready for change. The situation festered because the need for change was there but movement did not occur. In the other school system, the Board of Education mandated change. This was immediately followed up by all sorts of help to the staff to face the changes soon to come. Although anxiety levels were high, the ways to cope with these anxieties were clear. People moved rapidly to develop the skills that they felt they would need to cope with a problem they feared but unconsciously knew they had to face.

The critical question, of course, is whether the decision of the leader reflects these unconscious wishes of the public, wishes which demonstrate their own attempts to live up to the picture of the person they strive to become but fear they may never achieve.

To the degree that we can use a group setting to help people gain the support they need to face stress from within and without, to that degree we make it possible for democracy to succeed.

As a nation we face some unprecedented changes. We are becoming increasingly mobile, heterogeneous, and technically oriented. Some of the guide posts that used to come from tradition will have to be redefined by each group as they cope with new conditions.

It should be clear that my philosophy is biased toward describing personality as an ever-changing thing and holds that in dealing with an individual it is impossible to divide your relationship into levels. Accordingly, it is possible to use terms like teaching, counseling, or psychotherapy interchangeably without doing violence to the kinds of relationships that need to be developed in a group to achieve the goal of individual growth.[39] With this point of view it is possible to draw from both the fields of education and psychology in our attempts to explore the problems and skills associated with group leadership skills. The following hypotheses about the nature of personality and way to achieve behavior change represent my theoretical position.

1. To help people we need to start with their perception of a situation.

2. Help is most useful if it is initially directed toward the problem causing an individual (or group) the most immediate concern.

3. Individuals (groups) have an innate capacity to heal themselves, if they are provided a setting where they can feel secure enough to examine their problems.

4. As an individual (group) is helped to feel more secure, his need to shut out unwanted bits of information decreases. As he broadens his perception of the problem, he must by necessity include the values and attitudes expressed by society. Particularly in a group setting,

this means that the solution to a problem, although it starts out as egocentric, must ultimately resolve the paradox that man can only get his needs met through others. The following sequence may explain this concept.

> I want you to meet my needs.
> For you to be willing to do so, I must give you
>   a reason for doing so.
> It therefore follows that I can only meet my needs
>   after I have first considered yours.
> I have learned then that I can start out being
>   as selfish as I like, but I cannot achieve
>   my goal without considering how others will respond.

5. A change in any part of an individual's life affects all other aspects of his being. A new perception today can cause all past experiences to have a new and different meaning.

Certainly these assumptions are not original. As indicated earlier they can be traced back to the works of such people as Rogers, Wertheimer, Rank, Taft, Bergson, and Rousseau.

Since any belief is manifest only by the way it employs tools and techniques, the following chapter will consider just how people can be helped in group situations.

Discussion

This chapter provided many ethical and philosophical concepts worthy of further study. For the reader who is intrigued by the question of the appropriate role of the therapist or educator in our society, two books are especially recommended. Both Lindner's *Prescription For Rebellion*[40] and DeGrazia's *Common Errors in Psychotherapy*[41] will force you to examine your own beliefs.

If you find yourself somewhat confused by the brief survey of psychological theories, reading *Individual Behavior* by Snygg and Combs[42] will be helpful. Some may be disappointed by the absence of any specific discussion of learning theory. Its absence is not due to any question of the technical help learning theory has offered to practitioners. As a philosophy, however, except for the Pavlovian mechanistic approach to people, learning theory has made its greatest contribution when it has been used to explain phenomena within differing psychological systems. The symposium by Shoben,[43] Shaw,[44] and Combs[45] as well as the works of Dollard and Miller[46] provide examples of how these relationships are conceived from different frames of reference.

The question of where education ends and where therapy begins is highly controversial. An entire issue of *Progressive Education* (May 1955) has been devoted to this topic. Included are articles by philosophers, psychiatrists, group workers, educators, and psychologists. Also in this area, and presenting differing points of view, is the Volume VII, January 1957, No. I issue of the *International Journal of Group Psychotherapy* covering Group Dynamics and Group Psychotherapy.

Although not discussed in this chapter, the question of the need for adopting a theoretical position rather than developing a smorgasbord of techniques conveniently labeled an eclectic approach, deserves the careful attention of the serious student in the area. To help in an understanding of a philosophical stand which reflects personal consistency rather than rigidity, Carl Rogers' *Client-Centered Therapy* is highly recommended.[47]   On the question of a philosophical eclecticism, the article the author wrote in *Occupations* (now the *Personnel and Guidance Journal*) entitled "A Reply to a Plague on Both Your Houses,"[48] may amplify why eclecticism of philosophies is considered impossible.

Common to both of the last two references is the work by Lecky[49] on the importance of self-consistency. Also helpful is the discussion by Corsini[50] on the relationship of a leader's personality to the methods he will employ.

For teachers, Arthur T. Jersild's *When Teachers Face Themselves*[51] carries out the same themes in the classroom setting.

A good historical summary of writings defining group work, group therapy, and group organization can be found in a book of readings edited by Dorothea F. Sullivan entitled *Readings in Group Work*.[52] It contains articles printed in a journal entitled *The Group*, which is now out of print (New York: Association Press, 1952).

It is suggested that the more mature reader will enjoy browsing through *Group Dynamics* by Dorwin Cartwright and Alvin Zander.[53] This book and *Dynamics of Groups at Work* by Herbert Thelen[54] present excellent descriptions of the philosophy and techniques employed by members of the National Training Laboratory. Readers seeking more information about the T group should read *T-Group Theory and Laboratory Method* edited by Leland Bradford, Jack Gibb, and Kenneth Benne.[23]

A rather delightful way of broadening one's cultural experiences and increasing one's understanding of people having different problems can be achieved through leisure reading. The following books are just a few that can provide enjoyment along with increased sensitivity.

Algren, Nelson. *The Man with the Golden Arm*. Garden City, New York: Doubleday, 1949.

Baruch, Dorothy W. *How to Live with Your Teen-Ager*. New York: McGraw-Hill, 1953.

Baruch, Dorothy W. *One Little Boy*. New York: Julian Press. 1952.

Baruch, Dorothy. *New Ways in Discipline*. New York: Whittlesey House, 1949.

Beers, Clifford. *A Mind That Found Itself: An Autobiography*. Garden City, New York: Doubleday, 1935.

Bettelheim, Bruno. *Love Is Not Enough*. Glencoe, Illinois: Free Press, 1950.

Bisch, Louis E. *Be Glad You're Neurotic*. New York: McGraw-Hill, 1936.

Cozzens, James. G. *By Love Possessed*. New York: Harcourt, Brace, 1957.

Davis, W. A., and Havighurst, R. J. *Father of the Man*. Boston: Houghton Mifflin, 1947.

Deutsch, Helen. *Psychology of Women* (Volume 1—describes development to maturity; Volume 2—deals with salient phases of adult life). New York: Grune and Stratton, 1944.

Dunbar, H. Flanders. *Mind and Body*. New York: Random House, 1947.

Engstrand, Stuart. *The Sling and the Arrow*. New York: Creative Age Press, 1947.

Eysenck, Hans J. *Uses and Abuses of Psychology*. Baltimore: Pelican Books, 1953.

Freeman, Lucy. *Fight against Fears*. New York: Crown Publishers, 1951.

Fromm, Erich. *Forgotten Language: An Introduction to the Understanding of Dreams, Fairy Tales, and Myths*. New York: Rinehart, 1952.

Gerber, I. J. *Man on a Pendulum: A Case History of an Invert*. New York: American Press, 1956.

Jersild, Arthur T. *In Search of Self*. New York: Bureau of Publication, Teachers College, Columbia University, 1952.

Josselyn, Irene. *The Adolescent and His World*. New York: Family Service Association of America, 1952.

Levy, John, and Monroe, Ruth. *The Happy Family* New York: Knopf, 1938.

Maslow, Abraham H. *Motivation and Personality*. New York: Harper, 1954.

Menninger, Karl A. *Man against Himself*. New York: Harcourt, Brace, 1938.

May, Rollo. *Man's Search for Himself*. New York: Norton, 1953.

Packard, Vance. *The Hidden Persuaders*. New York: McKay, 1957.

Peters, Arthur A. *The World Next Door*. New York: Farrar, Straus, 1949.

Redl, Fritz. *Children Who Hate*. Glencoe, Illinois: Free Press, 1951.

Redl, Fritz. *Youth in Conflict*. Glencoe, Illinois: Free Press, 1955.

Reik, Theodor. *A Psychologist Looks at Love*. New York: Rinehart, 1948.

Reik, Theodor. *The Secret Self: Psychoanalytic Experiences in Life and Literature*. New York: Farrar, Straus, and Young, 1952.

Schulberg, Budd Wilson. *What Makes Sammy Run?* New York: Random House, 1941.

Selye, Hans. *The Stress of Life.* New York: Macmillan, 1956.
Steiner, Mrs. Lee. *Where Do People Take Their Troubles?* Boston: Houghton
     Mifflin, 1945.
White, Robert W. *Lives in Progress.* New York: Dryden, 1952.
Wolfe, Thomas. *You Can't Go Home Again.* New York: Harper, 1940.
Wright, Richard. *Black Boy.* Cleveland: World, 1950.
Wright, Richard. *Native Son.* New York: Harper, 1940.

Each author recommends books he has found helpful to him in broadening his horizon. Few authors have done as comprehensive a job as Carroll E. Kennedy in relating readings to basic questions human relations workers have to face. With the kind permission of both Carroll E. Kennedy and the publishers of *Counselor Education and Supervision,* we are reprinting here excerpts from an article entitled "Considering the Social Processes in Human Development."*

The writer has observed that consideration of the social processes of human development often finds students asking questions somewhat along the lines of the ten questions listed below. Selected references that have proved useful in such discussions are also included to illustrate an approach to the questions.

1. What Does It Mean to Be Human?

Is there such a characteristic as humanness to distinguish man from other animals? How do we make this distinction? Is such a distinction a matter of degree—of quantity or quality? Are there criteria for humanness? If so, are they universal or does the concept humanness vary with time and nation? Are we more human today than we were two hundred or two thousand years ago?

Animal stories such as those of Singh and Zingg's "wolf children" in India (88), Cathy Hayes' report of rearing a chimp in her home (39) and Kortlandt's article "Chimpanzees in the Wild" (52) are popular reading material associated with this question and stimulate the discussion of ways of "evaluating data." The Alorese natives' lack of ability to project themselves into the future (49), the effect of

---

* This article is excerpted from *Counselor Education and Supervision,* Vol. III No. 2, Winter 1964, pp. 84–97.

Carroll E. Kennedy is Counselor and Assistant Professor of Family and Child Development at Kansas State University, Manhattan, Kansas.

The numbers in parentheses are Kennedy's references and can be found at the end of this chapter.

social isolation on young children (30), the educated Dr. Nyiszli's (74) use of his medical skill to boil meat off the bones of fellow Jews in a concentration camp and Kierkegaard's analysis of a Biblical patriarch evidencing the highest faith and hallmark of human courage in offering his son as a human sacrifice (50) illustrate some controversial reading.

Speaking of the Stone-Age natives who killed her husband and with whom she has since been living, Elisabeth Elliot states in *The Savage My Kinsman*. "The Acua has not a reason in the world for thinking us his betters, and he probably has some very valid reasons for thinking us his inferiors." (33) Their search for criteria of humanness often finds students comparing the Acua of South America with Roy Heath's Princeton College student, *The Reasonable Adventurer* (40) or considering Wang Lund, the Chinese farmer who finds his meaning in the soil (19), and Arthur Miles, the British Physicist for whom the fullest expression of human nature is in the laboratory quest (90).

2. What Are Some Physical Influences in Social Development?

How does our native endowment influence our personality and performance? Are some people at birth more emotional than others? Are some races more intelligent than others? In what way does his physiological inheritance limit an individual? Can we predict and prescribe an individual's physiological inheritance? Are you happy or unhappy about this?

In a study involving people in prison, an investigator took those who were twins and located the other twin. He then searched the records to see if that twin had a prison record. Results showed that in only thirty-four per cent of fraternal twin cases did both twins have a prison record. In seventy-two per cent of the cases of identical twins, both twins had prison records. In many cases they were in prison for similar crimes conducted in different parts of the country after the twins were separated. This and similar twin studies reported in Charlotte Auerbach's *The Science of Genetics* (6) bring the age old nature-nurture controversy into student discussions.

Typical of other "provocative" studies relating physical and social processes are those reporting the bizarre food tastes of a patient with Addison's disease (10), an analysis of the onset of a growth of beard in a lovesick girl who happened to have an endocrine balance more susceptible to emotional upset than that of the average individual (20); and Professor Guhl's report of the physiological components in the pecking order of hens (36a).

Scientific American (73) and *Life magazine* (55) layouts help the student appreciate something of biochemistry's expanding study of man's inheritance. Roger J. Williams' declaration (103) that the tendency to down-play inherited differences leads to a negating of the importance of individual liberty—with uniformity, what is good for one is good for all—stimulates student philosophers. Philip Carey, born with a clubfoot in *Of Human Bondage* (62) and Bernard Marx viewing the development of test-tube babies in *The Brave New World* (46) present in fiction form questions of physical influence on social development.

3. What Do We Inherit Socially?

What of the social mileau into which a child is born?   In what ways do the sounds, sights, people and plans surrounding an individual influence what he is or becomes?   To what extent would an individual be the same regardless of where he was born?   How true is it that culture gives us eyes to see with, tongues to speak with and hearts with which to feel?   To what extent do we inherit a social niche and to what extent is our a classless society?

Shades of the sober Zuni, the ecstatic Kwakutil and the dour Dobu (12) flit in and out of discussions on this question and of the consideration of articles reporting that Norwegians seem to be more "conforming" than do Frenchmen (67); or the prevalence of multiple sclerosis is 2.4 times greater in Halifax County, Nova Scotia, than in the somewhat comparable community of Charleston County, South Carolina (4).

Students having looked at Reisman's *Lonely Crowd* (79) of "inner" and "other" directed people, and their 1960 reconsideration (58), may move from economic determinants of socialization to think again of the physical dimensions in social influence recalling Hebb's "The Mammal and His Environment" (40a) and Calhoun's "Population Density and Social Pathology" (21) or they may consider psychological environments of the type Wendell Johnson mentions in his discussion of the parental anxieties that may create climates conducive to stuttering (48).

Reports that boys from homes of different social classes perform differently on the Guilford Zimmerman Temperament Survey Test (89) and the suggestion that career-oriented girls are more likely than home-making-oriented girls to come from homes where the father is absent (100) bring the thoughts of school counselors more directly to bear upon the social forces relating to decisions of youth in counseling situations.

Eliza Doolittle and Professor Higgins may be characters of fiction (85) but Sister Mary Amator's (5) report of similarity in teacher-pupil personality makes the shaping of Eliza a lively topic for discussion.

4. How Do We Appropriate Our Social Inheritance?

By what mechanism does what is outside the individual get into or direct the organism? Are there principles that can describe the ways in which the behavior of an individual is changed through contact with his environment?

The learning theorist O. Hobart Mowrer becomes conversational in his article "What Talking Birds Taught Me" (70). Escalona's familiar report of "Feeding Disturbances of Very Young Children" (34) helps students think in life-like fashion about the ways of learning. *Hidden Persuaders* (76) and "Teaching Machines" (42) and electric typewriters (75) dramatize learning processes. Lovaas rewarded young children for aggressive *verbal* behavior and seemed to find that this resulted also in increased aggressive behavior in *nonverbal* play situations (61).

"A pheromone is a substance secreted by an animal that influences the behavior of other animals of the same species." Worker ants use it to direct other workers to food sources. The queen honey bee regulates the reproductive cycle of her colony by secreting a pheromone which, when ingested by the worker bees, inhibits development of their ovaries and also their ability to manufacture the royal cells in which new queens are reared. The *same* pheromone serves as a sex attraction in the queen's nuptial flights. Mature human females are more able to smell certain substances such as Exaltolide, a perfume fixative, than are men and young girls. A male subject becomes more sensitive following the injection of estrogen (104). Are pheromones "learning agents"?

Rosenzweig and Krech (82) suggest that experience and training significantly alter the concentration of brain cholinesterase and Gaito

(36) has hypothesized changes in DNA coding associated with learning.

5. What Are the Forces That Shape the Socialization Process?

If there is a social flux or enveloping climate which shapes the individual, how does this climate change? Does the physiology and personality of the individual have any influence upon the effectiveness of the environment—does either change the characteristics of the environment? To what extent is the socialization process independent of geological and technological processes in the environment?

The ratio of work to be done and number of people available to do it may influence the socialization process. Barker (9) sees the achievement-oriented people of the American frontier as growing out of the environmental demands made on a sparse population. He compares the roles of the youth and the elderly as "needed persons" in an American frontier community and as "marginal" in an English community.

Communities experiencing dramatic cultural change highlight some aspects of this question. Anthropologist Norman Chance (25) found that seventy-five per cent of the men in an Eskimo village were earning six hundred dollars a month working full-time at relatively permanent occupations associated with military defense installations. A few years previously these Eskimos earned a migratory living by hunting, fishing, and trapping. Chance attributes, in part, the smoothness of this cultural transition to the fact that the change was far reaching and rapid (as contrasted, for example, with cultural changes in progress in the South of this country). In "The Shelter-centered Society" (99), a group of social scientists speculate regarding the effects on the American people of a large-scale peace-time defense program.

At the Age Center of New England (96) it was found that *age* makes a difference in an individual's judgment of time. Time moves more rapidly for older people. There are some communities in the world where the median age is twenty and some where the median age is fifty.

Toynbee philosophizes on the forces of social change (94); Margaret Mead (64) tells "how to do it." Poetic descriptions of societies in transition are presented in *Hawaii* (66) and *John Brown's Body* (13).

6. What Are the Evidences of Socialization?

Is there a uniformity of behavior or a consistency of expectation that reflects the socialization process? How do the ways of perceiving and believing resulting from socialization processes in this country differ from those of other countries? Along what continua can we note social difference among the people of our own country?

College students seem to have a sterotyped way of viewing older people (8) and children seem to have a common way of ranking the effect of physical handicaps in other children (78). Children (87) as well as adults seem to have sterotyped views of occupations and industries (16).

The "administered" society lamented in the *Organization Man* (102) was found to so dampen competitiveness and individuality that leisure time activities such as social parties are a deadly bore (80).

Gordon Allport's classic on *The Nature of Prejudice* (3) may be supplemented by articles such as "The Stimulus Qualities of the Scapegoat" (14) and illustrated by the child's-eye view of Jean Louise (Scout) Finch in *To Kill a Mockingbird* (53a).

During the six year period while children were growing from eleven year olds to young adults, Havighurst and others recorded evidences and effects of socialization on the youth in a city of 45,000 population reported in *Growing Up in River City* (38).

Research at Harvard suggests a commonality of attitude that segregates the sexes with women being more "conservative" than men (97). Special supplements in *Harper's Magazine* (15) and *Life* (54) have looked at the evidences of socialization which constitute "The American Female". Dairies of Ruth Benedict (65) reflect her experiences in relation to the social roles of women.

7. What Is the Significance of the Family as a Socialization Agent?

To what extent does emotional climate of the family parallel the emotional pattern of the child? In what respects is the socialization function of the family unique? Who determines the objectives of the family's socialization program—to what extent is this possible or desirable?

Having reported in *Patterns of Child Rearing* interviews with 379 mothers of five-year-olds, Robert Sears and Eleanor Maccoby report their follow-up of these five-year-olds at ages eleven and twelve in "Relation of Early Socialization Experiences to Aggression in Middle Childhood" (84).

Class differences seem to prevail on matters of child rearing although what is characteristic of working class and middle class child rearing now is not the same as it was two decades ago (17).

Child rearing seems at times to be filled with paradoxes. One study suggests that homes which are *coercive* while allowing the child considerable *autonomy* are likely to produce boys who are successfully assertive in academic performance, in social influence and in friendship (44). Another study suggests that it is not the fact of the mother's working outside the home but it is rather how *she* feels about it that determines the effect such employment will have on the development of her children (43).

A Death in the Family (1) is a Pulitzer Prize novel dealing with autobiographical material in the childhood of James Agee. *The Letters of James Agee to Father Flye* (2) allow us to see this child as a youth and in adult life. *Diary of a Young Girl* (35) and *Mothers and Daughters* (45) are two other books from the rich store of literature providing vicarious introduction to the family as a socializing agent.

8. *What Is the Significance of Religious and Ethnic Factors As Socializing Agents?*

To what extent are these factors an extension of the family? To what extent is it possible and helpful to identify distinctive socializing effects of religious and ethnic groups? What are some ways in which the preservation of ethnic differences adds to a nation's richness? How may such uniqueness retard development?

A recent *Look* article (59) presents the Bar Mitzvah of a Jewish boy becoming a man in Cincinnati. *Current* considers racism in America (51). James Baldwin's essays collected in the book *Nobody Knows My Name* (7) and the *Time* (92) *Newsweek* (72) coverstories highlight the Negro artist and intellectual's concern with the problem.

The Ecumenical Council and the death of Pope John XXIII (93) gave occasion for religious leaders to consider developments within the Catholic Church and to speculate on added vitality in the relationship of individual Catholics with their cultural environments. Protestants looked at Catholics and Catholics looked at Protestants in succeeding issues of *Harper's Magazine* (29) (23).

Influence of ethnic and religious background is often a leading factor in lives of fictional heroes and heroines: Maria, the Puerto Rican Juliette in the 1960 version of Romeo and Juliette called *West Side Story* (86); Barach Ben Canan, patriarch of Israel whose story extends from the pogroms in Russia to the kibbutz that claimed new fruits from the waste land of Palestine (95); Beneatha Younger (37), Negro college student aspiring to be a physician, attracted to the nationalism of an egotistical Nigerian, deeply loyal to her family whose dream of a home of their own runs aground on integration conflicts in Chicago's Southside; Elmer Gantry, a sensational and sensual evangelist. (53)

When compared with other people in one Southern community, those who stated they have no fear of death also tend—more than do other older people—to state that they read the Bible, to express fewer feelings of rejection and depression and to show some tendency to have more leisure time activities. (47)   Children of Seventh Day Adventist families in some communities seem to have less dental decay than do other children in general in those communities. (71)   Such studies promote consideration not only of research technique but of the extended, interrelated implications of religion and ethnic factors in human development.

9. *What Is the Significance of School and Community Organizations as Socializing Agents?*

> *To what extent is school distinct from home and other community organizations as a socializing agent?   How may the community activities influence self-concept?   What are some socializing functions of government agencies?   What concerns do urbanization raise?   Are there any respects in which the State may be seen as a large self?*

The Child Buyer (41) helps guidance workers ask whether the talents of youth exist for the government or whether government exists for the people.   "Automation" forces the issue of whether work should be viewed from the standpoint of meaning and dignity it provides to individuals or whether it should be viewed from the standpoint of the gross national product (57).

Catherine Bauer Wurster employs the lyrics of Winston Churchill, "We shape our buildings and then our buildings shape us," to express the problem of urbanization. Today's metropolitan area: ugliness and noise in the center, monotony and inconvenience in the suburbs, purgatory of the immigrants, dreary lives of the aged, lengthening journeys to work, racial conflict, juvenile delinquency. Two-thirds of the people in this country will be metropolitan residents by 1970. Urbanization is inevitable, the question is what kind of urban environment do we want. Wurster plugs for a "balanced net-work of strong cities," something in between centralization and dispersal in city planning (105).

Community organizations, whether government, school or Soroptomist, reflect the community while moulding it. Pressure-group letters and lobbies are voices of the people. So too is the legislator—but how literal should be the translation? Is the legislator elected to use his good judgment and his independent sense of values or is he to carry out the specific wishes of his constituents? Emmanuel Celler says "Lobbies Are Not All Bad" (24). Senator Brig Anderson loses his life in search of an answer to this question in *Advise and Consent*. (31) Urie Bronfenbrenner's report of Soviet methods of character education (18) challenges educators to a study of "extrafamilial groups as socializing agents." Whitney Robbins, Acting President—aspiring to make it permanent—at Stacy Towers, fictitious western university, is aware of socializing forces from within and without the university, as is the coed who commits suicide (98).

10. What Is the Significance of Peers and Associates as Socializing Agents?

In what areas of the socialization processes are these influences most critical? What socializing functions do peers perform that others may not do so well? Are there some individuals who would be more influenced by peers than others would? Under what circumstances might we expect these influences to be most significant?

At Harvard Medical School, Rose Laub Coser found that junior staff members rarely make a senior staff member the target of their witticism. Her analysis of twenty recorded staff meetings of a mental hospital suggests that humor serves to reduce the social distance between persons occupying different positions in a social structure. (28)

The more a boy perceives that he has the attitudes and skills approved by members of his group the less he will desire to change himself. Furthermore, the more the group perceives that he has the desired skills and attitudes the less they will want him to change or develop, it was found in studies at a boys' camp. (91).

In *Street Corner Society* the leader is the focal point for communication within the teenage gang. His attention reinforces a conversation and his lack of attention squelches it. He knows more about what is going on in a group than does any other member of the gang. Positions of individual members in a group structure are linked to the leadership positions. Changes at the top may result in changes all the way down the line. (101) More contemporary, although less systematic, views of gang life are presented in *West Side Story* (86), in Arthur Miller's "The Bored and the Violent" (68), and in articles in popular periodicals such as "The Tense Generation" (60). Peer processes are also reflected in a Gallup Poll article on "Youth" (83), and in interviews with "College Dropouts". (56)

Do you remember Frankie Addams (63) the lanky twelve year old girl with crewcut and skinned elbows? Neighbor girls a year older left her behind while they moved into the age of Saturday night parties. Brandan Behan's autobiographical account of his teen years in prison gives a rather loud description of peer processes (11). Clyde Griffith's parents conducted a gospel mission in Kansas City. His sense of isolation and his striving to belong to a group are central themes in *An American Tragedy*. (30a)

Summary

The ten questions listed above are simply one way of summarizing some of the kinds of ideas with which students are concerned in their thinking-through of the processes of socialization. Similar types of questions are developed in discussion of physical and self processes in human development. The accompanying references illustrate some kinds of reading material the writer has found useful in such discussions.

The main point of the article is that counselors are working with social beings in a social context. It is important that *as students* they be encouraged in the lifelong task of attempting to gain some awareness of the process of socialization and some appreciation for its subtle beauty and far reaching implications. Such experiences seem to lead students to an increased sensitivity to and acceptance of themselves and others in the human situation.

REFERENCES FOR "CONSIDERING THE SOCIAL PROCESS IN HUMAN DEVELOPMENT," BY CARROLL E. KENNEDY

1. Agee, James. *A Death in the Family*, New York: Avon Book, 1956.
2. Agee, James. *Letters of James Agee to Father Flye*, New York: George Braziller, 1962.
3. Allport, Gordon W. *The Nature of Prejudice*, New York: Anchor Books, 1958.
4. Alter, Milton, et al. "Multiple Sclerosis and Climate," *World Neurology*, 1960, Vol. 1, pp. 55–70.
5. Amator, Sister Mary. "Similarity in Teacher and Pupil Personality," *Journal of Psychology*, 1954, Vol. 37, pp. 45–50.
6. Auerbach, Charlotte. *The Science of Genetics*, New York: Harper Bros., 1961.
7. Baldwin, James. *Nobody Knows My Name*, New York: Dial Press, 1961.
8. Axelrod, S. and Eisdorfer, C. "Attitudes toward Old People," *Journal Gerontology*, 1961, Vol. 16.
9. Barker, R. G. "Ecology and Motivation," *Nebraska Symposium on Motivation*, University of Nebraska Press, 1960. (See also "Psychological Ecology of Old People," *Journal of Gerontology*, April, 1961.)
10. Beach, Frank. "Body Chemistry and Perception" in *Perception and Approach to Personality* (Blake, R. R. & Ramsey, G. V. eds.) New York: Ronald Press, 1951.
11. Behan, Brendan. *Borstal Boy*, New York: Alfred A. Knopf, Inc., 1959.
12. Benedict, Ruth. *Patterns of Culture*, New York: Mentor Books, 1934.
13. Benet, Stephen Vincent. *John Brown's Body*, New York: Rinehart and Co., Inc., 1927.
14. Berkowitz, L. and Green, J. A. "The Stimulus Qualities of the Scape Goat," *Journal of Abnormal and Social Psychology*, Vol. 64, No. 4.
15. Bettelheim, Bruno. "Growing Up Female," Harper's Magazine, October, 1962.
16. Brayfield, A. H., Kennedy, C. E., Kendall, W. E. "Social Status of Industries," *Journal of Applied Psychology*, Vol. 38, No. 4.
17. Bronfenbrenner, Urie. "Socialization and Social Class Through Time and Space," in *Readings in Social Psychology*, (Newcomb, T., Maccoby, E., and Hartley, L. eds.) New York: Henry Holt Company, 1958.
18. Bronfenbrenner, U. "Soviet Methods of Character Education," *American Psychologist*, Vol. 17, No. 8.
19. Buck, Pearl, *The Good Earth*, New York: John Day Company, 1931.
20. Bush, I. E., and Mahesh, V. B. "Hirsuitism and Emotional Tension," *Journal of Endocrinology*, 1959, Vol. 18, No. 1.
21. Calhoun, J. B. "Population Density and Social Pathology," *Scientific American*, February, 1962.

22. Calitri, Charles, "Language and the Dignity of Youth," *Saturday Review,* July 20, 1963.
23. Callahan, D., "A Catholic Looks at Protestantism," *Harper's Magazine,* November, 1962.
24. Celler, E. "Lobbies Are Not All Bad," in *American Governments; The Clash of Issues,* (J. A. Burkhart et al., eds.) Englewood Cliffs, N. J.: Prentice Hall, Inc., 1960.
25. Chance, N. A. "Culture Change and Integration: An Eskimo Example," *American Anthropologist,* 1960, Vol. 62, No. 6.
26. Coleman, J. S. "The Adolescent Society," New York: Free Press of Glencoe, 1961.
27. Coon, C. S.: "New Findings on the Origin of Races," *Harper's Magazine,* December, 1962.
28. Coser, Rose L. "Laughter Among Colleagues," *Psychiatry,* 1960, Vol. 23, No. 1.
29. Cox, H. "A Baptist Intellectual's View of Catholicism," *Harper's Magazine,* December, 1962.
30. Davis, Kingsly. "Extreme Social Isolation of Child," *American Journal of Sociology,* 1940, Vol. 45, pp. 554–565, and 1959, Vol. 52, pp. 432–437.
30a. Drieser, Theodore. *An American Tragedy,* New York: Dell Publishing Co.
31. Drury, Allen. *Advise and Consent,* New York: Doubleday and Company, 1959.
32. Dugan, Willis. "An Inward Look: Assumption and Aspirations," *Counselor Education and Supervision,* Vol. 1, No. 4. Summer, 1962.
33. Elliot, Elisabeth. *The Savage My Kinsman,* New York: Harper Brothers, 1960.
34. Escalona, S. K. "Feeding Disturbances in Very Young Children," *American Journal of Orthopsychiatry,* 1945, Vol. 15.
35. Frank, Anne. *Diary of a Young Girl,* New York: Pocket Books, Inc., 1954.
36. Gaito, John. "A Biochemical Approach to Learning and Memory," *Psychological Review,* 1961, Vol. 68, No. 4.
36a. Guhl, A. M. "Pecking Order of Hens," *Scientific American,* October, 1954.
37. Hansberry, Lorraine. *A Raisin in the Sun,* New York: Random House, 1959.
38. Havighurst, R. J. *Growing Up In River City,* New York: John Wiley, 1962.
39. Hayes, Cathy. *The Ape in the House,* New York: Harper Brothers, 1951.
40. Heath, S. R. "The Reasonable Adventurer and Others," *Journal of Counseling Psychology,* 1959, Vol. 6, No. 1.
40a. Hebb, D. O. "The Mammal and His Environment," *American Journal of Psychiatry,* 1955, Vol. 111, pp 826–831.
41. Hersey, John. *The Child Buyer,* New York: Alfred A. Knopf, 1960.
42. Hilgarde, E. R. "Teaching Machines and Psychology of Learning," *NEA Journal,* November, 1961.
43. Hoffman, L. W. "Effects of Maternal Employment on the Child," *Child Development,* 1961, Vol. 32, pp 187–197.
44. Hoffman, L. W., et al. "Parental Coerciveness, Child Autonomy and Child's Role at School," *Sociometry,* 1960, Vol. 23, No. 1.
45. Hunter, Evan. *Mothers and Daughters,* New York: Simon and Schuster, 1961.
46. Huxley, Aldous. *Brave New World,* New York: Bantam Books, 1932.

47. Jeffers, F. C., Nichols, C. R., and Eisdorfer, C. "Attitudes of Older Persons Toward Death," *Journal of Gerontology*, 1961, Vol. 16, No. 1.
48. Johnson, Wendell. "Stuttering is an Avoidable Accident," *The Reader's Digest*, April, 1961.
49. Kardiner, A. *Psychological Frontiers of Society*, New York: Columbia University Press, 1945. (See also DuBois, Cora in *In The Company of Man*, Casagrande, J. B. ed., Harper Brothers, 1960.)
50. Kierkegaard, Soren. *Fear and Trembling*, New York: Anchor Books, 1954.
51. King, Martin Luther, Jr., and others. "Racism in U. S." *Current*, June, 1963, and August, 1963.
52. Kortland, A. "Chimpanzees in the Wild," *Scientific American*, May, 1962.
53. Lewis, Sinclair. *Elmer Gantry*, New York: Grosset and Dunlap, 1927.
53a. Lee, Harper. *To Kill a Mockingbird*, Philadelphia: J. B. Lippincott and Company, 1960.
54. Life Editors, "The American Woman," *Life*, December 24, 1956.
55. Life Editors, "Inside a Human Cell," *Life*, March 29, 1963.
56. Life Editors, "A College Majority—the Dropouts," *Life*, June 22, 1963.
57. Life Editors, "The Point of No Return," *Life*, July 19, 1963.
58. Lipset, S. M. and Lowenthal, L. *"Culture and Social Character—The World of David Reisman Reviewed,"* New York: Free Press of Glencoe, 1961.
59. Look Editors, "Jeffrey Becomes a Man," *Look*, August 13, 1963.
60. Look Editors, "The Tense Generation," *Look*, August 27, 1963.
61. Lowaas, O. I. "Interaction Between Verbal and Nonverbal Behavior," *Child Development*, 1961, Vol. 32, pp 329–336.
62. Maugham, W. S. *Of Human Bondage*, New York: Modern Library, 1915.
63. McCullers, Carson. "Member of the Wedding," in *Famous American Plays of the 1940's* (Hewes, H. ed.) Dell Publishing Company, 1960.
64. Mead, Margaret. *Cultural Patterns and Technical Change*, New York: Mentor Book, 1955.
65. Mead, M. *Anthropologist at Work*, New York: Basic Books, 1959.
66. Michener, James A. *Hawaii*, New York: Bantam Books, 1959.
67. Milgram, Stanley, "Nationality and Conformity," *Scientific American*, December, 1961.
68. Miller, Arthur. "The Bored and the Violent," *Harper's*, November, 1962.
69. Miller, Carroll. "Quality in Counselor Education," *Counselor Education and Supervision*, Vol. 1, No. 3 Spring, 1962.
70. Mowrer, O. H. "What Talking Birds Taught Me," *Parents Magazine*, February, 1958.
71. National Institute of Dental Research, *Highlights of Progress in Dental Research, 1960*, Washington: Government Printing Office, 1961.
72. Newsweek Editors. "The Negro in America," *Newsweek*, July 29, 1963.
73. Niernbery, M. W. "The Genetic Code: II," *Scientific American*, March, 1963.
74. Nyiszli, Miklos. *Auschwitz*, Greenwich, Conn.: Crest Book, 1960.
75. Pines, Maya. "How Three Year Olds Teach Themselves to Read—And Love It," *Harpers*, November, 1962.
76. Packard, Vance. *The Hidden Persuaders*, New York: Pocket Books, 1957.
77. Ramsey, C. E., and Smith, R. J. "Japanese and American Perceptions of Occupations," *American Journal of Sociology*, 1960, Vol. 65, pp 475 to 482.

78. Richarson, S. A. et al. "Cultural Uniformity in Reaction to Physical Disabilities," *American Sociological Review*, 1961, Vol. 26, No. 2.

79. Reisman, David. *The Lonely Crowd*, New York: Anchor Books, 1953.

80. Riesman, D., Potter, R. J., and Watson, J. "Sociability, Permissiveness and Equality," *Psychiatry*, 1960, Vol. 23, No. 4.

81. Rosen, S. et al. "Desired Change in Self and Others as a Function of Resource Ownership," *Human Relations*, 1960, Vol. 13, No. 3.

82. Rosenzweig, M. R., David Krech, E. L. Bennett. "Heredity, Environment, Biochemistry and Learning," in *Current Trends in Psychological Theory* (Dennis, Wayne ed.), Pittsburgh: University of Pittsburgh Press, 1961.

83. Saturday Evening Post Editors, "Youth," *Saturday Evening Post*, December 23, and December 30, 1961, Curtis Publishing Co., Philadelphia.

84. Sears, R., Maccoby, E. and Levin. *Patterns of Child Rearing*, Evanston, Illinois: Row, Peterson and Co., 1957. (See follow-up report Sears, R. and Maccoby, E. in *Journal of Abnormal and Social Psychology*, 1961, Vol. 63, No. 3.)

85. Shaw, G. B. *Pygmalion*, Baltimore: Penguin Books, 1942. (See also *My Fair Lady*, New American Library).

86. Shulman, Irving. *West Side Story*, New York: Cardinal Pocket Book, 1961.

87. Simmons, D. D. "Children's Rankings of Occupational Prestige," *Personnel and Guidance Journal*, December, 1962.

88. Singh, J. A. L. and Zingg, A. L. *Wolf-Children and Feral Man*, New York: Harper Brothers, 1942. (See also Montague, A. *The Directions of Human Development*, New York: Harper Bros., 1955.)

89. Singer, S. L. et al. "Temperament Scores and Socio-economic Status," *Journal of Counseling Psychology*, 1958, Vol. 5, No. 4.

90. Snow, C. P. *The Search*, New York: Charles Scribner's Sons, 1959.

91. Stotland, Erza et al. "Group Interaction and Perceived Similarity of Members," *Journal of Abnormal and Social Psychology*, 1960, Vol. 61, No. 3.

92. Time Editors. "The Negro's Push for Equality," *Time*, May 17, 1963.

93. Time Editors. "Vatican Revolutionary," *Time*, June 7, 1963.

94. Toynbee, Arnold J. *A Study of History*, (abridged by Somervell, D. C.) New York: Oxford Press, 1957.

95. Uris, Leon. *Exodus*, New York: Bantam Book, 1959.

96. Wallach, M. A. and Green, L. R. "On Age and the Subjective Speed of Time," *Journal of Gerontology*, 1961, Vol. 16, No. 1.

97. Wallach, M. A. and Kogan, N. "Sex Differences and Judgment Processes," *Journal of Personality*, 1959, Vol. 27, pp 555–564.

98. Walter, R. H. K. *Stacy Tower*, New York: McMillan Co., 1963.

99. Waskow, A. I. "The Shelter-Centered Society," *Scientific American*, May, 1962.

100. White, Becky J. "Relationship of Self Concept and Parental Identification to Women's Vocational Interests," *Journal of Counseling Psychology*, 1959, Vol. 6, No. 3.

101. Whyte, W. F. *Street Corner Society*, Chicago: Chicago University Press, 1943.

102. Whyte, W. H., Jr. *The Organization Man*, New York: Doubleday Anchor, 1956.

103. Williams, Roger. *Free and Unequal*, Austin: University of Texas Press, 1953.
104. Wilson, E. O. "Pheromones," *Scientific American*, May, 1963.
105. Wurster, C. B. "Framework for an Urban Society," in *Goals for Americans* (Report of the President's Commission on National Goals), Englewood Cliffs, N. J.: Prentice-Hall, 1960.

End of the Kennedy article.

BIBLIOGRAPHY

1. Hall, Calvin, and Lindzey Gardner. *Theories of Personality*. New York: Wiley, 1957.
2. Scheidlinger, Saul. "Group Factors in Promoting School Children's Mental Health," *Amer. Journal of Orthopsychiatry*, 22, 394–404, April 1952.
3. Slavson, Samuel R. "Common Sources of Error and Confusion in Group Psychotherapy." *International Journal of Group Psychotherapy*, 3, 3–28, January 1953.
4. Lifton, Walter M. "Group Therapy in Educational Institutions." *Review of Educational Research*, XXIV, No. 2, 156–158, April 1954.
5. Combs, Arthur W. "Problems and Definitions in Legislation." *American Psychologist*, 8, 554–564, October 1953.
6. Laycock, Samuel R. "Mental Hygiene of Classroom Teaching." *Understanding the Child*, 16, 39–43, April 1947.
7. Lifton, Walter M. "Group Classroom Techniques." *Progressive Education*, 30, 210–213, May 1953.
8. Super, Donald E. "Group Techniques in the Guidance Program." *Educational and Psychological Measurement*, 9, 496–510, Autumn 1949.
9. Wieder, Gerald S. *A Comparative Study of the Relative Effectiveness of Two Methods of Teaching a Thirty-Hour Course in Psychology in Modifying Attitudes Associated with Racial, Religious, and Ethnic Prejudice*. New York: New York University, 1951. (Doctor's thesis). Abstract: *Dissertation Abstracts*, 12, 163, No. 2, 1952.
10. Symonds, Percival. "Supervision as Counseling." *Teachers College Record*, 43, 49–56, October 1941.
11. Alpert, A. "Education as Therapy." *Psychoanalytic Quarterly*, 10, 469–474, 1941.
12. Baruch, Dorothy W. "Therapeutic Procedures as Part of the Educative Process." *Journal of Consulting Psychology*, 4, 165–172, 1940.
13. Ojemann, Ralph. "Basic Approaches to Mental Health: The Human Relations Program at the State University of Iowa." *Personnel and Guidance Journal*, XXXVII, No. 3, 199–206, November 1958.
14. Zlatchin, Philip. "Round Table: Education and Psychotherapy." *American Journal of Orthopsychiatry*, XXIV, No. 1, 133–140, January 1954.
15. Mahler, Clarence A., and Edson Caldwell. *Group Counseling in the Secondary Schools*. Chicago: Science Research Associates, 1961.
16. Jenkins, David H. "What Is Group Dynamics?" *Adult Education Journal*, 9, 2, 54–60, 1950.

17. Gordon, Ira J. "The Class as a Group: The Teacher as Leader—Some Comments and Questions." *Educational Administration and Supervision,* 37, 108–118, February 1951.

18. Gordon, Ira J. *The Creation of an Effective Faculty Advisor Training Program through Group Procedures.* New York: Teachers College, Columbia University, November 1950 (Doctor's thesis).

19. Pepinsky, Harold B. "An Experimental Approach to Group Therapy in a Counseling Center." *Occupations,* 28, 35–40, October 1949.

20. Trow, William C., and others. "Psychology of Group Behavior: The Class as a Group." *Journal Educational Psychology,* 41, 322–338, October 1950.

21. Lippitt, Ronald, Kenneth Benne, and Leland Bradford. "The Promise of Group Dynamics for Education." *Journal of the National Education Association,* 37, 350–352, 1948.

22. Benne, Kenneth, and Sheats, P. "Functional Roles of Group Members." *Journal of Social Issues,* 4, 2, 42–47, Spring 1948.

23. Bradford, Leland P., Gibb, Jack, and Benne, Kenneth D., (Editors). *T-Group Theory and Laboratory Method.* New York: Wiley, 1964.

24. Bradford, Leland P., Gibb, Jack R., and Benne, Kenneth D., (Editors). "Two Educational Innovations," *T-Group Theory and Laboratory Method,* p. 2. New York: Wiley, 1964.

25. Bradford, Leland P., Gibb, Jack R., and Benne, Kenneth D., (Editors). "Training and Therapy," *T-Group Theory and Laboratory Method,* p. 446. New York: Wiley, 1964.

26. Froehlich, Clifford P. "Group Guidance Approaches in Educational Institutions." *Review of Educational Research,* 24, 147–155, April 1954.

27. Driver, Helen, et al. *Counseling and Learning through Small Group Discussion.* Madison, Wisconsin: Monona Publications, 1958.

28. Caplan, Stanley W. "The Effect of Group Counseling on Junior High School Boys' Concepts of Themselves in School." *Journal of Counseling Psychology,* 4, 124–128, Summer 1959.

29. Wright, Wayne E. "Multiple Counseling: Why? When? How?" *The Personnel and Guidance Journals,* 37, 551–557, April 1959.

30. Thelen, Herbert A. *Education and the Human Quest,* p. 68. New York: Harper, 1960.

31. Freud, S. *Group Psychology and the Analysis of the Ego.* London: International Psychoanalytic Press, 1922.

32. Loeser, Lewis. *International Journal of Group Psychotherapy,* VII, No. 1, 5–19, January, 1957.

33. Illing, H. A. "C. G. Jung on the Present Trends in Group Psychotherapy." *Human Relations,* 10, 77–84, 1957.

34. Tillich, Paul. *The Courage to Be.* New Haven: Yale University Press, 1952.

35. May, Rollo. "Existential Psychiatry, an Evaluation." *Journal of Religion and Health,* I, No. 1, 1961.

36. Allport, Gordon W. *Becoming.* New Haven: Yale University Press, 1955.

37. Allport, Gordon W. "Psychological Needs for Guidance." *Harvard Educational Review,* 32, No. 4, 373–381, Fall, 1962.

38. Frenkel-Brunswick, Else, et al. "The Anti-Democratic Personality," *Readings in Social Psychology* by Newcomb, T., Maccoby, E., and Hartly, L. (Editors). New York: Henry Holt, 1958.

39. *Journal of the National Association of Deans of Women.* "Counseling and Group Work," **X**, No. 3, 99–124, March 1947.
40. Lindner, Robert. *Prescription for Rebellion.* New York: Rinehart, 1952.
41. DeGrazia, Sebastian. *Errors in Psychotherapy and Religion.* Garden City, New York: Doubleday, 1952.
42. Snygg, Donald, and Combs, Arthur. *Individual Behavior,* revised edition. New York: Harper, 1958.
43. Shoben, Edward J. "Counseling and the Learning of Integrative Behavior," *Journal of Counseling Psychology,* **1**, No. 1, 42–48, Winter 1954.
44. Shaw, Franklin J. "Counseling from the Standpoint of an 'Interactive Conceptualist.'" *Journal of Counseling Psychology,* **1**, No. 1, 36–42, Winter 1954.
45. Combs, Arthur W. "Counseling as a Learning Process." *Journal of Counseling Psychology,* **1**, No. 1, 31–36, Winter 1954.
46. Dollard, John, and Miller, Neal E. *Personality and Psychotherapy.* New York: McGraw-Hill, 1950.
47. Rogers, Carl. *Client-Centered Therapy,* p. 9. Boston: Houghton Mifflin, 1951.
48. Lifton, Walter M. "A Reply to a Plague on Both Your Houses." *Occupations,* **XXX**, No. 6, 434–437, March 1952.
49. Lecky, Prescott. *Self-Consistency.* New York: Island Press, 1945.
50. Corsini, Raymond. *Methods of Group Psychotherapy,* pp. 125–127. New York: McGraw-Hill, 1957.
51. Jersild, Arthur. *When Teachers Face Themselves.* New York: Bureau of Publications, Teachers College, Columbia University, 1955.
52. Sullivan, Dorothea, F. *Readings in Group Work.* New York: Association Press, 1952.
53. Cartwright, Dorwin, and Zander, Alvin. *Group Dynamics.* Evanston, Illinois: Row Peterson, 1956.
54. Thelen, Herbert. *Dynamics of Groups at Work.* Chicago: University of Chicago Press, 1954.

"No man can reveal to you aught but that which already lies half asleep in the dawning of your knowledge."

From The Prophet *by Kahlil Gibran.*[*]

3

The Tools and Techniques Involved in the Helping Process

Differences in philosophies, as described in Chapter 2 (Freudian, Rogerian, etc), affect the frequency with which some techniques are used over others, and certainly affect the manner in which the practitioner plays his role, interprets process, and plans for the future. But in the minute-to-minute operation it would be difficult to distinguish one philosophy from another. Since in the material which follows it would be helpful for the reader to be able to analyze the interactions described, a look at a few specific techniques is in order. These techniques are the same as those found in a one-to-one learning situation, although, as we will see, the group setting permits different ways in which they can be employed.

Before examining some of the more basic techniques, it is important to have a prior understanding of the way communication provides the key to the helping process. Essentially the major problem in our society is a breakdown in communication. Not only do people have trouble understanding each other, but frequently a person is not sure of himself. Actually this book itself is limited to the help that can be provided through the use of words. The first and hardest lesson for the beginner to learn is that you cannot assume that the other person meant what you assumed his words to mean. Not only do words frequently have a variety of meanings, but also the way in which they are said can vastly alter their intent. Shakespeare understood this well when he had one of his characters say, "The lady doth protest too much, methinks." One of the skills most desired by maturing youth is to know whether a girl really means no when she says it. To review, then, words are defined with a variety of meanings in the dictionary, they change meaning according to the setting, and they can reflect the exact reverse of their stated meanings. To further complicate the issue, people use ideas to express feelings that are important to them. It is almost as if words were a car, with the feelings being its passenger, and with the passenger being more vital than the car itself. The major problem, then, is to see how one can learn what the other person is trying to convey. Until one understands the feelings, one cannot begin to help him (or them) face the issue to be solved.

The first place where anyone can start is with his own experience. "What could the words I hear possibly mean?" Having explored the range of possible alternatives, a person next tries to examine the context in which the words occurred to select the most likely meaning. He still cannot be sure that his own needs are not causing him to distort what he has heard, so that ultimately all he can do is to check if his idea is what the other person actually meant.

Sometimes, however, understanding the meaning one has given to a word is not enough. In some situations, insight may depend upon experiences as yet unknown to the person. Words can cause insights to develop only if they can rearrange prior meanings into a new format.[1]

This attempt at precision of meaning is really at the very heart of the helping process in which several things are going on at once. To clarify the relationship in the helping process, the person being helped will be called the client. For the client who hears from another his idea exactly as he meant it, there is the wonderful feeling of being understood, of not being alone in the world, and of having someone else available who can help him see if he is getting across to others the things he desires. For the client who sees someone else trying to understand, but who finds that his words do not seem to convey the exact meaning he desires, there is still the opportunity to try to redefine himself. In this process of redefinition—this attempt to clear away ambiguity—frequently the speaker becomes clearer not only about what he wants to say, but also about what his true feelings really are.[2]

The skilled group worker needs more than a text to train his sensitivities to hearing and responding to others. The group leader not only needs to have knowledge of others, but also has to be sure his own house is in order. We do not hear others say things which, if we recognize them, would force us to see unacceptable things in ourselves. The more we need to block out from hearing, the less we can help others. Although this chapter can discuss techniques, no true learning can take place for the reader until he has a chance to see if he can use the ideas himself. He also needs help from others who can call his attention to the things he typically doesn't hear or respond to.

Thus, the primary goal in the helping process is to assist others in examining their words or behavior to see if they represented what the client wished to communicate. With this as our goal let's explore some tools which help people to clarify their thoughts. The process of reflecting back to the client the literal dictionary meaning of what he says is called "*reflection of content.*"

When we reflect back to the person what he is *trying* to say, or the latent desires in his words, the process is called "*reflection of feeling.*" Reflection of feeling is particularly tricky. If we can help put into words a feeling of which the person was dimly aware, but had not found a clear way to state, we will help him by this clarifying process. If, however, we pick up feelings which we feel are there but which the client is either not ready to examine or which represent our distortion of his feelings, we may be in for trouble. The attempt to reflect these unconscious needs or to link up past experiences with present behavior is called "*interpretation.*" Since any linking of past with present or any predicting of future behavior has to come from the perceiver's own experiences or logic, the success of this technique will be vitally dependent upon its accuracy and the concurrent help given to the person to face frightening or unacceptable ideas. Since interpretation is so dependent upon a vast experience and an ability to judge a person's readiness for threatening material, it is a device best reserved for only the most skilled person.

Since most helping relationships demand ways of relating that are not part of the typical social situation, a technique called "*structuring*" is used. In essence, "structuring" involves either a statement of the rules of the helping process or an understanding of such rules by the way the therapist or group leader does or does not act in specific situations. In a group setting, the initial group leader may take the responsibility of indicating the limits to be imposed on the group by the setting in which they are meeting or by the nature of the group. In other words, he is indicating the outside limits imposed by society. Rules developed inside the group reflect a philosophy along with its concept of how the leader can be most helpful. In this book, the leader's role in "structuring" is seen as that of assisting the group to become aware of problems they need to solve and helping them learn to work together in setting up the rules by which they will function together.

Because many people coming into a helping situation expect the expert to take over, it is important that the initial leader make clear early in the sessions what the group can or cannot expect from him. Since the group will be more responsive to his behavior than his words, it is vital that there be consistency between what he says and does. The leader or therapist has been referred to as the initial leader because, as early as possible, it is the leader's objective to have members of the group assume responsibility for directing and assisting their fellow members.

In the initial sessions of a group, structuring will include, among many others, such questions as, "What is the group going to do?" "What is the leader's role?" "How are people treated here?" "What are the acceptable things to talk about?" "How confidential will the contents of group sessions be?" "Isn't it a sign of weakness to admit confusion over ideas or goals?" Although most of the structuring occurs early in the group's life, structuring can continue as long as the group needs to develop ways of handling new situations.

Other more common tools that all of us have had a chance to experience include *questioning, supplying information, clarifying an idea* (summarizing all the points raised that bear on each other), and (probably most important of all) the use of *silence* to allow the other person to think his own thoughts in his own way. These are but a few of the techniques available. At the end of this chapter the reader will find references that can help fill in needed knowledge on the counseling process and tools involved.

Recently there has been a tendency in the field of counseling to believe that probably none of these tools in itself is of great importance. The touchstone of the helping process is, now more than ever, felt to be the way the person who is trying to help indicates to another that he really cares about him. It is a relationship that cannot be faked. One way to let others know that you feel that what they say is really important is to constantly look at them. To actually understand them, you need to see the facial expressions and gestures that go along with their words. For example, try the following experiment yourself.

Knowing that constant eye contact is helpful, try this on a friend: Tell him that you wish to have him help you learn how to convey interest in a client. Ask him to let you know when he feels you are with him and when he feels you are wool-gathering. For the first few moments try your hardest to listen to the feelings the client is expressing. Then, while still focusing your eyes on the client's face imagine a scene taking place behind him, and, in a sense, look right through him to the scene beyond. Return again to a real attempt to listen. This time, however, spend your time thinking of how you would like to answer him. In other words, although you are concerned with his problem, your major attention is on what it means to you. If you are successful in playing these roles you will discover to your dismay that when you are not really listening to what he is trying to express, you are fooling no one but yourself.

Part of the purpose of this chapter is to introduce you to the jargon used by professionals in the fields of counseling and therapy. Since the remainder of the book will focus on psychological skills coming from these professional fields, let us take a look at the teaching process so that we can recognize its similarity to the material which follows. The following analysis of teaching represents a summary of an excellent article on this subject by Louis Raths.[3] The comments about each heading, however, are my interpretation of their applicability to the helping process.

Raths has divided teaching into separated operations. We will specifically examine what he has called the "Clarifying Operations, the Show-How Operations, and the Security-Giving Operations."

Clarifying Operations

I.1. *Clarifying through reflection.* This has been partially covered by the preceding section.

I.2. *Clarifying through use of a definition or illustration.* For a person to understand an idea fully he must be able to communicate its meaning to others. Clarification is frequently best achieved by describing an applicable concrete situation. The group seeks to facilitate its understanding by requesting the person to illustrate his idea.

I.3. *Clarifying by pointing up what appear to be apparent inconsistencies.* Notice the word "apparent." What does not make sense to the hearer initially may be seen as related when the speaker draws up the relationship as he sees it. One good illustration of this comes in the popular refrain, "you always hate the one you love." A moment's thought will reveal the fact that it is hard to feel strongly about someone who is unimportant to you.

I.4. *Clarifying similarities and differences.* Particularly in a group where there may be a tendency to get support by either forcing a single stand or by the operation of cliques, this approach is very important. Because a pressure group forces opinion by presenting a united front, helping members of this subgroup examine their stand and pointing up areas of hidden disagreement as well as consensus within their group, causes the clique to disintegrate and join the total group. It also points up that the strength of the group can come from difference as well as agreement.

I.5. *Clarifying through questioning underlying assumptions.* This can be a dangerous tool. If the group by this device rejects all assumptions but those the majority believes in, it can have a threatening and restricting effect. If, however, it is used to help the person or total group define the assumptions they are making so that they can decide if these are beliefs they can really accept, then the approach has positive implications for growth.

I.6. *Clarifying through anticipation of consequences.* Since the response of others to our actions is a major concern, the degree to which the group helps provide possible results enables the person to determine his course of action. One rather popular way that is used to think through this situation is by having group members act out with a person a scene in which he tries his idea. The other members, by their behavior, give him concrete evidence of what the future effects of his approach might be.

I.7. *Clarifying through questioning meaning.* Is this what you mean? or, Do I understand you to say . . . ? The latter implies that the hearer could be misperceiving but wants to understand. Thelen[4] has pointed out that children are so imbued with the teacher's role as an authority that they may begin to believe that truth is the opinion of someone on whom you are dependent. Teaching people to question may be the first step toward helping them understand their right to their individual belief. The questioning process may also help them realize that as they question the ideas of a person in an authority role, their questions may cause the authority to modify and change his ideas, too.

I.8. *Clarifying by examining points of difficulty.* This could apply not only to an idea but also to helping the group examine their own group process. For example, sometimes a group seems at a loss as to what they want to do. Helping them examine the feelings or ideas that seem to be causing trouble is the first step in removing this road block. What's getting in our way? Why are we so upset?

I.9. *Clarifying if a personal statement was meant to show a personal feeling or one that the individual feels all people must hold.* This is one way of helping the group see demands that individual members are making on them. It also points up to the individual demands he is making on others.

I.10. *Clarifying by relating feelings to behavior.* By calling attention to the feelings which others are getting from a person's behavior, it helps the person accept responsibility for the way he expresses his emotion. "We all seem to be so angry at each other that we seem unable to let the other person talk."

I.11. *Clarifying through a review of the steps in a person's logic.* This concept is somewhat like I.5. Implicit is the idea that a review of the steps will help a person see the fallacy of the logic involved. Although this approach can sometimes work, it cannot help failing unless the motivation for his reasoning will be more effectively met by an alternative logic which is presently in the client's available repertoire of responses. For example, the group points out to a client that he is tired when he stays out late with the boys and that his health and school work are suffering. The client recognizes the truth of the group's statement, but the logic does not meet his need for peer group approval or the satisfactions he gets when he is out with the fellows.

I.12. *Raising questions of purpose.* What are you trying to prove? This is an attempt to help the person search for and recognize the underlying motivation for his activity. To the degree that he is secure in the group and has a motivation to get an answer, this approach may be helpful. Also, the question must reflect an attempt to help the person rather than be a belligerent challenge of his rights or goals.

I.13. *Seeking origins of an expression or idea.* Since nothing we think or do is unrelated to our past experiences, to the degree that we can integrate a present idea with the concepts that led to its creation, we achieve a fuller realization of the meaning of the idea to us.

The Show-How Operations

II.1. *Through demonstrations.* Although copying another's movements can be a helpful way of learning skills, the motivation to succeed through being like someone else is really a double-edged sword. The more the individual sees happiness as being achieved by emulating someone else, the more he will try to be like the other person. In the process he will tend to overlook the things that make him different from his idol. He will assume an equivalence in their interests, skills, personality, and goals. Since he can never be the other person, he never achieves a sense of accomplishment that he feels really reflects what he could achieve on his own two feet. Especially in a democracy, we seek to preserve the individual's right to his own life. The issue therefore really is: How do we help people incorporate into their own lives the values *we* feel are important? The answer to this is not a simple one. The author takes the stand that society has the responsibility of providing young people with many samples of roles to examine and try. It must then provide a setting in which each person can examine how the parts of each role will be consistent with his unique abilities and goals. The group, with its different members and opportunities for trial behavior, is particularly suited for this job.

II.2. *Use of resource persons and teaching aids.* The use of resource people and materials is closely tied to the meaningfulness of these sources of help to the goals of the group. The resource person who comes in to tell others what they should be doing will be useful only to the extent that he is supplying information that the group needs, wants, and is ready to use. The fundamental concept here is the difference between *information* and *advice*. Although many people ask for advice as one way of avoiding responsibility ("He told me to do it, it wasn't really my idea"), advice rarely works. If the adviser tells people exactly what they want to hear, it is experienced as reassuring. At the same time, people react with the feeling that they already knew the answer and that the resource person has added nothing. If, however, the adviser suggests ideas that clients cannot accept, a dilemma arises. In the event that they take advice that they basically cannot go along with, they experience the feeling that they are not very worthwhile people if anyone can persuade them to actions that violate their own beliefs. There is then a resulting decrease in feelings of personal worth and in ability to be responsible for their own behavior. On the other hand, if the group decides to ignore the advice of the resource person it is difficult for them to seek his help again, since by their actions they have demonstrated a lack of faith in the correctness of his advice.

Information, as contrasted from advice, then, is provided only when the people seeking a solution which clarifies their problem see need for knowing alternative ways to reach their goal and are willing to accept responsibility both for implementing their decisions and for accepting the fruits of their action.

The timing, then, when information is sought by the group, is vitally dependent on what has preceded their request and on their security in accepting responsibility for their behavior. Information volunteered before a group perceives a need for it actually works as advice, since it implies the direction in which the adviser thinks they ought to be going and his feeling that they ought to be ready to accept responsibility.

II.3. *Exploring alternative methods or ways to solve the problem.* Our security in feeling able to cope with our environment certainly is a function of the range of techniques we have learned to use in coping with a variety of situations. We facilitate security and growth of the individual when we provide both a secure setting and opportunity for trial behavior. In this type of group setting the client can dare to experiment with new methods since the price of failure is not the same as that which society imposes.

An example here might be helpful: Little Billy Smith comes home from school crying. He has been beaten up by another youngster. We could solve (?) the problem by taking action against the other child, but Billy will not have learned how he can cope with the next bully. He will have learned that if you go to someone else he will solve your problem for you. Suppose, as an alternative solution, that Billy had discussed this with the coach, and that the coach had offered to teach Billy to use judo. Let's imagine that Billy receives one lesson, and on his way home he again meets the bully. How will he fight? The way he did in the past. He will use his judo lessons only when he feels he can get results that are equal to or better than what he already knew. Incidentally, Billy was willing to try to develop his skills with the coach because he knew that while he was learning the coach would not hurt him. In his lessons he could make mistakes without suffering irreparable damage. The role of the school or therapeutic group is to offer the same opportunities to make mistakes without irreparable damage to the person.

Also involved in this area is the concept of failure. Typically, failure has come to mean that the person has not measured up to a preconceived standard. This is but one way of looking at the inability to achieve beyond a certain point. A more helpful way is to conceive of the point of failure as a concrete measure of all the person has achieved to that point. For example, how can a person discover how high he is able to jump? He keeps raising the cross bar until he reaches the point where he can no longer clear it. This point of failure is both the measure of how high he *can* jump and a concrete point against which to compare his hoped-for goal. Too often in our competitive society, we spend so much time in measuring the distance between where we are and where we feel we must go, that we lose sight of what we have already accomplished. If our goal in society is to help people feel a sense of personal worth, at some point they need to be helped to examine where they are, where they have been, and where they feel they need to go. It is in helping a person reconcile what he is and the bases he has used to decide where he must go that we are simultaneously providing motivation for learning and are improving his mental health.

Actually, in a true learning situation the goal of the people or person providing help is to help the individual discover which personal tools he possesses which he can use to solve problems. The ultimate goal of any therapeutic situation is *not* the resolution of the problem. Rather it is an attempt to teach problem-solving techniques.

Security-Giving Operations

III.1. *Meeting the need for belonging.* It has been said that all of us determine our personal worth through the eyes of others. Essentially we recognize that since each person wants to feel worthwhile, to the degree that we share things in common, we are sure of mutual acceptance. The fly in the ointment is, however, that while we can achieve acceptance by being a carbon copy of the stereotype, this role does not enable us to be recognized as a unique person. This need for group acceptance is strongest in the adolescent. Picture the typical high school girl of our day dressed in the uniform of the day. It may be leotards, bobby socks, or whatever the group has decided. Suppose this young lady should overhear two boys trying to decide whom to take to a dance. "I don't see what the problem is, Tom, these gals spend so much time together you can't tell one from the other." Young Miss walks away in confusion. What does she have to do and be, not to be considered a square? How different does she dare let herself be without risking group rejection as a queer? Although the example chosen was that of an adolescent, these questions are common to people at all age levels. What are the limits of our society? How can we meet our needs within these limits? And for the mature adult there is added the more difficult question; how can we help others see that the status quo needs changing without losing our group membership?

III.2. *Meeting the need for achievement and personal growth.* One way we prove to ourselves that we are worthwhile is by examining our day-to-day accomplishments. If we keep repeating what we could do yesterday, the glow of accomplishment fades. Personal growth involves a constant reassessment of the reality of the new goals we are setting up for tomorrow. Since we do not achieve in a vacuum, part and parcel of this assessment process is the support we get from the reactions of others. One of the rather unique characteristics of the group setting is that, as we observe other people solve problems and grow, it gives us courage to try to solve problems ourselves. Part of it might be caused by the feeling that if the other person, whom we feel is weaker, can achieve—we can, too. Along with this is the support that comes from knowing that other people are facing similar problems and that we are not alone.

III.3. *The need for economic security.* Although a group does not meet this specific need it can be very helpful in assisting the person in sharpening his skills in achieving economic self-sufficiency. Job security in our society involves more than just having needed skills. One of the major reasons people lose jobs is their inability to get along with fellow workers and to accept responsibility. Job security rests also on the degree to which the job gratifies basic needs. For some, job satisfaction depends purely on the money they earn. This is not only a status symbol but also a means to gratify needs that cannot be met through their jobs. For other people, the conditions under which they work are more vital. A group can be helpful in assisting a person in defining what he seeks from a job so he can decide if the job he wants will meet these needs. For many, the group can provide a setting in which to practice job-getting or interpersonal skills. The group frequently can help a person think through more effective ways of solving problems on the job. Not least of all, it can help a person examine what he needs in the way of economic security to meet his present needs for effective living in his society.

III.4. *The need to be free from fear.* Although the group can, within its own limits, set up rules that will protect the individual from physical and other threats, there is a real question as to whether freedom from fear itself is a good thing. Fear can be a motivating force to solve a problem. It can also be the basis for avoiding situations which realistically are dangerous and beyond the control of an individual. Rather than freedom from fear there ought to be substituted the ability to face fear. For example, many of us are aware of the fact that any day some trigger-happy person could fire a bomb that might precipitate the end of the world as we know it. This is a very real possibility. There are many things an individual can do to attempt to modify society so that this no longer will be possible. Immediate solutions are not likely. Living in daily fear could make a person unable to do even those small things which on a combined group basis might solve the problem. In other words, at some point we need to help people live in a society where security and the absence of fear can become a possibility. We need to build up individual security that comes from knowing that each person has used the full extent of his capacity. No more can be demanded of any man.

III.5. *The need for love and affection.* Raths has described this as showing others you are hurt when they are hurt. There is a real question if this is a helpful thing. To the extent that you are truly hurt each time another suffers, the trials and tribulations of the world can soon overwhelm you. As an alternative, the development of an empathic attitude might be considered. Instead of sympathizing and identifying with each pain of the other person, you attempt to let him know that you understand how he feels and that you want to help. In your own mind you recognize that *he* is feeling the pain, not you. Unless you are free of the pain, you cannot be objective enough to help him to look at his feelings. When the counselor identifies with his client, we have two clients instead of one. This augments the problem rather than lessens it.

There are many kinds of love. Many of you are familiar with what has been termed "sMother Love," or the possessive kind of attention that robs the person of his rights and personality. All of us tend to be suspicious of other people. A rather frequent question is "Why are you being so nice to me?" People basically recognize that all behavior is motivated by some need of the individual. Understanding the needs the "loving" person is trying to meet helps the recipient decide if this is helping or hindering his own desires. The more honestly we express our motivations for being concerned about others, the more secure both they and we will feel. In the group this problem is somewhat simplified. Very quickly groups come to realize that they will sink or swim together. The growing awareness of how interdependent they are on each other makes very clear that from what may appear as a selfish basis, each person wants the others well and happy so that the other people can meet his needs, which they couldn't do if their abilities were impaired.

Feeling important to others in and of itself demonstrates your value. The security of love works two ways. It proves that there are others who care while at the same time increasing your esteem in your own eyes.

III.6. *The need to be free from guilt.* Feelings of guilt can so immobilize a person that any positive action is impossible. Guilt feelings can be alleviated in several ways. One common method is for an authority to remove guilt by providing punishment that will pay for the action that is causing guilt feelings. A common example of this is the little boy who confesses to misbehavior and feels relief when he is spanked, since he then considers the score has been settled. A group sometimes acts this way, but generally they do not want to sit in judgment. In the group setting there is a more effective method to deal with guilt feelings. As members of the group feel able to share their feelings with each other, they frequently discover that they are not alone in their perceived misbehavior or guilty thoughts. Part of the weight of guilt feelings comes from the sense of being different in one's behavior or problems. Each person feels alone. As he discovers that others face the same situation, although his feelings haven't changed, each person feels better able to cope with his problem. Realizing that others have faced and solved the problem gives support. Knowing that there are others with whom you can feel free to discuss the situation also is a source of security. You are free to talk with them because you feel they are no better than you, and you do not lose group acceptance by admitting your feelings.

III.7. *The need for acceptance of the other person.* A group soon learns that each person in his turn will ask questions that are very naive in the eyes of others. Accepting the "naive" person's need for information and his right to use the group to clarify his own thinking causes the group members to examine questions, not in terms of their sophistication, but rather in terms of what it means to the person who is asking.

III.8. *Ways of controlling conflict situations.* Groups develop a sixth sense in judging when a group member is being pressed beyond his ability to cope with the situation. Since taking a problem out of someone else's hands implies a lack of faith in their capacity to handle the problem, group members hesitate to take overt action. Rather than have the person retreat from danger, or remove the danger, group members provide support to the person under attack so that he has additional strength to face the situation. It is not uncommon for the group to take overt action toward a member who seems to be unfairly treating another. Learning that the way that he treats other group members will affect how the rest of the group will treat him causes each person to carefully consider his effect on others.

These are a few of the characteristics that Raths covers in his article. Although there are many other aspects of teaching, those presented here should demonstrate the communal focus of teaching and therapy.

Discussion

In the chapter which will follow, the reader will have an opportunity to get the feel of a group in action. To get the most out of
the protocol and the marginal comments, it would be wise for the
newcomers to the field of counseling to do some outside reading to
improve both their technical skills and their depth of understanding.

To gain insight into the counseling process, texts by Arbuckle,[5]
Porter,[6] Tyler,[7] Thorne,[8] and Rogers[9] are recommended reading.

The books mentioned above plus Wittenberg's[10] *So You Want to
Help People* will describe the nature of the helping relationship.
These books also will help in preparing the student to identify differ-
ent techniques.

Implicit in the description of the teaching operations is the question of the role of the group leader. Questions of identification of
members with the leader certainly carry overtones of the problems
associated with the transference relationship. Although the nature
of the leader's role will be covered in detail later, reading material
on transference now will enable the reader to have a more fundamental conception of the variety of relationships that occur simultaneously in the group. The term transference covers feeling and
behavior directed toward another person which may be due to the
effects of earlier experiences. Specifically, the chapters dealing with
transference and countertransference in Patterson's[11] text will provide
a summary of the literature in this area and a résumé of the issues
involved.

Although I have not always agreed with the categories suggested
by Raths as appropriate to the teaching process, basically I hope that
this chapter provided the last needed bridge to demonstrate the essential similarity in the various aspects of the helping process.

BIBLIOGRAPHY

1. Thelen, Herbert A. *Education and the Human Quest*, Ch. 3. New York:
Harper, 1960.
2. Bordin, Edward. *Psychological Counseling* (chapters dealing with concept
of the role of ambiguity in counseling). New York: Appleton-Century-
Crofts, 1950.
3. Raths, Louis. "What Is Teaching?" *Sociatry*, II, No. 3, 4, 197–206, 1948.
4. Thelen, Herbert A., *Education and the Human Quest*, Ch. 4, p. 71. New
York: Harper, 1960.

5. Arbuckle, Dugald. *Teacher Counseling.* Reading: Addison-Wesley, 1950.

6. Porter, E. H. *An Introduction to Therapeutic Counseling.* Boston: Houghton Mifflin, 1950.

7. Tyler, Leona. *The Work of the Counselor.* New York: Appleton-Century-Crofts, 1953.

8. Thorne, Frederick. *Principles of Personality Counseling.* Brandon, Vermont: *Journal of Clinical Psychology,* 1951.

9. Rogers, Carl. *Client-Centered Therapy.* Boston: Houghton Mifflin, 1951.

10. Wittenberg, R. M. *So You Want to Help People.* New York: Association Press, 1947.

11. Patterson, Cecil. *Counseling and Psychotherapy: Theory and Practice,* chapter 9, "Transference and Countertransference." New York: Harper, 1959.

4

A Group in Action

In any training program there are several ways of helping the participants become involved on a more intelligent basis. The whole area of group process is so involved that it appears helpful to give the reader the feel of what a group sounds and acts like.

For our purpose, it does not matter why the group convenes or how logical or rapid their deliberations are. The skilled group leader learns to go below the surface chatter to see the ever-present needs of each individual. At the first session he will expect to structure his role and to have the group test him out. One measure of the leader's sophistication is his ability to see the interplay among members in the group setting as they try to meet their needs.

This chapter is a transcription of an actual demonstration presented at the American Personnel and Guidance Association Convention in April 1955. This group, although artificially assembled for demonstration purposes, goes through many of the typical growth pains of any new group trying to jell. In addition, the group raises issues and problems that form the basis for the major portion of this book. To assist the reader, the actual protocol is on the left-hand side of the page. To the right are comments on process, pinpointing of issues, and discussion of controversial issues raised. The material that follows is taken from a tape recording and has been edited for greater ease of reading.

One of the problems that we will be facing here today, as you may very well guess, is that if we are to be able to try to have some fun, and at the same time relax, we have to make this as natural as we possibly can. We have our mikes down on the table and although people will try to talk to each other so that you can hear us, if we're not talking loud enough, I'm afraid that the responsibility will have to be yours to move up. Our ability to try to do what we are attempting depends upon our relaxing, and believe me, we're pretty anxious right now. Let me try to describe to you what we think we are doing, and then maybe, when we get into the discussion section you can help us know if we achieved our objective.

Some of you have been at sessions recently where we've been talking about counselor training, and how counselors find their own values get in the way of doing the things that are important. We have also discussed how counselors use different techniques to avoid facing clients. At the U. of I. we have felt very strongly that we must spend considerable time during counselor training in helping the person who is to be the counselor get a chance to see what some of his needs are, and to begin to understand what it feels like to be in the roles which he will be holding later on. When the trainees have clients, their ability to empathize will partially depend upon their understanding of what it feels like to be in the client's role. We believe that the way you learn group techniques is not by hearing about them, through lectures or in books, but by seeing what it feels like right down here. Our course is, therefore, structured in the following way. When the students arrive at the very beginning of the course they are greeted by my smiling face, welcoming them. The class is limited to 12 people, that's a luxury that I know many of you cannot afford. But this makes a very real difference in what we can hope to accomplish.

The group is told that the purpose of the course is to help them learn how to work with groups, what they want to do in groups, and what it feels like to be in a group. They are also told that the contents of the course and the way the group will achieve its goal is left completely for the group to work out, with whatever help from me they want to have. The net result is, as we will try to help you see, a relationship which becomes fairly informal and also one where we begin to look at each other as people and begin to tie in some of our experiences that are quite beyond the classroom.

The people seated around this table were all students in courses in group guidance.

Now I'd like to go around the table and let you know who we've got here—some of these folks are looking for jobs, so I surely want you to know who they are—starting to my left is Elizabeth Mullins. She is a director and counselor trainer at Indiana University in the Residence Halls. Across from me is Mary Ann Pelican; it's kind of hard describing what her job is. She works for the Chicago Council on Foreign Relationships. She was trying to describe her job to me before. She said when people come from other countries, she takes them around and shows them the Wrigley Building. (*Laughter.*) Mary Ann is also a person who has had considerable training in counseling, and she'll be glad to talk to any of you afterwards, since she is interested in a new job. (*Laughter.*)

Curt Stafford is at the U. of I. as a research assistant, working at the Office of Teacher Placement in charge of the follow-up studies where we attempt to see how effective we've been in helping people in our Teacher-Training program. Bill Lewis is a counseling psychologist working at the Danville V. A. Hospital, while he is completing his work on his doctorate at the University of Illinois. Dorothy Farris has got some interesting things going on, and I hope she shares some of them with us. She's the YWCA program director in Alton, Illinois.

Bill Carlson is a teacher and counselor working with junior high and high school students at Weldon, Illinois. Louise Sharpe, Dean of Women at Central Michigan State Teachers College, is our recorder for today. She will have a rough time because this won't go according to protocol.* Dominick Mazzitelli formerly was a psychologist at Manteno State Hospital. He now is on the campus at the U. of I. While he is taking his work there, he is working as a counselor in the Elementary Education Teacher Training Program. Last of all, Rita Newton, whose field is Art Education. So as you see, we've got quite a diversified group.

I might indicate that this is something that we want. Unlike some people who see group therapy as being most effective when you have a homogeneous group, we strive for heterogeneity. If this group is to reflect the world of reality, it ought to contain different people with different needs, interests, and different ways of expressing themselves. If we can learn to communicate among each other in the group, then we've learned something that will be a skill that we can use in other groups where we will have as great a diversity as we have here.

I think at this point I will not say any more—except just to indicate this: that we will try here to have what is rather a typical session for us. How typical it may be of the usual classroom is something we would like to discuss with you later. There is just one other thing I'd like to mention to you: I indicated to you that the goal of the course

---

* Dean Sharpe was assigned by the convention to cover our session. She was not part of the group, although she was seated with them.

is indicated to the students at registration and at the initial class session. There are only two other limits imposed in the course. One is that every session, like this one, is to be tape recorded; after every session students are required to listen to the recording so they can have a chance to hear what went on in the group that they didn't hear, because they were so personally involved. We have one other gimmick. Right after each session the students write logs on their impression of what's been going on in the group. They then have a chance when they listen back to the recording to discover what they failed to perceive in their initial impressions.

Generally, when we listen back to a tape, we do it in a group so that we can all share our perceptions of what's going on. It gives us a chance to compare what one person is seeing and the other is not. At this point I'm just going to leave it to the group to carry on. I might tell you that we did not plan this session before and so have no idea of what's coming up. (To the group)

Comments

1. Where do you want to start?

1. An open-ended question indicating immediately to the group that the responsibility is theirs.

2. CURT: Well, we noticed one thing right off, Walt; as soon as you stood up, way back, you notice how the group kind of quieted down. Boy, they perceive you as an authority figure. Well that's your last chance.

2. Continuing of structuring by group redefining initial leader's role.

3. LIZ: I, uh, I don't like the recorder (pointing to Louise Sharpe) down there at the end of the group.

3–17. Group sets about task of developing security with each other. The presence of a nonparticipating and nonvulnerable observer has to be resolved. The group recognizes that Dean Sharpe's presence has both positive and negative effects. They examine ways to incorporate this person so she will not be a source of threat.

4. DOM: If she was not down there then I'll have to be down there, and I don't like being at the end of the group.

5. CURT: You mean this is something different from what we've had before?

6. LIZ: We've never had a member in the group before that wasn't a part of the group.

7. DEAN SHARPE: Well, the recorder doesn't write legibly, so maybe that will help.

8. WALT: Dorothy. Are you trying to say something?

9. DOROTHY: I was uh, well, when you were talking about the recorder down here, I thought that maybe we could pull her in and make her be a part of us. Or did you mean that you just don't, you don't like anyone writing stuff as we . . .

10. LIZ: Oh no, it's not the writing, 'cause we write ourselves.

11. SHARPE: This is something personal, between you and me. (*Laughter*)

12. DOM: The role, huh?

13. LIZ: I'll see you after class . . .

14. DOM: You leave her here 'cause I need some support on this.

15. BILL L: I think it's the role that she's not comfortable with, not the personality.

16. BILL C: Is it a matter of her being up here with us physically, but not being with us as part of the group?

17. LIZ: That's right.

18. DOM: I have a different idea on this. I think we're going to take out on Dean Sharpe what we would like to take out on the rest of the group watching because we're scared, 'specially the ones behind me. Real paranoid. (*Laughter*) (To Dean Sharpe) So don't take it personally. (*Laughter*)

18. An interpretation of underlying hostility coming from being in a threatening situation. Attempt to help Dean Sharpe see the hostility is not directed toward her, but rather what she represents.

Comments

19. CURT: This is certainly something unique from the way we've been used to functioning in class. We haven't had all these externals to try to get over with. . . . I hope we get over them in a little bit. (*Laughter*)

19. Having faced the underlying feeling, the desire is expressed to move on.

20. MARY ANN: Have you noticed how we are deferring getting started?

20–22. Awareness of the fact that this topic is also serving the purpose of delaying the group from having to face the threats from within the group.

21. BILL: Yeah!

22. CURT: Yeah, we're very much aware of their presence.

23. WALT: We haven't gotten started?

23. Question designed to point up that (20–22) are really subterfuges since they, too, are part and parcel of the steps a group goes through to achieve security.

24. LIZ: We've started, but we're ahead of ourselves. (*Laughter*)

24–26. Another reflection of the underlying anxiety and tension.

25. BILL L: All this laughing shows some tension.

26. DOM: That's an understatement!

27. MARY ANN: (*Jumble of voices*) We got started awfully quickly for a beginning session. It usually takes us quite some time. I think one of the reasons is that I don't think I could stand much silence with so many people around, where I would be comfortable with about 30 seconds of silence in the classroom. No more than 30 seconds.

27. After recognizing feeling, group is again able to examine reasons for tension. Definition of how silence in this context is a source of threat.

28. WALT: Then it's not only the person who is using writing differently, but also silence has taken on a different meaning for us in *this* group.

28. Reflection of two feelings recognized as sources of threat.

29. MARY ANN: The thing is that I've often found silence to be

29–34. With acceptance of feeling, they move on to see

a very comfortable thing . . .
and here, all of a sudden, it
scares me to death!

what these feelings really
represent.

30. BILL C: I wonder if we had
only the people at the table we
could comfortably be silent, but
we feel some other pressures.

31. BILL L: Well, we're supposed
to be up here to show something, to prove something, and
we feel that the silence won't
prove anything.

32. RITA: In radio the worst crime
is over 5 seconds of silence.

33. DOROTHY: Yeah, and we also
realize that we won't have too
much time to do it in, so we try
to make the best use of the time
that we do have.

34. MARY ANN: I feel a terrific pressure to perform . . . and say
something.

35. CURT: And we've all gone
through the experience in the
actual class setting. You can't
hurry the thing along. That's
what really makes it bad.

35. Recognition of the limits
of time along with an ac-
ceptance of limits of hu-
man abilities.

36. WALT: Sort of a conflict for us.
On the one hand we see that we
can't speed it up . . . and yet
we feel that we've got to put
across a point.

36. Reflects ambivalent needs
that are in conflict.

37. DOM: What are we trying to
put across? We're trying to
condense in a half hour the experiences we've felt, and I believe it's very close to all of us,
a whole term's work or a whole
year's work in a half hour and
show these people that we've
got something *good* here! How
can we do this in a half hour?
I feel defeated before I start.

37–38. Sees a need to define problem prior to an attempt at
resolution.

38. LIZ: Dom, that's a big problem
I've run into in my work . . . I
want to convince them that
here's something good . . . and
words can't describe it. You al-

most have to go through the session to do it, but if you have to go to Illinois and take this course to start using it, it's not going to go very far, very fast.

39. LIZ: It's a frustrating situation!

39. Reflects tension and frustration in problem solving.

40. DOM: Yeah, this is something similar to this meeting I was sitting in on yesterday . . . where we were talking about something, and the thing that they seemed to be talking about was: how do you convey, or how do you describe, how do you *tell* a person about what he feels in a client-counselor relationship? No one seemed to know how to say it. This is the problem we have now, how do we show what we're feeling? How could we describe this? How can we tell them that when we were in this particular class—and I'm using this because there was security there—how can we tell them that this was a good thing? You just don't describe it . . . the words that we use, I forgot the topics we talked about, except the sex life of the Eskimo. (*Laughter*)

40. Sees problem as difficulty in communication of personal feelings, along with a recognition that the content of the words used may be very foreign to the feelings they are communicating.

41. MARY ANN: That was a good discussion!

41–44. Awareness that content cannot serve as easily as feelings as a basis for providing a common denominator. Also present is the right of the individual to help the group see the effect of its behavior on him.

42. CURT: You're excluding me from the group now. (*Mixed voices*)

43. CURT: How many different classes do we have represented here now?

44. WALT: Yeah, I think that's one point that we might clarify and

that is that the people here were
not all in a group together and
that we have several groups represented. The people at the table
today represent a new group
that has never really worked together. We are going through
some of the growing pains of being a group even at this time.

45. Liz: Wait a minute Walt, hold
on.

45. Leader made the mistake
of trying to speak for the
group without either being
so delegated or being sure
he represented their position.

46. Bill C: I think we are simply
saying that the security we get
can be gotten from the groups
that we were once in, but we
have to get it from the group we
have here.

46–56. Group recognizes need to
find security. Initially
they seek security in past
experiences. From this
grows the recognition that
whatever the basis of past
security, to be really useful it must be used to help
develop a new basis for
security in this new set-
ting.

47. Dom: Until I get it here, I'm
going to use my other group as
a basis. (*Laughter*)

48. Mary Ann: The only thing is,
though, that the support that
we once had . . . for example,
the four of us . . . pardon me,
Walt, the five of us . . .
(*laughter*) and the security that
we had together, can be a basis
to begin reaching out to these
folks that we don't know as well.

49. Bill L: Yeah, but why
can't . . .

50. Liz: If they feel left out, what
then? How do you pull them
in?

51. Dom: What you're saying is that
we should pull them into our
group. Why shouldn't they pull
us into their group?

52. Bill L: Why don't we just
realize this is a different group?

53. Dorothy: Yes!

54. Dom: O.K.

55. BILL C: But it's this group here that we're working with now.

56. DOROTHY: Uh huh.

57. Walt: This is kind of hard for us to face at this time.

    57. Reflection of difficulty in facing present threat rather than past security.

58. BILL C: It's nice to look back, but our problem isn't in looking back . . . it's looking here.

    58. Acceptance of these feelings.

59. DOM: I think one thing we can do, though, although they are different groups . . . there were similar types of experiences in the sense that the structures were similar, and we are trying to understand each other and ourselves through this structure, and I think one of the ways in both groups or the three groups that are represented here, is that we are looking for some kind of support so that we could feel less threatened and talk about ourselves. I think we could start in terms of that. If I know what I'm talking about. (*Laughter*) I'm not sure.

    59. Having faced threat, the group now tries to seek a solution. The idea being confused, the words reflect ambiguity. A good example of an attempt through words to search for the idea.

60. MARY ANN: It's hard to talk. Will you try again?

    60. First overt effort of a group member to provide specific support to another person. Support is offered through acceptance of the feeling plus an offer of continued acceptance.

61. DOM: Yeah, I think that one thing we've experienced, is that when we did get a group going . . . ah . . . we had enough support from each other so that we could deal with problems that we wanted to deal with, that were pressing, whether they were . . . ah . . . manifested in the group. Or . . . ah . . . seemed peculiar to the group, or they were really something we brought in from outside. We had something we wanted

    61. Recognition of effect of group support on enabling a person to think through an idea.

to talk about to somebody. Ah
. . . however, we did this didn't
make any difference to me. I
got a good feeling going . . . I
felt that somebody was understanding what I was saying.

62. CURT: The thing that still bothers me about this, Dom, is the
thing that was brought up a little
earlier, this time pressure. Ah
. . . I'm in the class right now
. . . and uh . . . we've had
something like 12 sessions, 12
2-hour sessions, and just *now*
we're getting around to the point
where we're dealing with some
things that have really been
bothering a lot of people. Well
that's 24 hours of work. Here
we are pushing on this 15 minutes to ½ hour and it still bothers
me.

62. A return to a previous
strong feeling which, at
least for this person has
not been resolved. Group,
however, accepts the right
of the person to return to
an idea he has not worked
out for himself.

63. RITA: But some of it transfers
from one of the 427 (number of
group guidance course) groups
to another, because one of the
people in your group happens
to be the minister at our church;
and he thinks . . . because he
knows I took the course, he's
able to say . . . just one sen-
tence . . . "Rita, we've become
a group!" (*Laughter*)

64. LIZ: You understand what he
means . . .

65. RITA: Yeah, and so he singles
me out to tell this to. So that
in a way, if you were in 427,
there are a lot of things like
that I could say to you, and
I'd know you'd understand.

66. DOM: I have the same experience with one of the girls . . .
this girl in your class now . . .
she looked at me and said she
was taking 427 . . . and I said
"Uh huh" . . . (*laughter*) I
didn't have to say a word.

63–67. The group returns to an
issue which will be a ma-
jor issue for some time.
The question is whether
transfer of experiences to
new situations is possible.
This ability to see the abstract ideas which are common to both old and new
situations is the height of
mature understanding and
learning.

67. DOROTHY: But you know, on the other hand, uh . . . there can also be some people who maybe . . . haven't had 427 . . . that you can be talking about some of these things to, and they, too, can understand. And they can know the thing you're trying to do and even be helpful.

68. MARY ANN: I think the thing that's so hard to in any way demonstrate to people is the kind of relationships we establish with each other, that are so abnormal . . . in the college community, in the graduate school . . .

69. RITA: 427 makes us abnormal? (*Laughter*)

70. MARY ANN: No, I mean the ways we acted toward each other were different in the ways we could talk and feel . . .

71. BILL L: Such an in-group feeling.

72. LIZ: But is this necessarily the result of the college community . . . or can you do this anytime you put a collection of people together in the proper atmosphere and create a group?

73. DOROTHY: We are trying to understand something together.

74. LIZ: That's right, you can do this anywhere, whether it's on a college campus or (*group adds names of other settings*).

75. MARY ANN: What I mean though, Liz, let me try to clarify this, is . . . in the business world, or in the academic world, people *don't* act toward each other the way you and I act toward each other in our groups. It's a stripping of a lot of things.

76. DOM: It's a real different structure.

77. MARY ANN: That we carry around all the time.

68–69. Beginning of acceptance of underlying sex components of feelings and the difference between the appropriateness of expressing these feelings in different settings.

70–77. An exploration of the limits and relationships which distinguish this type of group from others.

78. DOM: When we walk into an ordinary classroom we usually have someone standing up at the front of the room. We don't look at each other, but we look at someone standing there who is going to give.

79. CURT: Even if it isn't this situation, Dom, even if you've got a group sitting around a circle in the classroom, you don't necessarily have the kind of thing we have here. You're not baring your soul to your neighbor, necessarily.

80. MARY ANN: Let me throw this in, if I may, if it means anything. I was talking to an advertising executive the other day. He was . . . Oh, all interested in this kind of attitude . . . and he said, "Well, of *course* we have people seated around in a circle!" As if this was the thing that made for the kind of attitude to relate one person to the other. You can set up the vehicle but . . .

81. LIZ: You mean the physical setup without the feeling?

82. MARY ANN: He was still "Boss," and people were still cautious about what they were saying.

83. LIZ: Are you saying that what we've got here is an unreal situation, as far as reality goes, with the barriers down and security present?

84. MARY ANN: It's real, very much real.

85. LIZ: For us . . . but I mean . . . take it up to the Wrigley Building, if you will. (*Laughter*) Then what you get from the group we can carry with us, but you can't go up there and have the same thing talking to "Joe Blow" in the advertising game.

78–85. Examination of differences between past group experiences and present. Group looks at physical organization, role of initial status leader, security needs, and problems of communication.

86. DOM: Oh let me get a word in. (*Laughter*)

86. Upset, needs to verbalize his feelings.

87. WALT: You're real upset about this.

87. Acceptance of feelings as reflected in his behavior rather than words.

88. DOM: Ah . . . ah . . . what I hear you saying is that first of all we had a completely different structure. One of the things that's very important is that when you're not set for this kind of structure, it's hard to see it. How long did it take us to realize what this guy's role was? (*Pointing to Walt Lifton*)

88. As before with Dom, idea presented by person who provided help is incorporated in Dom's thinking. Specifically he focuses on the differences in perception that are gained through words versus behavior. Emphasis is on importance of behavior.

89. MARY ANN: A long time.

90. DOM: He told us point-blank we could take care of the marks, the grades, important. Every class we go for grades. They go up to the Teacher Placement Office and they are on our records, and if we're looking for jobs someone's going to look at them. We think. Sometimes they don't. How long did it take us to work out the idea that he wasn't suddenly going to snatch away this function that he was handing us, and leave us high and dry?

91. MARY ANN: What I'm *trying* to say is that in a normal situation in business or somewhere else people don't have the security to do the things that we do here.

91. Recognition that ability to perceive is a function of perceptual defense. Concept of perceptual defense (you see what you can stand seeing) with increased security people see more of the world around them.

92. BILL L: That's right. It takes so long to get the feeling for the group. . . . Like we were talking about "we've got a group now." It took how many weeks to understand what it meant? Whereas, in the business world if things don't go like that (*snapping his fingers*) or in the class-

92. Again a repeat of an earlier theme of the inability of society to recognize the realities of both time and human ability.

room if things don't move right
along, well generally the instructor or the students are so insecure they can't stand it.

93. Liz: Didn't we become a group
after we hit the wall, and when
we hit it and fell, they picked
us back up and that's when we
became a group?

93. This comment points up
the fact that the height of
group security is achieved
when the person falls in
his own eyes, yet contin-
ues to be accepted by others. It is the beginning of
the feeling that they are
accepted as people, not
just because of their ideas
or behavior.

94. Dom: I still have the scars.

95. Dorothy: Mary Ann: are you
really trying to say that in groups
outside of this class this thing
can't happen?

95–100. Recapitulation of trans-
ferability concept now
combined with the role
security plays in under-
standing.

96. Mary Ann: No, I don't mean
that at all . . .

97. Rita: No, but you can't expect
it.   Sometimes you leave the
classroom with a sense of ex-
pectancy.   I would leave 427
and dash down to a very small
seminar group, and we all sat
around a table just the same size
and boy did I get into trouble
day after day!

98. Mary Ann: What I mean is this
. . . I'm not saying it's not possible; as a matter of fact it would
be fine if it were able to be put
into use.   I'm saying that people, in business or somewhere
else, can't say kind or nasty
things to each other, without
having a reaction that is negative.   Here we can do both of
those things.

99. Liz: Well, isn't that why you
created this kind of group for
teaching purposes?

100. Bill L: Well, it really doesn't
become a group until the anxiety gets so high about this sort

of thing and then there has to be the cohesiveness.

101. WALT: You mean we became a group because we were so afraid of something else?

102. BILL L: We were so threatened if nothing was going on, we'd have to get together.

103. DOM: I think what we're saying here . . .

104. LIZ: Dom!

105. DOM: Wait a minute Liz— (*laughter*). I think what we're saying here is that people are not used to perceiving each other this way or reacting to each other this way and what it takes is a complete reorientation. Ordinarily, when anyone walks into a classroom, he's set, he's been trained, I remember when I sat in elementary school, this way, (*showed his hands clasped in front of him*) everytime the teacher walked down the aisle, it was hard for me to *un*seat myself this way . . . and . . . outside of groups that are planned this way . . . it's a difficult thing to set up. It takes time for people to realize and to become comfortable. They're comfortable in a role where someone gets up and tells them something. They're used to this, and it's very threatening to take on the responsibility of a group member and to be responsible for the other person sitting on the other side of the desk or the chair . . . desk or the chair, I'm confused! (*Laughter*) . . . The table, I'll get to it Liz. Ah . . . it takes a lot of time to take on this responsibility of somebody else's needs and to say if I'm going to get my own

101. Reflection that group is perceived as a means of dealing with threat.

103–105. Resurgence of former relationship where these two people competed for leadership. Although Dom cuts Liz off, he indicates his awareness of what he has done, and his feelings of responsibility to her.

needs satisfied, I'm going to have to help someone else! We just don't work that way ordinarily . . . it's hard to shift!

106. MARY ANN: But . . .

107. RITA: Wait! Liz, you had one oar in, this is the supreme sacrifice for me. (*Laughter*)

108. LIZ: I know! The thing that threw me now was when people use the word "group" they generally mean something entirely different from what we have here. And the same word being used on two things, and the only way I could differentiate was the way I felt in the two places, and this I couldn't explain. It was terrible.

109. CURT: This is what I was wondering about your group, Mary Ann, are you thinking of a group as setting out to do something . . . say get a certain job lined up in business?

110. MARY ANN: Well . . . I . . . certainly . . . people aren't going to group around nothing but, still, does that mean that there doesn't have to be some sort of relationship established?

111. WALT: There's something here that bothers me, as it must. Are you saying that when we are related on a feeling level, we got no tasks done?

112. MARY ANN: Thank you.

113. CURT: No, there's a difference between going specifically at a task as, say, the stereotype which I have, in which you might be doing something in business, as opposed to the way we approach it here.

114. LIZ: I think we ought to let Rita come in with what she has . . .

107–108. Very interesting by-play. Rita is indicating to the group not only how she has changed but is also demonstrating how "time" —time to talk or think— is now seen as "giving" rather than just submission. Liz is re-raising problems of semantics and communication.

109–111. Exploration of concept that goals of groups whether they be work or "people" oriented would effect group relationships. Raises the basic philosophical issue as to the reason for the existence of groups. As a means toward an end or as an end in itself.

112. Support obtained through identification.

114. Having been helped Liz now wants to help Rita use the group, too.

115. RITA: You know, this is a real change for me from last year. And it operated back in New York two weeks ago when I gave up the floor in the midst of twenty-five people, when I'd been trying to get in all morning! Ah . . . now I forgot what I was going to say! (*Laughter*).

116. CURT: You lose your thought when you wait.

116. Support through reflection of feeling while also indicating an interest in what she is trying to say.

117. RITA: If you've got the ability to structure this kind of thing in other groups, it can be done in other groups. It doesn't have to be a counseling department of a college for it to work. It can work in other groups, but it has to be planned for, and worked for, and wanted. The limits have to be set; it has to be explained. I lived with a minister for awhile, two years ago; this always floors people! She was a *girl* minister. (*Laughter*) . . . and she had a youth group, and it was in a church that was fairly authoritarian about its other relationships . . . at least didn't have this kind of orientation, and she was able to set up a group, of people which included me . . . and it was a church with which I had very little sympathy for. She included me as sort of "Devil's Advocate," and I got the warmest, most wonderful, secure feeling from that group! And they were people whose ideas I ordinarily could not tolerate.

117. People can be accepted for themselves not just their beliefs.

118. MARY ANN: I wanted to tell an experience. I didn't think I'd get a chance to say anything beyond the Wrigley

118. Mary Ann returns to her attempt to reconcile work groups and therapeutic groups.

Building. We designed study groups to work in different geographical and political areas. My pride and joy is the Latin American group, who wanted to study like crazy for weeks. We started in September. We are just getting to the point now, when one of the ladies in particular, who is only there not to learn about Latin America, but to have some *friends,* is making her friends. The group leader is just becoming aware of this. We've begun doing work, and we're learning about *Latin America.* She's not worrying about her friends anymore, 'cause she has them. She's gotten away from all this other junk, which is no longer important.   And . . . what I'm saying is . . . it took me from September to April to get this idea across. 'Cause this was a man who's in the insurance business who *told people what to do!* (*Laughter*) And no one seemed to realize . . .

119. Dom: You know, the funniest thing just happened . . . I didn't hear a word you said. I was just so pleased to hear your voice again. (*Laughter*)

119. Indicates support from relationships and strong feelings of affection that develop in groups. It was remarks like these that caused some members of the audience to be concerned about the possibility that group members would "act out" their needs with each other, in out-of-group sessions. Briefly, this problem was faced by the group in class and techniques developed to deal with it. Actually it has never represented a problem since basically a respect for the other person's need led group mem-

bers to be very careful about the effect of their behavior on others. Dom's comment also demonstrates that the relationships are effected by more than just the words used. Mannerisms and physical gestures became a language in themselves.

120. MARY ANN: You see this is what you can't explain to people.

121. LIZ: Aren't we trying to describe what exists here that doesn't exist many places, a climate that permits you to use this kind of group in any way you want to?

122. MARY ANN: Yes.

123. LIZ: We can use it to learn group dynamics, or counseling, or "basket weaving," or . . .

124. DOROTHY: (*Jumble of voices*) That we can take it out into groups that possibly are in situations or places where people have never heard of this type of thing before, and apply some of the principles that ah . . . that we have gained, that we have experienced eh . . . as you were talking a little while ago Dom . . . we actually experience these things in this group. Well, all right, we've experienced them, so we can go out in situations and . . . begin making these things *work*.

125. CURT: That was what was getting me. You were mentioning things like "basket weaving," and I got to thinking of that, and I didn't hear all of what you said Dorothy, so I had to pick up the tail end. It's more than what you learn about

125. Picks up idea of learning problem solving rather than the solution in a specific situation.

Comments

Latin America. It's well, "here's me," "here's how I function," "I'm learning some new things about how I function." "It gives me this greater freedom."

126. RITA: Here's something I thought about when you were saying "Go forth and do likewise." The thing I found in my sort of work was that I *couldn't* go forth and do likewise. And I'm still not capable of working with my Art Ed classes in the way that this group works . . . but I'm a different person, so I'm working differently with the classes.

126. Understanding the concept frees the person to express his idea in his own way.

127. CURT: Are you different, Rita, or are you seeing yourself differently?

128. RITA: Oh well, let's not go into that!

129. BILL C: Are we saying that we can't possibly jump from what we have in the security of a group like this immediately to other groups, but that we have to work for some kind of security with them? Sometimes we have to start quite a ways down the "totem pole" to work on up towards the top.

130. BILL L: It seems like you're expecting too *much*, if you're expecting every group to have this sort of feeling about it.

131. LIZ: It takes a long time to get it, but I think the big problem, at least I found it was going as a member of this group to a leader of another group. The thing that made us a group actually was getting rid of Walt as a leader and pulling him in as a member.

132. DOM: It's an interesting thing we are saying . . . how do

129–132. Here we have one of the major problems in a democracy. Having solved a problem once, it's hard to accept that each new group demands the right to develop in its own way, even if it involves making mistakes others have made before them. This is the eternal cry of the adolescent who resents parental domination and wants the right to shape his own life. As the group matures they are better able to use other's past experience as a basis for making their decisions. They cannot accept this information until they feel sure they are secure enough to not let the data itself guide them in directions they may not wish to go.

we tell people about this? Do
we go in as a leader and try to
describe this and yet when we
came into the group and Walt
described it to us, I thought
he was talking Chinese! The
conclusion I come to is wherever the specific places that we
want to initiate this type of
relationship, and you can't do
it everywhere . . . it's not the
panacea for relationships, it's
specific. . . . The only way
we can do it is by going out
and living it, because you can't
do it just by saying it. You
have to go out and instead of
explaining it, just like we didn't
understand it, how do we expect them to understand it?
It's a feeling, thing, it's a . . .

133. LIZ: A big problem I ran into
was . . . here I'm accustomed
to saying what I'm feeling.
You've clobbered me back
down whenever I've gone too
high, and I have . . . and I
got into a group this year that
when I *did* it, I scared some
of the people and they backed
away. And it really frustrated
me because I wanted to say
what I was feeling, but if I
did it, I destroyed what grouping they had to begin with.

133. Just expressing feelings
isn't enough. The setting
where it is done, and the
way it is done both will
effect a person's relationship to a group.

134. BILL C: The group didn't have
enough security to accept what
you were doing.

135. MARY ANN: For the first time
I found out the tricky problem
Walt probably had, because
first of all, here I am . . . I
am the leader, and there were
people there that were 30 years
my senior! And yet they referred to me as an authority
figure, and this isn't what I
wanted! And then, I tried to
"group it up" and be a member

135–136. Being a leader may put
you in a conflict situation
where what you want to
be does not always coin-
cide with a group's per-
ception of your role. It's
not comfortable to be misperceived.

(*laughter*) . . . and I felt rejected and I drove home with my "tail between my legs" feeling "nobody likes me!" (*Laughter*) You suddenly have to try to find out where you *do* fit in this group.

136. Liz: I think part of the problem is, we expect the other members of the group to perceive what we're doing, and to see what we're doing as we are just expressing ourselves. They take the common, ordinary way of perceiving it. "They're directing this at me personally."

137. Bill L: Well, one of the big things that Mary Ann was talking about, seems to me, is that when you're taking the course, it's not until we're really *into* the course that we really understand. We get real threatened in the middle, and that's probably what's happened to you . . . now . . . you're right in the middle of it and it's pretty hard.

137–143. Part of the group process includes periods of threat. The group can face the threat only as they provide support to one another. During threat people regress to a more dependent kind of role.

138. Liz: But we held together so we could get to the end.

139. Mary Ann: Yeah!

140. Bill L: Yeah.

141. Liz: Sometimes they collapse around you when the first threatening occurs. And then they escape into an authoritarian setup.

142. Mary Ann: That's what they did.

143. Liz: That's exactly what they escape into . . . because it holds security for them.

144. Bill L: Well, Mary Ann's going to have to have a pat on the back once in awhile. (*Laughter*)

144–147. Until the group develops an acceptance of the leader, he needs a basic personal security to accept

145. MARY ANN: Who's gonna give *me* security?

146. LIZ: You're kind of by yourself on it because you're the only one that's there!

147. WALT: Aren't we saying that a part of the problem of the leader's role is to help the group cope with him and give him the support to do the role that he wants to have?

the hostility and rejection he may experience. Leader's role may be to help group learn how to deal with the leader.

148. DOROTHY: Yeah.

149. MARY ANN: Uh huh.

150. LIZ: That's the problem we keep having trouble with.

151. MARY ANN: Now the point is, how are we going to implement this? Solve my problem please! (*Laughter*) I can't stand another one of these Latin American sessions. (*Laughter*)

152. RITA: Well, you'd have to solve mine, too.

153. LIZ: Mine, too.

148–153. In facing this problem group is providing each other support as they identify with each other. Feelings of guilt based on fear of personal inadequacy are alleviated as they are shared.

154. RITA: I have one group that just doesn't want to be a group. (*Laughter*) And uh . . . I am learning how to use myself in a different way from what I used to be. I think 427 didn't teach me how to use myself as a group leader the way 427 used a group leader. I have become a different kind of group leader, and it fits me, and I can do it that way.

154–166. With an acceptance of problem group now is free to examine different ways members could solve problem.

155. BILL L: What . . . what's your concept of a group leader?

156. RITA: In one group I don't . . . this didn't work either and I haven't got any technique for it.

157. LIZ: What's a group leader?

158. BILL L: Look at the way Walt's leading this group. (*Laughter*)

159. LIZ: Yeah . . . but he's not leading it.

160. BILL L: That's what I'm trying to say.

161. RITA: Can you picture me leading a group this way? (*Laughter*)

162. DOM: I think it is a bad comparison because Walt isn't leading this group and . . .

163. BILL L: Well, that's what I mean, she's saying . . .

164. DOM: We have already had other experiences with Walt. We have him sort of controlled in our own minds. (*Laughter*) However we did it, we did it, but Rita is talking about going in with a new group, and I think this is a different situation. I don't know . . .

165. WALT: Are we saying that there is no leadership in this group?

166. BILL L: No.

167. LIZ: No, we're saying no one person holds the role of leadership.

168. BILL L: But . . . apparently . . . it seems to me that she is perceiving it differently.

169. DOM: (*Everybody said no*) Why not . . .

170. LIZ: Because leadership is a quality of the group, and we shift it back and forth as we go. You had it a minute ago; I've got it now. Bill's gonna get it.

171. CURT: I think one thing we can . . . (*Jumble of voices*) (*laughter*)

172. CURT: Uh . . . this business of leadership I think it's been a group leadership on this one point. Now compare our

167–170. Group explores idea that leadership doesn't need to be the prerogative of only one person. Concept that leadership can include verbal passivity is examined.

171. Play on words "who's going to get it" reflects anxiety over hostility expressed by group members when a leadership role is assumed by a person.

172. Facing anxiety, group examines how with less tension their behavior is changing.

group here. We're a first . . .
an initial group here. This is
our first session, and you compare it with the first sessions
you remember from 427
and . . . uh . . . boy! We
went through a period here
where everyone was trying to
get into it so (*gesturing cutting
each other off*). In the beginning it was fast and furi-
ous . . . but we have slowed
down a little now. I am starting to recognize some of you
as I normally know you outside . . . I . . . (*laughter*)
I . . . we're talking a little
more slowly and also we've
moved off . . . uh . . . uh . . .

173. Dom: A good indicator of this
is that we haven't bothered Dr.
Sharpe here. (*Laughter*)

174. Bill L: Let Curt finish.

175. Liz: Yes . . .

176. Mary Ann: Let's let Curt finish.

177. Dom: Well, I . . . if you insist . . . (*Laughter*)

178. Curt: The things we have been
getting into here at the end of
examining these things that
have been happening to us
since then. We have moved
a good bit from the opening.
I . . . I think we've grown.

179. Dom: I see what you're saying,
what you are saying is that we
have reached the level where
people don't bother us as much
as they did, and one of the
indicators is that we didn't
bother Mrs. Sharpe. She's sort
of faded in the background.

180. Mary Ann: I only want to
say one thing . . . uh . . .
and that was what Rita said.
I want to try to figure it out,
if I can . . . uh . . . she was

174–178. Almost because of 170
and 171 group fights to
protect the rights of the
individual.

180–188. Growing awareness that
new roles are possible, and
that new behavior in some
situations is valuable.
Also present is the realiza-

giggling when she said, "Try to imagine me being quiet as Walt has been." Try to imagine *me* being quiet as Walt has been, but I have done it. And it's completely amazed me. I mean . . . under particular circumstances where the only thing you could do was to shut up, you shut up.

181. CURT: You know, we're . . . we're loaded here in one thing. Now . . . looking around at the table. I don't know Dorothy and Bill too well from seeing them in class, but the rest of you I have seen in action. There isn't anyone here who is noted for his silence.

182. BILL L: Well, we can't all be talkers. (*Laughter*) We can't imitate Walt. We have to relate in the way we feel most comfortable.

183. MARY ANN: It depends on what at that point is the thing one must do.

184. LIZ: But . . .

185. BILL L: Uh hum.

186. RITA: Mary Ann, I can do what he does by being quiet, and I can do it by talking, too. I found this out just a few weeks ago. I was leading a group and uh . . . uh . . . I got the same kind of results, I think, in terms of people being able to come out with highly unacceptable opinions in a group that had never seen each other before and never would again.

187. DOROTHY: Are we saying in a sense that. . . .

188. RITA: Uh . . . but I did it by doing more talking than he would do. I did it Newtonian instead of Liftonian, I guess. (*Laughter*)

tion that real growth comes not from identifying with and copying someone else, but in developing one's own way of doing things.

189. Liz: Yes . . . but . . . no . . . there were times in our classes when Walt carried a large verbal part of the 2-hour session.

190. Mary Ann: Yes, but what always happened? He'd get slugged at the end.

191. Curt: Wait, wait, I'll tell you.

192. Dorothy: Just a minute. I . . . I was wanting to say . . .

193. Dom: Bang the table, kids. (*Laughter*)

194. Dorothy: Maybe there are many, many ways of being a group leader.

195. Group: Yes . . . sure.

196. Bill C: For example, uh . . . if we could go on long enough, we might guess that people who had been most aggressive here might find themselves in rather . . . find themselves in certain leader roles . . . that the group would react to. I remember this happening in our own group that uh . . . uh . . . after the group settled down after some of the beginning sessions, and then some of the individuals in the group began . . . began to pick up bumps because Walt . . . the group had . . . well, I guess Walt took it first, didn't you?

197. Walt: Uh huh . . .

198. Bill C: And then . . . then it got passed around to some of the others.

199. Curt: Walt, do you mind if I mention a little bit about . . . about the way you were using the group . . . uh . . . as a member yourself?

200. Walt: Uh huh.

201. Curt: You *would* mind?

202. Walt: No. (*Laughter*)

189–198. Repeat on theme that leadership carries with it possible group hostility and rejection. 196 may be in response to Dom's statement that to be recognized one needs to bang the table. The idea here is that the group has a mellowing effect. It subdues the too aggressive while encouraging the more subdued.

199–202. Reflects concern for concept of confidentiality.

203. CURT: Something that pointed out a lot to us . . . uh . . . Walt's wife has been sick, for those of you who have been away . . . she's been sick for 3–4 weeks in the hospital now and boy! We could . . . we could just see his behavior in class. He wasn't a leader at all. I mean, he was in there. . . . "I've got some problems." Boy, "my home is all shook up and all." I think everyone in the group was aware of this after a very short time. He was . . . he was just using the group to help himself out. And uh . . . this I think, is above all is the thing that . . . oh . . . which destroyed any ideas that anyone may have had that he was still an authority. He was just using us for himself.

204. WALT: It is a real question, now, Curt, as to whether that's a good thing. Certainly people differ on this.

205. LIZ: Isn't that the . . .

206. CURT: Well, I know that . . . oh . . . the way . . . we had been discussing his role so much, trying to find his role and all. Not the fact that it came out and here it was . . . uh . . . we were doing his role, I mean. It was defined by his actions.

207. BILL C: Is this suggesting that to the extent that the leader can himself get help from the group, he can then help other people?

208. LIZ: I think it's also saying that to the extent that the leader is seen as an authoritarian . . . uh . . . it's related to how much the group will become a group as we speak of it here.

204–218. Controversial issue as to whether initial group leader ought to allow personal needs to enter into group situation. The concept present here is that since initial leader provides, through group identification with him, clues as to ways to behave in a group, the more roles he is able to play with honesty, the larger the range of possibilities of behaviors are made available to the group. Group seems to react to behavior as described in 203 with the feeling "If it's all right for him to admit these feelings and weaknesses it surely ought to be O.K. for me to do the same." Along with this is the idea that if a group can accept a leader as having human

Comments

209. MARY ANN: Well . . .

210. BILL C: I think you are turning it upside down. To the extent that he's *not* an authority, he can be helpful.

211. LIZ: That's right.

212. MARY ANN: Yeah, the point is that . . . that he is not the only therapist, that each one of us, in our turn, we are equal to serve when we are able to be a therapist.

213. LIZ: But it is terrifically frustrating to people, and I know 'cause I was one of them . . . that have relied on an authority for security.

214. CURT: Uh hum.

215. LIZ: And to have it pulled away . . . why you hit hard. I bounced back up, though, fortunately.

216. DOM: That's an understatement.

217. BILL L: That's where the (*laughter*) where the group leader, the one who is initially the group leader, has to be very secure because the group members when they first start out say "where's the authority; where's the security," and they all start griping and complaining.

218. LIZ: And if you can't find it in him, you turn and look to each other for it, and the minute you get it or get a taste of it, why that's when the group rolls.

219. MARY ANN: Yeah.

220. BILL L: Yeah, that's when it's worth all the anxiety and frustration.

221. WALT: I have a problem at this point . . . I wonder how we want to solve it. We didn't set any finite limits on this group. Do we want to keep

weaknesses, rather than being perfect, they change their concept of what to expect from a leader. It also changes their concept of the ways in which they should relate to him. Concurrent with this changing concept which permits the leader to be imperfect, is the growing willingness on the part of group members to assume a role they feel they now can measure up to.

218. Awareness that group members, too, have potentiality for giving leadership and support provides the security that promotes group growth.

221. Setting of limits is a group function. Time is a major limit. In deciding on limit, group, as usual, examines its own needs as

rolling, or should we let the
other people have a chance?

the basis for making a decision.

222. LIZ: Let's let them have a
chance.

223. BILL C: Yeah.

224. WALT: How about it?

225. CURT: I think so . . . because
there's only so much that they
can get from listening.

226. DOM: I would like to let the
rest of the people in on it.

227. WALT: O.K.

228. DOM: They have been so *quiet.*
(*Laughter*)

229. WALT: Well, I am going to
stand up so at least I can see
people. Also, with the session
over, my authority role won't
get at me so badly. Thanks
a lot. I would welcome any
questions or comments that any
of you (to audience) would
like to raise. We would feel,
I am sure, much more comfortable if we could have a chance
to explain what we . . . yes?

From audience:

230. DR. MARGARET BENNETT: The
young lady directly across from
you . . .

231. WALT: Rita Newton.

232. BENNETT: A moment ago . . .
uh . . . made some statement
about a person expressing a
highly unacceptable opinion,
and I'd like to raise a question
and hear the group discuss.
Uh . . . whether in a real
group therapy class you can
ever say anything that is highly
unacceptable or whether what
you say may not be a means of
your helping to understand
yourself.

232. Question of the nonjudg-
mental nature of a thera-
peutic group.

233. RITA: What . . . what . . .
what . . .

234. BENNETT: Or . . .

235. RITA: I'd like to answer.

236. BENNETT: Or allowing the group to help you understand yourself. I wasn't quite sure what she meant.

237. WALT: Rita.

238. RITA: When I said unacceptable I meant . . . this was a human relations conference, and people went with the expectation that they would talk in favor of brotherhood. People . . .

239. BENNETT: Oh, I see, you were speaking about . . .

240. RITA: People came out saying things that sounded very . . . unorthodox as far as what one is supposed to believe about brotherhood if one comes to a brotherhood conference. (*Laughter*) There was a great deal of hostile feeling; there was a great deal of Chauvanistic type feeling, and it was getting expressed by people. People were saying . . . I noticed that the leader of the entire convention was sitting facing me and they had asked me to lead this particular small group. And when anyone said anything which was not part of the brotherhood party line, uh . . . uh . . . a frown would come over her face, whereas I was sort of saying, "No, keep going . . . I see what you mean. I see the frame of reference, I think, in which you're saying this. And even if you say it and no one agrees with you . . . they at least now know that there are people who think this." So that's what I meant when I . . .

240. Focus on acceptance of person rather than his idea or behavior.

241. BENNETT: Yes, but in a real group therapy class I wonder if you can ever say anything that is highly unacceptable.

242. WALT: Not in a value sense or judgmental sense. Whatever you say hasn't a value of being acceptable or unacceptable, but rather in societal terms, these are some of the things we don't usually talk about because they're threatening.

242. Attempt to distinguish between role of group in helping others see what "society" would reject, as contrasted with what the group will permit to be expressed.

243. WALT: Dr. Wrenn?

244. DR. WRENN: What is the so-called leader's role? Now, I grant you that this is a leaderless group (*laughter*) . . . leaderless group in the sense . . . in the fact that the leadership shifts . . . uh . . . as a teacher in a situation like this for instance . . . when somebody sticks their neck way out . . . and says something that others resent. Maybe it's a statement of hostility toward the so-called leader, you see. Then is it possible that it is the leader's role to try to relieve a little of this hostility against the one person or rather should we leave it to the group to take care of that over a period of time?

244. Therapist has responsibility for welfare of group members. Question raised as to if this does not include controlling experiences and threats the person faces in the group.

245. WALT: I think I can answer that. It's a function of the leader's own security and his feelings of confidence in the group. But . . . uh . . . for myself, I think that at the beginning I tend to be more anxious, wondering whether this group is really going to jell. And . . . I don't always have the confidence I ought to have. But my role then becomes not pulling the pressure off a per-

son, but trying to help clarify the feeling that we're facing. "We seem to be pretty mad about something here. I wonder whether we can take a look at what's happening and what we can do about it." Uh . . . as a matter of fact, I had another kind of role that sometimes the group found helpful and sometimes not. It almost might be called didactic. "What's going on now?" I would say. "What are we doing?" "Do we like it?" So that we could all not only label what was going on and see it for what it was, but possibly begin to take a look at the way we wanted to deal with it. And this I did fairly actively. But, as I say, this is me and some other person might . . .

246. WRENN: In a well-jelled group somebody else might take over and try to fix the situation.

247. WALT: I think that there is something that's very important here . . . that uh . . . might be clarified. My role as a leader . . . uh . . . as I perceived it anyhow, was to help the group set up a structure with me in which they could work. It was not in terms of the *way* they would work. I would try to help them. But because folks like Liz and others had feelings about authority figures, I had to be destroyed as an authority figure before there *could* be other leaders in the group. That's what happened in the group that Dom was in . . . that after I was . . . chopped off . . . Dom was next. And after Dom, Liz was next. You see, we were all three author-

ity figures, and we had things in our personalities that made us this. And when the group disposed of some of our needs that were getting in their way and they learned how to cope with them, then things really rolled. I think there is one concept here I'd like to make clear. Uh . . . there are many weaknesses as a person that I am sure that I have. Uh . . . I'd like to live with them. I'd like to be aware of them. But I think that my ability to work with a group depends not upon being a perfect person, but trying to set up a setting where my weaknesses won't get in the group's way. And I recognize that I have some of these needs that aren't always helpful to the group. It, therefore, to me appears more important that I give the group a device to get me out of their way when I am not being helpful. But . . . just . . .

248. UNKNOWN MALE VOICE: Walt, I would like to get some ideas about the original problem that was brought up by the group here. That is, this business of getting some identification since they were more or less strangers from the three different groups. And I noticed some cohesion and some division here, one particular physical one which seems to be . . . uh . . . uh . . . by chance. That is, there is a brief case between two people, and they are seated apart. . . . (*Laughter*) This man here has had his back turned practically the whole time on one group member.

249. WALT: Uh hum.

248. Focuses on importance of group cohesiveness as relating to the degree members relate with one another. Demonstrates the way the physical setting can effect the nature of the relationships.

250. (As IN 248): She, in turn, has been sitting on the opposite side of her chair. Could we get a poll of the people around here to see how they feel identified with each other in this group relationship between each other?

251. WALT: How about it? Do you want to speak to it?

252. GROUP: Yes! It's all right with me. I . . .

253. LIZ: I . . . I feel quite well identified with everybody. I completely forgot the recorder. (*Laughter*) Umm . . .

254. SHARPE: Is that a compliment?

255. LIZ: I have become identified with Miss Farris (Dorothy) and Bill on the end I have less identity with. Now, I've never met these two people before 10:30 today. Uh . . . I didn't . . . I feel quite well identified with both of these people, and then the others I have known from the group I was in and so I automatically picked that up, I think.

256. WALT: I think there is one point I'd like to raise. I . . . I feel a certain mission involved in this session. The things that you are describing are the things that came out in the logs. These are the things that people began to perceive and recorded in their written impressions of each class.

257. WALT (*to Mary Ann*): I . . . do you remember one of the things that you did? May I tell about it?

258. MARY ANN: Sure, I don't care. (*Laughter*)

259. WALT: In one session, Mary Ann . . . for whatever her rea-

251. Group is still given responsibility of making decisions.

257. Vital that confidentiality be preserved. It is the member's right to decide what can be shared with people outside the group.

son was . . . (*laughter*) . . .
made a wall chart of how many
times people participated.
Boy, did the group clobber her
with that. She was raising the
question as to whether or not
we were worthwhile people.
If we weren't . . .

260. Liz: It was how she presented
it.

261. Dom: Yeah.

262. Mary Ann: Yeah! It was the
manner in which I did it.

263. Walt: You carry on . . .
(*Laughter*)

264. Mary Ann: Well, it was . . .
uh . . . (*laughter*) . . . and . . .
the tapes, and I took down the
number of responses of each
party in the group. And . . .
uh . . . (*laughter*) . . . and
. . . uh . . . as I did this . . .
uh . . . I found . . . uh . . .
to some extent, the people who
I thought were not talking were
actually responding. Well, I
came into class on my white
horse (*laughter*) . . . and uh
. . . instead of . . . I certainly learned a lesson.
(*Laughter*) Uh . . . I put it
on the blackboard without saying anything to anyone in the
class. And 15 minutes of the
session went by and somebody,
I guess it was Liz, made some
crack about "What is this ba-
loney on the blackboard?" And
then they all climbed down my
throat, and I had to try to explain what it meant and I also
. . . the thing that was most
important in my regard is that
I realized the personal, emotional reason why I had done
it. And uh . . . it was a matter of terrific antagonism toward me. And yet it was fol-

260–264. Demonstrates again effect
of "consultant" or infor-
mation giver who volun-
teers data group has not
sought. It was not the
data itself that was re-
jected, but rather what the
presenting of the data implied about the group
members' capabilities of
recognizing problems on
their own.

lowed up by *so* much security and support afterwards that I was able to face it, and . . . uh . . . personally was almost raised rather than diminished.

265. WALT: What we're suggesting here is that through this action which threatened the group, the group became responsible for helping an individual see what it meant to them. And in doing this, the person who had been threatened got support.

265. Despite hostile nature of the act, group accepts the person while rejecting the act.

266. MARY ANN: Uh huh.

267. WOMAN'S VOICE IN AUDIENCE: I'm interested in the language used here . . . and I would guess that perhaps you found this in the beginning sessions . . . uh . . . perhaps that such words as "threatened," "external security," or "insecurity" were quite frequently used in class discussion, and then began to drop out. Do you find this in the regular class session as a kind of barrier? How is that handled in your group?

267. Communication being a vital issue, part of a group's growth comes in developing a "language" which is commonly understood. Part of the role of slang in the adolescent is that this is a clearly understood language.

268. WALT: Dom, I wonder if you want to talk on the question of jargon and what happens in the group when you do use jargon? (*Laughter*)

269. DOM: Uh . . . the question of jargon came up quite abruptly with me. I had a lot of clinical background, and in the class I used quite a bit of the specific terminology of the clinician. And . . . uh . . . for a while I threatened the group with this because they felt . . . first of all, they didn't understand, and second of all, they . . . uh hum . . . it sounded like I knew so much more than everyone else until

finally when they got a little security, I started getting my head banged in. Until . . . I had to leave this realm, otherwise leave class bloody every day. Uh . . . but . . . the jargon comes up not in terms of this internal and external security and threat, it wasn't, I would say, part of the vocabulary of the class . . . until we would have sessions, part of the sessions in which we would try to find out . . . just as we did here toward the end, we were trying to say where have we gone; what have we done. And uh . . . these were the best words we could find to . . . uh . . . describe the process that had gone on previously, if someone said, "I didn't like what so-and-so said." Well, in this session where we were trying to pull things together and understand what went on, someone said, "You might have felt threatened." And this was a good word to express the feeling. And this is how the words developed, because actually when you come into the class with jargon you have such a diversified group, you tend to run into the "wall." I developed the word "wall" because I felt I was running up against it quite a bit. I kept bouncing off it for a while until the group felt secure with me. And I was insecure with the group, and this is why I was using it, let's face it!

270. CURT: Uh . . . I would like to speak on two points, one right along with this and another that is somewhat new here. We haven't brought it in yet. I can't describe too

270. Demonstrates that this is a common problem.

much about a similar instance going on in the class now, because there's a problem of confidence in this group and . . . uh . . . this is one of the things that you don't come out with in one session . . . about how sacred are the things that we say in here? How far should they be carried? One of the persons in the present group is sitting out in the audience now. And so . . . uh . . . I can be reported back on this by this other one in class. (*Laughter*) I'll be very careful about what I say, but I would say almost 100% the same problem has come up in the present class now, Dom. We have a person who is being accused of being a Freudian, and throwing his Freudian terms around. And . . . uh . . . boy, it wasn't about two sessions ago it happened.

271. Dom: I'd like to add another thing, by the way . . . that when the group felt secure with me and I felt secure with the group, they didn't hesitate to ask me when I did use a word that I was using as part of my ordinary vocabulary because of the setup I was in. It didn't . . . they didn't hesitate to ask me what I meant. They allowed me to use it after they understood what I was . . . my own problem, and they accepted me this way.

272. WALT: One of . . . I'm sorry. Go ahead.

273. Dom: Don't interrupt me! (*Laughter*) In fact, in fact, there were times when they asked me about different things that I have had in my own experience, which was related to

271–277. The group language is a growing thing. They will tend to try to share each person's unique language as long as they feel it will help both the person and the group.

this, which they had clobbered me for previous to this. So that it was strictly a matter of relationship and counter threat . . . and threat. That once we worked this out, it . . . this didn't constitute a threat any longer, so it was all right to do this.

274. CURT: There's something else that bothers me, Dom, this word clobber that you use. I think this is part of our jargon.

275. RITA: We made a new jargon.

276. DOM: Very descriptive term. I'll show you the bumps. (*Laughter*)

277. CURT: Clobbered is more than getting hit over the head with a baseball bat, but it is with soft pine because, after you have been hit over the head, there's security in this group so that you can take a hit over the head and you can grow from it.

278. WALT: Well, I think the thing we learned from it was that we get hit because people care enough about you to try to do something about it.

278. Repetition of theme that honest feeling reactions from group, rather than being seen as source of threat, provide comfort since they not only let the person know where he really stands but also show others' concern about him.

279. MARY ANN: Let me, let me say something about what Dom said in his use of jargon in our group. And that was . . . we certainly clobbered Dom, but good! And then he found out that he could be a man that could explain things to us. After the threat was gone to both Dom and to us, he could explain his words to us and help us understand. I think part of this was in my counting responses, this same thing happened to me. I found I could help people if we both felt well enough about it.

280. WALT: Part of what we're saying here is an important concept. "How can the group learn to use people as resource people, but not as advisors who will tell them what to do?" And I think that when anyone came in with jargon or anything similar to that which by implication said to the group "This is right, this is the way it is, this is your label," the group resented it. But when a person came in and provided something that the group needed and he had, the group was very, very accepting of him. And that was a hard lesson for us to learn.

281. RITA: I'd like to say something about the value of learning your vocabulary this way. If you . . . if you learn what the words mean by feeling them first, and then maybe using words like "clobber," "the wall," and all the slang we put into it, it isn't awfully hard to pick up the technical jargon when you start reading. Because when you read all of the technical words, you know how they feel inside. And somebody else could have been taught the vocabulary in a straight academic class and never know what the words really mean.

282. WALT: Yes? (*to woman seeking question*)

283. WOMAN'S VOICE: I noticed that these two people were sort of left out of the group (*referring to Bill C. and Dorothy F.*) What would you as a leader do about this?

284. WALT: Nothing, absolutely nothing. I want to explain something about that, because

281. Words to be truly meaningful need to be incorporated into each person's personal frame of reference.

284–286. Role of isolate is a common source of concern. Idea is presented that this

I think that's kind of interesting, too. In several groups now, I have had members who have said almost nothing, and as the group continues one of the things they discover is that their security with each other depends on knowing what the other person is feeling. Communication, incidentally, I might indicate, goes on in other than just a verbal level. People who are indicating their feeling by their affect, by their faces, by their movements · or in any way, are accepted by the group, but the individual who seems to be isolated forms a threat to the group and the group takes it up as a problem. And then the individual who doesn't talk becomes quite anxious because his status in the group depends upon his . . . and his acceptance . . . depends upon his giving to the members what the group needs for security. And so the pressure is not my asking them to talk, but the person's seeing that they'd better talk if they want to use the setup.

285. WOMAN'S VOICE: Dorothy seemed to have a lot of the answers in her mind so she gave out this feeling to the rest of them so that's probably the reason she was accepted more by the others than he was and yet she didn't ever say very much. She perhaps could be frustrated in the group. Would you as a leader have shown this?

286. CURT: Walt, you wanna . . , (*Laughter*)

287. DOM: Wait a minute. I think one of the things that will explain this is a question that was

is both a problem for the person and for the group, rather than being solely the responsibility of the leader.

raised by this gentleman here. We only have met for a half hour. I am very close to the girls because . . . (*Laughter*)

288. DOM: Good enough, maybe I shouldn't say more. I have been in class with them in particular situations. I could sit here and I know what they're talking about. Dorothy has the same experience because she's been in with this group. Now Carlson . . . I don't know whether Carlson . . . I met Carlson here yesterday. I don't know if Carlson has been in a class with any one of us here, you see. Curt I know from around the campus, but I haven't been in classes with him so I didn't feel as close or as understanding because I hadn't shared this experience with either Bill Lewis or Curt.

289. CURT: One of the problems here is the fact that I was blocking you (to Mary Ann) out because I was concerned. I was picking this up. Most of your talk was directed down in this corner and Bill off in this corner was getting sort of shut out.

290. MARY ANN: Let me . . .

291. CURT: It was kind of hard to get around to see him, so in trying to pull him in I was shutting Mary Ann off.

292. MARY ANN: Well, let me just try and answer this lady's question. We had this occur in our group . . . uh . . . and it was a matter of sometimes there would be a daddy who would say, "All right now, Mary Ann wants to talk." So I would always depend on Dom making

289. Indicates some of the motivations for physical "blocking behavior.

292–293. Comment provides illustrations of how people learn to be responsible for own behavior. On a symbolic level it also shows how a single person can be perceived as representing to others, a variety of important figures in their

Comments

room for me to talk. I took
no responsibility on my own.
But he mothered me along the
path.

293. WALT: (*to Dom*) Now you are
a mother too. We seem to
play many different roles for
each other.

life. To the degree that
one group member can
use another to work out
significant relationships,
and to the degree these
relationships are perceived
as being common to other
situations, to that degree,
incidents in the group,
have a major effect on the
person's total life.

Discussion

The protocol you have just read represents just one of many different
approaches using groups in the helping process. Corsini[1] has included
sample protocols in his text from each of several different philosophies.
Bach[2] demonstrates his approach in great detail while relating his
theory to psychological systems. Sample protocols involving groups
in educational settings can also be found in Hinkley and Hermann,[3]
Gordon,[4] Moreno,[5] and Hobbs.[6] If films are available to you, the
following titles are worth considering:

Role Playing in Human Relations[7]
Activity Group Therapy[8]
Meeting in Session[9]
Belonging to the Group[10]

Despite the differences a reader can find in the sources cited, there
are many group characteristics he will discover that are common to
almost all approaches. An examination of what happened in the group
we just explored may be helpful. Although the demonstration con-
tained many elements which are not present in the normal setting, by
the nature of its membership there are provided characteristics to be
found in both initial and mature groups.

As all beginning groups this group starts out by trying to answer
several basic questions. What are the limits within which we are
allowed to function? What do we have in common that can serve as
a basis for providing group cohesion? What needs do we have which
are pressing and must be dealt with immediately?

The group resembles a mature group in that they are less concerned over the role of the initial group leader, they are ready and

willing to express their feelings to each other, and they are ready and able to accept their responsibility to the group.

As all groups, this one actually moved on three planes simultaneously. One level represents the actual manifest content of the topics they explored. The second level comes from the feelings being expressed through a diversity of content. The last level is represented by the learnings which occur through the actual relationships they establish with each other.

In some ways a group may be likened to a symphony. There are several basic themes that keep winding their way in and out of the fabric of the total piece. Separate instruments try out the theme for themselves. The theme is changed and modified and sounds different as either instruments are combined or two themes are joined together. When we listen to a symphony we enjoy the repetition and embellishments. Unfortunately, in most groups, progress is judged by the newness of the content and the lack of repetition. If the group worker could accept group process in terms of an ever-tightening spiral, he can then begin to perceive how during the repetition of the content new individuals join the chorus, and how associated ideas are integrated with one another.

Topics will not become the focus of the group's attention if they are not meeting the needs of several members of the group at the same time. The topics themselves tend to be less important than the way they are used. To some degree the extent to which a topic is continually prolonged may provide a clue as to the degree to which the conversation is being used as a way of delaying facing something else.[11]

When topics appear loosely related to the objective of the group it is more helpful for the leader to help the group explore what it is doing, rather than switch topics or inhibit discussion.[12]

Just as the content repeats, so too do the underlying feelings crop up again and again. The idea that a person's ability to perceive is a function of his security is the basis for this phenomena. Members of the group move at different rates. They require different relationships to provide security for them. As each person reaches the threshold of security he needs, he suddenly perceives what others may have already understood. Not only is this new insight something he wishes to share with others, but he needs the chance to concretize his insight by testing out if he can use words to communicate his idea to others. The acceptance of individual differences in growth and insights is vital to the atmosphere in a group.

Typical themes in groups include feelings of hostility or warmth toward authority figures or peers, fear of personal inadequacy and the threat of admitting the need for help, confusion over responsibility for self or others, ambivalent feelings of dependency vs. autonomy, and confusion over what constitutes reality.

An illustration of the relationship of content to movement on a feeling level may be useful. In the group session there is reference to a class session where the group explored the sex life of the Eskimo. One could wonder, and appropriately, what relationship this has to a course in group guidance. The actual discussion evolved in the following way. A member of the group commented that she felt the group was getting very close to home because they had begun to discuss their feelings about the difficulty in expressing their anxieties over death, birth, and other phenomena that could not be easily explained. At this point several members of the group related incidents in their lives that were important to them. One told of her concern with a practice near her home in North Dakota. It seems there were times during the winter when the ground was too hard to be able to dig a grave. Bodies were, therefore, stored until the first warm day and a mass burial was held. Another person expressed his attitude toward the loud wailing of his relatives at a funeral. The overt expression of emotion by the Italians led the group to think about the part culture plays in determining how feelings are expressed. Basically, several things were happening. Not only was the group broadening its acceptance of cultural differences, but as each person revealed his own cultural heritage, and found the group able to accept him and his heritage, a more basic security within the group developed. It was after this session, which included the discussion of peoples as culturally distant as the Eskimo, that a silent member of the group participated for the first time. She was a Negro who had migrated from the South. She had learned not to express her feelings and to avoid Negro labels as they led to rejection. In this group she, for the first time, began to feel that maybe she could be accepted as a person. When she began to talk the group became very quiet. They recognized how difficult this was for her. After she finished speaking, person after person told her how much they appreciated her confidence in *them*, by being willing to share her feelings with them. This floored her. She had never believed she had anything of worth to others.[13,14]

One way in which the group succeeded in relating content to feelings was through the use of its daily written logs. Since the log was essentially a personal document it provided each person a chance to record feelings he was secure enough to see in black and white but feelings he may not yet have been ready to share with others. In a sense the writing of these logs formed a kind of rehearsal that enabled group members to discover a way of expressing feelings in a manner they could accept yet in a form others could perceive. Frequently the ideas written in a log one day were expressed verbally in the group the next session.

Because the logs were available over a period of time, it was possible for each person to see how his feelings in relation to specific content shifted. He could also see different types of content discussions that evoked similar feelings in him.

The third level, represented by the relationships in the group, is illustrated by the members' references to each other as sister, mother, or daddy. It also can be seen during the group's exploration of the leader's role and how identification with the leader was only a first step in developing their own leadership pattern.

In many philosophies the use of time is an essential part of the therapeutic process. The protocol provides several examples of concepts related to time: time as giving, time as a limit on doing, time as representative of something you cannot change (a minute is 60 seconds, no more no less), and the use of time as a way of accepting responsibility for oneself.

There is an interesting concept demonstrated by members' reaction to others' use of time. The counting of frequency with which members participate occurs commonly in groups where I am involved. Typically the person who decides to do this is an individual who feels he has been too verbal and resents the fact that others do not talk more, since that would free him from feeling he is being unfair to the group. As the group deals with this situation several insights usually develop. The group tends to agree that to use the group a person must share his thoughts with others. Identifying with verbal members is seen as only one part of a total process. The group then becomes aware of a peculiar phenomena. Although measuring a person's increasing use of group time may provide a measure of behavior, since the total amount of time available in any one session is limited, the theoretically optimal share for each person is obtainable by dividing the total time by the number of group members. It is at this point that the group discovers that the instrument not only has theoretical weaknesses but also it postulates that in a democracy everyone *must* have an equal share of everything. Desiring to preserve the right of the individual to talk or to be silent, the group reaches the understanding that although the person has a theoretical right to equal time *he also has the responsibility of asking for this time if he wants it.*

In other words, where freedom of choice is present, silence can be interpreted as assent. This brings home an associated important lesson. *If you do not exercise your rights you cannot be resentful of others who meet their own needs.* Responsibility to others is predicated on knowing the needs of others. Since we have no right to assume their needs, it remains the responsibility of each individual to make his needs known to the group.

An examination of the way group members were interrupted or supported will provide an example of how a group tends to limit a person they may feel is monopolizing the discussion, while encouraging the less verbal person.

Basic to the use of any group is the feeling on the part of the group members that what they say in the group will not be used against them in outside settings.[15] To insure this security every group rapidly develops ground rules covering the confidential nature of the sessions. This is not as simple a problem as it would appear. Group members are very anxious to use their new found insights in other settings. Typically, groups decide that concepts or feelings can be shared with outsiders, *if* the specific content is not divulged nor the people involved identified. An associated issue is the right of group members to meet together in subgroups outside the group sessions. Although no breach of confidence is involved here, the group discovers that any insights they develop outside the group are not useful in the group, if the group does not understand these ideas. Many groups therefore suggest that, where appropriate, outside discussions of group members be reported in the group so all can share in the thinking process. It is this attitude, among others, which makes it difficult for group members to act out their needs outside the group, rather than in the group session. It is also this attitude which inhibits the development of cliques.[16]

One of the most important aspects of group therapy is the tendency of the group to strive together to solve a problem. They seek to become more self-reliant and less lonesome.[17,18]

Foulkes[19] has presented an interesting rationale as to why group therapy works. He points out that although group members reinforce each other's normal and neurotic reactions, collectively they represent the very norm from which individually they deviate. Redl[20] has pointed out that group therapy, unlike individual therapy, includes elements of societal reality, not the least of which is societal retaliation for perceived misdeeds. Probably one of the most comprehensive descriptions of group life can be found in a series of articles by W. R. Bion.[21] His analysis and presentation has stood the test of time. It is well worth exploration by the reader.

Of all the issues raised by this demonstration, the question of the role played by the leader has major significance. It is within the leader's role that one can find evidence of the psychological theory that a group is using as a basis for operation and evaluation, and within an examination of the leader's behavior lie basic clues as to the skills and personality characteristics found most useful by a group.

I have taken the position that for a variety of reasons it is helpful for the initial leader to lose his position of authority as soon as possible. As he seeks membership status by changing roles in the group, he is then in a position where he must contend with others on the basis of equality. Such a role serves well, after the group has learned to cope with its leadership needs, in preventing the initial leader from using the group to meet his own personal needs in a fashion detrimental to the group.[22]

Acceptance of the group of a leader on a membership basis carries with it loss of any right to maintain special privileges. Readers will note that members of the group refer to the author by his first name. Early in the relationship the question of how to address the author provided the basis around which the group could express its feelings toward authority figures. The way group members fluctuated in using Professor, Doctor, Mister, or Walt provided a sensitive barometer as to how that person perceived the author at that moment.

The protocol should certainly demonstrate the vicarious thrill members seemed to get in controlling an authority figure, at the same time they express concern for the individual in the role.

Basic to the security of any group leader must be the recognition that much of the hostility the group directs toward him is not meant for him personally but rather what he represents. Knowing that all groups go through common stages helps the group leader recognize when the group process he observes is a normal development or is a function of something he is doing.

The chapter that follows is designed to help the reader learn about some of the typical problems faced in groups.

BIBLIOGRAPHY

1. Corsini, Raymond. *Methods of Group Psychotherapy.* New York: McGraw-Hill, 1957.
2. Bach, G. R. *Intensive Group Psychotherapy.* New York: Ronald, 1954.
3. Hinkley, Robert G., and Lydia Hermann. *Group Treatment in Psychotherapy.* Minneapolis: University of Minnesota Press, 1951.

4. Gordon, Thomas. *Group Centered Leadership*. Boston: Houghton Mifflin, 1955.

5. Moreno, J. L. (Editor). *Group Psychotherapy*. Beacon, New York: Beacon Press, 1945.

6. Hobbs, Nicholas. "Group Centered Psychotherapy," Chapter 7 in *Client-Centered Therapy* by Carl Rogers, Boston: Houghton Mifflin, 1951.

7. Film: "Role Playing in Human Relations." Washington, D. C.: National Education Association.

8. Film: "Activity Group Therapy." New York: Columbia University Press.

9. Film: "Meeting in Session." New York: Bureau of Publications, Teachers College, Columbia University.

10. Film: "Belonging to the Group." Collaborator R. Havighurst, Encyclopaedia Britannica Films.

11. Talland, G. A., and Clark, D. H. "Evaluation of Topics in Therapy Group Discussion." *Journal of Clinical Psychology*, 10, 131–137, 1954.

12. Thelen, Herbert. *Dynamics of Groups at Work*, p. 57. Chicago: University of Chicago Press, 1954.

13. Slavson, S. R. "Racial and Cultural Factors in Group Therapy." *International Journal of Group Psychotherapy*, VI, No. 2, 152–165, April 1956.

14. Wittenberg, R. M., and Berg, Janice. "The Stranger in the Group." *American Journal Orthopsychiatry*, 22:89–97, 1952.

15. Lindt, Hendrik, and Sherman, Max A. "Social Incognito in Analytically Oriented Group Psychotherapy." *International Journal of Group Psychotherapy*, II, 209–220, July 1952.

16. Slavson, S. R. "The Nature and Treatment of Acting Out in Group Psychotherapy." *International Journal of Group Psychotherapy*, VI, No. 1, 3–27, January 1956.

17. Powdermaker, Florence. "Psychoanalytic Concepts in Group Psychotherapy." *International Journal of Group Psychotherapy*, I, No. 1–4, 16–21, 1951.

18. Frank, J. "Some Determinants, Manifestations and Effects of Cohesiveness in Therapy Groups." *International Journal of Group Psychotherapy*, 53–63, 1957.

19. Foulkes, S. H. *Introduction to Group Analytic Psychotherapy*, p. 29. London: W. Heinemann, 1948.

20. Redl, Fritz. "Group Emotion and Leadership." *Psychiatry*, 5, 573–596, 1942.

21. Bion, W. R. "Experiences in Groups." *Human Relations*, 1, 314–320, 1948; 1, 487–496, 1948; 2, 13–22, 1949; 2, 295–303, 1949; 3, 3–14, 1950; 3, 395–402, 1950; 4, 221–227, 1951.

22. Wittenberg, Rudolph M. *The Art of Group Discipline—A Mental Hygiene Approach to Leadership*. New York: Association Press, 1951.

5

Typical Problems in Group Process

For the beginning group worker there is real value in being able to recognize typical recurrent experiences in group behavior. To the degree that the leader can anticipate group movement, he is better able to know when members of the group are responding to his needs rather than reacting to their perception of what he represents. Although groups differ both in the speed of their movement and in the ways they develop to express their needs, there are definable phases through which almost all groups go. This chapter is designed to provide the reader with the chance to think through typical problems of group process.

The Initial Leader

All groups depend on a catalyst to merge the individuals into a cohesive unit. The steps involved in achieving cohesion are very much a function of how the initial leadership in the group develops. Studies in leadership[1-3] have demonstrated that no one can become a leader if he represents ideas or behaviors that are beyond the group's present knowledge or acceptance. The best leader is the one who helps the group achieve their desired goal. To do this, he needs to help the group examine each of the following ideas:

1. What common goal exists among group members?[4]
2. What can they expect from him as a leader?
3. What group roles does the group need? In many groups these roles are defined and acted out on an unconscious basis. Generally all groups seem to need people who seek help, those who are willing to provide help, and those who represent societal reality. In the pre-

vious chapter, the group labeled these roles as those of client, therapist, and "wall" respectively. Other groups have had their moralists,
seducers, advisors, etc.

4. What can the group members expect from each other?

5. What limits does the group wish to set on their own behavior?

6. What limits exist which set boundaries on group actions or
goals?

It would be relatively simple if all the leader had to do was to
raise each of the questions above for discussion, have members vote,
and record the group's decisions. Unfortunately, for those seeking
simple solutions, groups get the answers to the above questions
through observing each other's actual behavior rather than the words
being spoken. This means that what the leader does from the very
first moment describes to the group the leader's actual desired role
in the group. He must be willing to let the group make their own
mistakes. Benne[5] describes it as follows:

> He must be willing to let them try and fail as well as succeed. He
> cannot protect them from reality if his goal is to support them in facing
> the reality of self and others in all of its complexity and in handling
> such reality more rationally than before. What he can insist on is that
> realities be recognized, named, and analyzed, rather than ignored, denied,
> or oversimplified. But his version of reality is not reality, and he must
> be strong enough to have his version of reality challenged and changed
> if he is to be permitted to challenge the versions of others.

One way for the leader to demonstrate his concern for the group is
by providing them with an immediate opportunity to express their
feelings and problems. Typically, groups start by expressing their
insecurity over unclear boundaries. (Are we supposed to . . . .?)
From the very beginning, groups will need to test out the leader's reaction to their needs. The earliest needs to appear in the group will
be those of dependency-independency, love-hostility, and the need
for acceptance by both the leader and the group.

Each person will try to cope with the group situation by using his
existing repertoire of defenses. If he can get others to respond to
him in the expected customary fashion, he has no need to consider
change or to examine himself. Since change is threatening, part of
the leader's initial job will be to develop in the group sources of security to meet these threats.

The major role of the initial leader is to be able to recognize the
needs expressed by group members as being a function of both the
person and the group setting, rather than merely a reaction to the

leader personally. The leader not only tries to reflect the feelings being discussed, but also, probably of greater importance, helps point out the similarity and differences in feelings among group members. By showing how different members using different content are expressing similar feelings, he helps the members see their common concerns and facilitates identification between members.

Gordon[6] has clearly articulated the functions of the leader in providing links between the thoughts and comments of different group members:

> Another important function which the group-centered leader serves in the group is the "linking" function. In face-to-face discussion groups, it often happens that one person will say something, then a second person will add a new idea but without conveying the relationship of his idea to the first contribution. The thought of each member remains independent or unlinked to other thoughts. Occasionally, someone may enter in and relate his thought to that of another, but usually we can observe several currents of thought in a group, each going its own way. If, however, the group-centered leader makes an effort to perceive the linkage between the separate comments and then conveys this relationship to the group, the discussion then seems to flow in one current, building up force as each new contribution is linked to it.
>
> The "linking" function of the group-centered leader is related closely to his function of reflecting the meanings of members' statements. This is because the meaning of a member's comment often *is* the link to the main stream of thought or to the previous comments. Its actual linkage is frequently hidden by the content of the comment. Thus, by clarifying the meaning of a comment, the group-centered leader makes clear to the group how the new contribution is related to the previous discussion.

In similar fashion, by accepting feelings of hostility directed toward him and by not responding with hostility, the leader helps the group learn how to help others look at their feelings without the need to be defensive.

An interesting study by Thibaut and Coules[7] found that communicating back negative feelings to the source of the feelings reduced interpersonal hostility and overt acts of aggression.

Basically, the leader's initial job is to help the members of the group learn to direct their attention on each other rather than on a leader. He achieves this by continually focusing on:

1. The meaning of an idea to the group.

2. The issues that the group seems to be in disagreement over and that they feel a need to resolve.

3. The feelings they are expressing through their behavior rather than their spoken words.

4. The ways they are forcing others into roles or behaviors.

5. The actions or problems which the group raises and needs to solve.

6. The continuity between group sessions and themes raised.

The following protocol may demonstrate these ideas.

(A few minutes chatter and discussion about the tape recorder.)

W: Where would you like to go today?
   Laughter
Dɪ: What did we do yesterday? Somebody take a quick five minutes to summarize.
L: I nominate you.
M: _____ didn't take part too much yesterday so he should do it.
Dɪ: The person who didn't take part yesterday summarize.
Do: Who's going to volunteer for that?
Dɪ: Who's going to volunteer?
   Short silence
Do: Sort of putting someone on the spot.
   Laughter
Do: I felt like I didn't take much part yesterday.
Ro: Don't forget the difference between oral and mental participation.
W: This is a point—can we be part of a group and yet not have the group feel that we are sharing? (*Short silence*) Putting it another way—can you have a group on a purely mental participation basis?
Rɪ: The Quakers seem to be able to feel that.   And I feel it when I'm among the Quakers.
M.L.: Sure, deaf people have groups.
W: We are raising the question, really now, as to what is a group.
E: I think even more basic than that is the idea of whether you can participate in anything without actively participating. You can listen to a record and participate, some can participate and listen, and some can just shut up for a minute.
W: You have a full house of people at the Virginia Theater all participating in watching the movie—do you have a group?
L: Yeah—the environment is the same and the goal is the same—it's an awfully loosely knit group though.
E: And yet all their emotions will be tied up in the same thing.
Rɪ: More so than if they were all sitting listening to a lecture.
Ro: Depends on the movie.
M: Is that spectator kind of thing a group?
Ro: Of course, we are all spectators at some time in the group.
Dɪ: Are they interacting now, or are they only reacting to a common stimulus?
Ro: Well do you have to have interaction for a group?
M: I think so. You could have people writing letters to each other in different parts of the world—they have some commonality but there is no actual change—I think you should have a face-to-face relationship, don't you?—a give and take, if not orally at least gesturewise.

Ro: You think then a group has to have a face-to-face relationship to be a group, M?

M: I think so.

Ro: That would be limiting the group to an awfully small (*interrupted*) . . .

E: Wouldn't you say in regard to religion that everybody in a religion no matter where he is, is more or less a group?

M: Yeah, but sort of secondary—just because people think alike does that make them a group?

E: Well, some people it does—it depends on how strongly they feel about what they are thinking about.

B: Would you say the spectators at a basketball game were a group?

B: They were all actively participating in a certain way not in the actual game; they were all having the same goal.

L: During a period of the game they would be a group.

W: Seems to me we have two or three ideas that have been presented. One is that a group is defined as any, I'm trying to pull out some of the common elements as I think I heard them, ah, any collection of people who have something in common. We have also said that a group is any collection of people who are reacting to a common stimulus. We have also said that a group, and this is somewhat different from the others, is a group only when the people are interacting with each other, and then we further defined that this interaction is predicated on a face-to-face relationship and that they cannot interact unless they can perceive one another. We have had several different ideas expressed here.

E: I would like to carry this religion thing a little farther too. You take the Jewish religion. Some people who feel strongly about their religion will do some things for other people that they have never seen before, so long as they are the same religion, or orphan groups, or clothing for Israel, or whatever else. And there is something there. I don't know if they are really a group; there is something there that a mixture of other people without the same kind of goal wouldn't have.

W: I'm wondering if you are saying this, I'm reading into your remarks now, that isn't exactly what you said—I'm adding something to this— are you saying people feel a group if they identify with the others?

E: Yeah (*hesitatingly*).

W: I wonder whether it is necessary to identify with people in order to have a group?

E: No, it isn't necessary (*interrupted*) . . .

W: But this is one possible way of getting it.

L: I was going to ask, on this interaction with a face-to-face relationship, when the people disband such as when we meet here—then the group no longer exists?

M: No—I say it still does—ideally.

L: Yes, now in a case where it still exists ideally, you would incorporate her idea, ah, whether it be religion or a common goal in a schooling situation.

M: I'm beginning to . . .

L: If it disbands every time—if every time it disbands, it dissolves, then the next time they met face-to-face, would they have to start from rock bottom again to become a group? And how can you ever form a solid group, if when one disbands, the group dissolves? (*Short silence*)

L: Now like the group at the game last night—they dissolved and will never be a group again until there is another athletic situation where there will be stimulation of the formation of another group, which is not the kind of group which we are really interested in. But you take the group like the religious group, or, ah, within a school. If you develop school spirit you are trying to develop a group actually, and you are trying to develop a group that will maintain this group feeling outside of the school building. If that can't be done, I think you are sort of lost before you start in a school situation.

M: I think that my differentiation is that the people in the group not only have to identify with the people in the group and with the group as a whole, but they have to work together to do something.

L: Still that could be incorporated under any collection of people with a common stimulus or something in common—a common goal.

W: Let me ask this question. I don't know whether it will help in the thing we are talking about, but when people form in a group in the sense in which you are talking about it now, does this entity represent something different from the people involved? Is the total more than the sum of the parts?

R: Definitely. I think so.

L: I think it's the melting of the parts rather than the sum of the parts.

W: Is this something we are all in agreement on?

In the preceding protocol, group members were using an attempt to define what constitutes a group to achieve several goals at once. They were forcing other members to define their ideas so they could see if their own ideas would be acceptable. At the same time they were testing the limits *this* group would impose on group membership. (Do I have to talk to be considered a participating member?) Less obvious, but also present, is the group's concern over the possibility that group membership in some unclear way may have effects on them in other situations. At one point, the leader appears to have the need to point out the importance of members identifying with each other. Since it is his need and not the group's, they ignore him and continue on.

The leader can check his own behavior by asking himself the following questions.[8-12]

1. Have I defined societal limits to meet my needs, or is greater flexibility possible?

2. Have I used words or behavior which force others to look up to me and accept my knowledge and control?

3. Was I aware of the feelings people were trying to express, or did I become more interested in the content or ultimate goal?

4. How did I respond to hostile, affectionate, or other disturbing needs members expressed toward me?

5. How did I relate to a group member who represented my ideal?

6. Was I more accepting of group members who were helping the group more than I was of those whose needs prevented them from relating to the group as a whole?

7. Have I been hostile or sarcastic or critical toward any group member?

8. Did I have a personal goal I would have liked to see the group accept?

9. Was I reacting to sexual charms of the opposite sex?

10. How did I react to emotional demands of members of my own sex?

11. Did I foster total group decision, or did I support a subgroup?

Since answering these questions demands a level of self-understanding all of us may not have, other cues may be easier to locate. The leader can ask himself

1. Was there any time when I found myself perspiring? What was the group talking about at that time?

2. Did I ever raise my voice? Why?

3. Were there points at which I was uncomfortable and wished the group would move on?

4. Did my mind ever wander to things outside the group discussion?

5. Are there members of the group I'd like to spend more time with?

6. Are there members of the group whom I wish would drop out of the group?

If any of a leader's answers to the above questions were in the affirmative, he needs to re-examine the needs he has which would best be met in other settings. In the event the initial leader can comfortably handle the problems raised, he will find the group increasingly taking over responsibility for individuals and group process.

Although all groups do not develop in the same way, after the first period spent in orientation and testing limits, there usually will be a sharp rise in tension and hostility. It is almost as if the group must discover if members will accept each other at their most obnoxious levels. It is helpful to realize that groups tend to permit well-liked members to deviate from group norms while they demand exact obedience to limits from members they tend to reject. Where this behavior occurs, it is sometimes helpful for the group leader to report factually the differences in the group's treatment of members.

The following two excerpts demonstrate rising tension and hostility while the group members are attempting to discover ways to relate to each other.

M: I wonder—are we picking at each other intellectually or not?
Do: What?
M: Are we picking at each other intellectually?
Do: Well . . .
E: Yeah, I kinda get the feeling that we are not doing anything. We are just talking to pass time.
M: Using big words—that's about it—or not—I don't know.
W: Talk accomplishes nothing?
E: Well it all depends—I just don't feel that we have a goal. I think that everybody is just saying something to get the tension out, and doing a very good job of it.
Ro: I think it's increasing rather than decreasing.
Ri: I was just putting down (in her notes) that every time somebody says something, someone interrupts and that this isn't going to get us anywhere.
Do: I didn't feel that we were picking at each other, I feel that we are getting tense and anxious because we can't solve our problem.
E: Well, what is the problem? I don't even know what the problem is!
Do: The problem is what we are going to do . . . what . . . we found that . . . I hate to use the word define—we're trying to define what this group is going to be—trying to come to some kind of a conclusion. A. has given his conception of what he thinks it should be. I gave mine, ah, . . . we are throwing out things actually to try to get some kind of problem solving here, and we seem to be complicating it more than anything else.
W: At this point we are pretty clear on what everybody else doesn't see *our* way, but we are not quite sure what we see together.
L: And I think, even in this group, when somebody takes the role where they become a professional analyzing the core group feeling in the group, even we resent this.
A: Because we realize that they're just as involved as the other members.
L: It's just that we don't like someone putting themselves in a position to say "Well Daddy will look at you and decide what he thinks is wrong with you."

In groups meeting two hours weekly, the author usually finds this happening after 10–16 hours. If, at this point, the leader remains calm and helps the group face its anxiety, the group rather rapidly breaks loose and begins to define problems to be solved. It then continues on to seek causes and possible solutions.

Frequently, after helping a member work out a rough problem, the group will appear immobilized. If the leader explores this apparent plateau with the group, it frequently is defined by the group as a sort of breather. During this calm spell the group recoups its strength to face the next issue.

As the group grows with maturity, leadership functions are so consistently carried by group members that an outsider observing the group would be unable to determine who was the initial leader.[13-16] Each person who serves as leader needs to discover ways of communicating to the group his desire to help but not to direct. No one behavior is the answer, but the following illustration may serve as a clue to help the reader decide what his typical behavior might be.

As was indicated in Chapter 4, the author discovered that people in his group tended to look visually to the leader for guidance. He, therefore, began systematically to shift the place where he sat each session. He not only made it difficult for the group to develop a set place to look for help, but by changing his seat he also forced group members to shift their seats as well. This brought many members into contact with each other who had not really perceived each other before. Symbolically it also demonstrated the initial leader's desire to be free to become part of the group and his desire to have mobility of thought and action.

It has been pointed out that a group seeks security by discovering the societal limits within which they must function. This question of society versus the group, with the group seen as a subculture, has been described very ably by Beck.[17] For readers interested in the sociological implications of group psychotherapy, her article will be of particular interest.

Initially, the leader is treated as an authority figure despite his own desires.[18,19] It is the author's belief that a verbal structuring by the leader is helpful. As illustrated in the protocol in the preceding chapter, the group members hear the words used in structuring but do not accept an idea until they experience the behavior that goes along with it. One might ask then, why bother talking? Why not just start right in and let actions speak for themselves? This might work if group members are familiar with the helping process. If, however, a person's behavior does not coincide with the group's past experiences, their ability to recognize what is happening in the group makes his behavior less threatening. Now, having both words and action, the concepts can more easily be integrated into the group's own storehouse of ways to relate to others. Within the context of learning theory, connecting words with behavior develops cue responses which in the future can cause the words to carry new meanings and stimulus value.

The role being suggested for the leader is an active one. To the degree that the leader feels a need to structure every eventuality, he will so limit members' perception of their freedom to act that nothing he does later will convince them that they are free to act. It is here that sensing the feelings of the group provides the leader with clues as to what information the group wants rather than what he feels they eventually might need. If he is to be the leader in the true sense, the people who make up the group will define for him the goal and the needs which must be met.

As the group matures it will begin to recognize the necessity of exploring more effective ways of meeting its needs. In the following protocol we see the group struggling with this problem.

E: The thing is, a need doesn't always have to be solved in a certain way— say the need for recognition—a kid might use a loaded pistol. . . . A kid might also draw a picture to get his need satisfied. But it is frustrating to him if you sit down and discuss with him that guns aren't so nice to carry around and that he'd better draw a picture. (*Several people talking*)

Ro: In the first place, he has this need to carry the gun or the pistol or to draw the picture; that's what we're talking about. Some place he's been blocked if he has this need. Does he not?

E: What you are saying is that in order to have a need you have to have first been blocked, which I don't agree because when you are born you have needs.

Ro: No . . .

Do: Let me ask this question. Whose thinking through which answer is better? Is it yours or the child's?

E: Both.

Do: No. You see you are saying it is better for him to paint a picture because he'll get recognition. You see this, but he may not see it.

E: I'm not saying I'll say "You paint the picture."

Do: Until he does see it, until he does go through it, he's still feeling a frustration of some need until he finds a substitute or sublimation.

E: The point is, say that he's carrying this loaded gun, and so he's satisfying his need he thinks. And you don't take away the gun. Wait a week and then say "Paint a picture." But it's a process that's continual, and you don't take away something and then replace it, but you do both at the same time.

Do: You see *you* are doing the replacing, not the child. The child may not see this connection you are telling him exists.

E: Yeah, that is why I'm saying it is a slow process.

Do: And until he sees this —what I'm saying, in this transition period, until a person learns to satisfy his needs in a socially acceptable manner, he's not going to feel that he is satisfying his need, and he is going to be frustrated. And he may be hostile and he may have anxieties about it because . . . until he is able himself to realize that this is connected up to him in some way . . .

E: I don't know whether I'm wrong in what I am saying or you just aren't understanding what I am saying.

E: Just that it's not a process where you break and then support, but it's a process where you are breaking and supporting at the same time. You are not pushing, I mean you are not forcing. And as the kid begins to see that he is doing something that is not only socially unacceptable but it is also something that is causing him more difficulty, then you begin replacing it with a more constructive kind of activity. (*Several people talking*)

Ro: But what if the kid doesn't recognize the support—therein lies the frustration.

Do: I'll agree with the process and transition, but what I'm trying to say— how do you perceive the child in this process of transition? How does he feel?

Voluntary and Involuntary Groups

One of the first questions one raises in looking at a group is the nature of the group membership. Is this a voluntary or an involuntary group? In other words, although the group members may share a common concern, did they come together of their own volition or were they forced to belong by some societal agency? Although there is little doubt that groups desiring a vehicle to meet a common need have the edge over involuntary groups, since there is no problem of motivating members to cooperate, it is unwise to assume that any other kind of group must of necessity fail.

To better understand the problems associated with the character of a group it might be helpful to examine a group where the initial motivation for membership was not present. During World War II the author was assigned to serve as a Psychiatric Social Worker at Welch Convalescent Hospital.[20,21] Welch was an Army hospital specifically designed to help rehabilitate patients suffering from combat fatigue. The labels change with time; in World War I the patients would have been called shell-shock cases. Despite labels, these were confused, hostile men with a variety of psychosomatic complaints, with guilt feelings about their inadequacy, and with a common desire to be discharged from the Army. Recovery carried with it the possibility of return to harsh Army discipline, and even more frightening, a return to possible combat and death.

The hospital setting represented the stereotype of the place where rich men go when they wish to retire. Situated in Daytona Beach, Florida, it included several swimming pools, athletic facilities, well-equipped shops and classrooms, and it had access to deep sea fishing and other forms of entertainment. The men were assigned to treatment battalions where a team of psychiatrist, psychologist, and psychiatric social worker tried to provide help. It was the psychiatric social worker's job to help the men plan their day's activities and, in group settings, to examine their problems and to suggest possible solutions. Initially, because the men focused all of the hostility caused by their troubles on the Army, they were freed of as many assigned duties as possible. Given the freedom to use or not use the camp facilities, large numbers of men preferred to lie on their beds, dreaming and isolating themselves from each other. After a period of time, all professional personnel realized that some changes were needed. An order outlining a schedule of activities for a day was issued. Men were forced to go to the activities but were then *free* to decide on the level of their involvement. Some interesting things happened.

The men were lined up in Army style and were marched to the occupational therapy shop. Once inside, they were free to spend the hour as they wished. Initially, they wandered around making hostile remarks to the patients who were busily engaged. Several questioned a man working on a bracelet as to why he bothered. He told them he had been successful in selling the bracelets. It suddenly hit some of the men that if they, too, could sell bracelets they would have money to get liquor. The shop suddenly became active.

What were some of the dynamics beneath the behavior described in the foregoing experience? There seem to be several concepts that emerge:

1. For all groups, but especially for involuntary ones, society's demands must be clear and pressing.

2. Given the freedom to explore ways of relating their needs to society's demands, people will tend to meet their most consciously perceived needs first.

3. In the process of meeting primary needs within a societal framework, clients learn that, at least at that simple level, they have the capacity to help themselves. Their attempt to prove even this level of competence is the first step toward tries at more difficult problems. In other words, people can only develop confidence in themselves by experiencing success that is meaningful in their own eyes. This last idea is frequently misunderstood. The teacher who wishes to provide

success to a youngster by giving him honorary jobs or frequent compliments may find his efforts to no avail. The compliments have to be perceived by the youngster as having been merited by his behavior. The jobs have to be ones perceived as desirable by the youngster and not just by the teacher. In other words, manipulating the environment fails when the client does not perceive the new setting as the manipulator had anticipated he would. Rather than guess at desirable experiences, the helping person should help the client to relate content and meaning within the client's frame of reference.

In planning for social change, a more fundamental step is required. It is vital that the people who will be affected by the change share in developing the plans designed to help them.

Community after community desiring to participate in the Federal Economic Opportunity Act of 1964 has discovered that eligibility for funds to develop a Community Action Program depends on proof that the indigenous poverty population plays a meaningful role in the development, administration, and operation of the community program. Many social agencies, much to their chagrin, are discovering that their perception of their clients' needs and the perceptions of the clients themselves are worlds apart, and that there exists a gap in communication. Clients express their resentment at the dependency status implied when they are not given a share in planning. Being independent implies freedom of choice.

One of the female members of a group guidance class phrased it very well when she said: "I enjoy having a boy take my arm to cross the street, but if I felt he did this because he thought I couldn't make it across myself, I'd resent his action."

Membership in an involuntary group can also be a source of security. A group of men in the stockade at an Air Force base explored their feelings about being in the stockade. Although, to a man, they would have preferred freedom, they admitted some ambivalence. While in the stockade they could not easily get into more trouble. Most of their primary needs were being met. They could allow themselves to be quite dependent people and not have to feel guilt about their lack of responsibility, since they could blame society for their presence in prison. To put it another way, not being secure enough to face their own need for help, the men found it comforting to initially be able to get help while pretending they accepted it only because of outside limits.

The issues described in involuntary groups raise the following general questions:

1. At what point does society have the right to place its demands before those of the individual?

2. When will society's demands serve as a basis for help and not interfere with the helping process?

3. How can a group resolve the confusion arising between their conception of the demands coming from society and the demands which will represent their own needs?

Unfortunately, there are no neat answers to these questions. They do, however, represent the common starting place for groups, regardless of whether the groups initially are composed of voluntary membership or not.

The nature of membership in groups has been presented as but the first step in a client's acceptance of responsibility for his behavior. The nature of his group affiliation also may involve his acceptance of the limits imposed by society and his acceptance of his own limited individual capabilities.

Group Composition

If the group atmosphere is a function of the composition of its membership, the question of who shall be included in the group is of importance. Slavson,[22] working from a psychoanalytic point of view, believes a potential group member must be evaluated in terms of (a) having had at least minimal satisfaction in his primary relationships during his childhood, (b) not being too sexually disturbed, (c) needing a quantity of ego strength, and (d) having minimal development of his superego. Bach,[23] working from a different orientation, excludes people from the groups he leads if (a) they have insufficient reality contact, (b) have culturally deviant symptomology, (c) are chronic monopolists, or (d) have psychopathic defenses of an impulsive nature.

Both of these authors, thinking essentially in terms of severely disturbed people, seem to be saying that they are looking for people who can relate to others, who do not have mannerisms others find too disturbing or offensive, and who will not by their aggressive nature present the group with problems of setting and maintaining group limits. Bach[23] and Powdermaker and Powdermaker[24] seem to agree that admitting at least two of any one kind of personality is helpful, since it will prevent the person from feeling isolated. They also seem to agree that when the differences between group members are not too radical, learning tends to be facilitated, since the client is exposed to a wide range of experiences.

A quick rereading of the preceding two paragraphs should demonstrate that the emphasis is not so much on the presence of a characteristic as much as it is one of degree. Unfortunately, the author has not been able to locate any dependable device that both calibrates the quantity of the characteristics discussed and suggests the number of adverse traits any specific group can assimilate. In reviewing the literature in this area one always discovers that the ultimate composition of these groups reflects "clinical judgment" and in some cases more likely reflects what the leader believes *he* can tolerate. Studies like the one by Ash[25] certainly raise questions about the reliability and validity of clinical judgment.

Certainly if one is developing a group for therapeutic purposes, he has every right to try to develop a group which he believes will be most effective. Unfortunately, most of us will find ourselves in group situations where membership would not be open to our approval even if we were sure about the criteria we ought to use. Does this mean that groups with an unselected membership are bound to be untherapeutic? In the author's opinion, nothing could be further from the truth. The degree to which any group can represent society as a whole certainly will affect the usefulness of that group as a testing ground of ideas. The issue then is not so much one of how to limit people from membership as it is how to achieve a heterogeneous group that has the tools to control the elements within it that may lead to disintegration.

It is on this basis that it is felt that the primary basis for membership ought to be common concern over a situation or interest. Cartwright[26] has pointed out that for a group to be effective as a medium for change it must first of all be important to its members. Thelen,[27] following up this idea and summarizing research in the area, indicates that groups composed of friends are likely to have more energy to spend in participating. Being initially secure with each other, they are free to use energies in other ways. He also points out that groups composed of friends are more likely to deal with whatever problem they need to, whether it centers around school achievement or another area of concern.

For a group to be therapeutic there must be help given to enable members to discover the need for different roles than those typically played in friendship groups. Generally, we want friends to see things our way; we want their sympathy and support. Friends serve as a source of comfort rather than threat. As was pointed out in Chapter 3, however, the helping role demands empathy not sympathy, information not advice, and both support and reality factors instead of dependency relationships. These understandings are the tools of the initial leader. It is illogical to expect a group to know how to relate most helpfully without prior experience. It is only as the initial leader himself relates to others in the ways to be learned that group members have a chance to know, evaluate, and use these therapeutic tools. As groups try to set limits, like the group below, friendship versus therapy becomes an issue.

A: In other words, I don't have to worry about my interpretations or my response to his actions if it's friendship.

Do: Can you be a therapist part time and a friend part time? Can you switch roles?

A: Inasmuch as, in my opinion, these people tend to pick out friends that satisfy certain types of needs.

Rɪ: Friends can have therapeutic effects.   (*Chorus of "Oh, yes!"*)

Dɪ: But are they therapists?

Do: No!

Dɪ: This solves what I was going to say to M., because what I was hearing in M. is that all a counselor does is give support, and I'm sure she didn't mean it. (M: "No!") But this is all your argument . . . your whole argument was . . . all a counselor does is give support

M: That's right, Di, you know this is something that we talked around . . . a little different angle . . . if you are in love with someone—your wife, or not your wife or sumpin (*laughter*), and, ah, is that love relative to the reciprocal need satisfaction (*laughter*), I mean if you love somebody . . . You know what I mean?

Do: Say it. It's better to say it out loud than just think it. (*Laughter*)

M: Love means getting your needs satisfied and helping another person satisfy his needs.

E: Or is love something ethereal . . . ?

M: Which you *just* feel!

Do: I don't believe in ether.

M: You don't?

Do: I don't believe love is ethereal.

E: No, he said he didn't believe in "ether" [not either].

M: No.

A: Somebody once defined love as a state of mutual dependency.

Do: I think that is part of it. I think it can even be the whole relationship. But I don't think it's necessary. People go through life doing this—I know people that have done it. I wouldn't want it for me though.

A: Well essentially though is this any different than choosing a friend because he satisfies a need? When I'm saying dependency, I don't mean it in dependency types of needs, but any type of need satisfaction.

Dɪ: You're pushing it pretty far . . . (*Laughter*)

Ro: If you choose your husband to satisfy your needs or your friends to satisfy your needs, I disagree with that.

M: Don't you though?

E: How else would you choose a husband?

The protocol above provides a clear illustration of the group member's fear of the price he may have to pay to get his needs met. The play on words and the underlying sexual connotations of the discussion show the importance of the need for affection and concern over the appropriate way to express these feelings. Group laughter is a helpful clue to point out areas of tension and hidden needs.

Out-of-Group Sessions

Confusion over how to preserve the confidential nature of the group, while recognizing that in most societal settings group members will have occasion to meet outside of the group, causes groups to examine early in their life how best to handle the multiplicity of relationships group members may have. This area is one of marked disagreement among writers in the field. Some authors insist that it is necessary that group members do not see each other outside of group sessions. For isolated therapy groups this may be possible, but when groups are formed as part of an existing institution, such a limit is unreal. Although the simpler the relationships are between people, the easier it is to cope with them, it is rare in society for a person to be able to so purify his relationships with others. If, on the other hand, the group can develop clearly defined roles for in-group and out-of-group relationships, group members have a chance to learn the basic idea that different behaviors are appropriate in different settings.

The following protocol illustrates the awareness of the group of their desire to maintain the group atmosphere in other settings, and then their awareness that this may not be possible. Being concerned over the effect of these out-of-group meetings, this group set up a rule that obligated group members to feed into group settings the ideas or relationships developed outside the group between members in order to achieve group security and cohesion.

R_I: I always wanted to be the first one to arrive in our dorm at college and the last one to leave, and I didn't want to miss a thing. (*Laughter*) Even if I had an important committee meeting or class, I would feel threatened if I didn't go out for coffee because I've always been that compulsive about it. I sat at one of these big tables, and at another table a lot of people were talking and I didn't know what was going on . . .

E: I just thought when Ro said that—God, I wish I was that normal!

Do: (*To W*) This is what you meant when you said that your wife wasn't going to see you all semester.

Ro: I also missed E. not being there.

M: We go out for coffee a lot, and I think part of it wasn't there.

RI: I don't think we can stop these between class meetings because we can't stop seeing each other, and if I were to see M. and if you were to see E. and have coffee this would be a subgroup of our group, and we can't make a vow that we don't see each other in between time. It may be we can learn how to deal with it. Personally, I don't know how you felt about it, but when we left yesterday, I said something about, if you want to know what we talked about the other time we had coffee I'd be glad to tell you, although it wasn't particularly related to class.

B: Well that's why I said it, because I was interested in the type of things you talked about.

E: This kinda reminds me of a family now we're getting so close it's kinda like a mother and the mother doesn't want to let go of any of her kids.

Do: Who's the mother? (*Laughter*)   The group.

DI: I think one thing we can do to reduce the threat about some of these meetings is geared to what W. said he would like for us to do. We do not discuss class at the luncheon. (*Refers to session where confidential nature of group was explored.*)

L: But, Di, I don't think it's only a matter of discussing class. It's a matter of people liking you and . . .

Ro: A group feeling.

Do: I think we are going to have to live through it a while.

It has been suggested that specific situations represent a helpful core around which people can learn to relate to each other. Because interests and behavior of people change with age, it is logical that the basis for group formations will differ at varied age levels. It is also to be expected that the manner in which the groups choose to communicate will also change. Little children still accustomed to acting out their needs may find play and activity groups most natural to their typical behavior.[28,29] Adolescents form a special problem in group counseling. This is a period of very rapid growth in both their emotional and physical drives.[30,31] It is a stage where their speech is highly developed. They have a growing ability to express themselves verbally with less need for physical activity to release their needs. Because adolescence is a period of rapid shift, however, group activities may not remain stable in one mode or the other.

Thelen[32] has suggested that the major need of students is to find their places in the group. They are also concerned about their ability to adjust to authority and to explore and define their assets and limitations. He believes that these needs primarily color what students learn in class and the meaning to them of the material learned.

Certainly parenthood, with its concomitant increased sense of responsibility, forms a ripe basis for group help.[33] As parents see themselves through other parent's eyes they may be able to better evaluate their own behavior. As their own information increases and as they are better able to empathize with their children, their total adjustment improves. To the degree that they discover that other parents share their feelings and anxieties, they feel less guilty and can feel better able to relate more positively to their children and mates.

Although society and peers are important at all ages, the role of group counseling with older people deserves special attention. The growing sense of isolation experienced by people as their families grow up and become self-sufficient, when added to the isolation caused by both the death of friends and the loss of physical contacts, increases the sense of loneliness of the older person. Inability to hear, see, and travel all form special problems to be explored when working with "senior citizens."

There are two other important concepts associated with group membership, namely, size and the length of the group's life.

Group Size. Size has a direct relationship not only with the defined purpose of the group but also with the possible relationships between group members. In a two-person "group" there is no escape from the need to react to each other. With the addition of each member to the group it becomes increasingly possible for a person to diminish his interactions with others. At the very least he can participate by identifying with active members. Since the security of the group depends upon the ability of the members both to communicate and to receive a sense of acceptance, a point is reached where it becomes physically impossible to be aware of all people present. Because visual cues are part of communication, too, the increasing size of the circle needed to accommodate more people creates greater distance; words need to be shouted and too many people lose the chance to express their ideas, since the time available for the total group is limited. Authors differ on when this magical point is reached. The popular upper limits are between 8 and 15. When the group gets beyond this size the group may find the need to operate in subgroups at critical points in order to re-establish the conditions needed for emotional involvement and release. Under good conditions, where group involvement is high and large numbers of people in the groups tend to identify with each other, it has been possible to have members of groups of as large as 25 work and help each other despite the size. Certainly the larger the group the more difficult it is to achieve the level of group security needed to explore threatening ideas or behavior. A review of the suggested relationship of group size to group purpose found in Tables I and II in Chapter 2 may be helpful.

Aggressive, talkative participants should be encouraged to sit next to each other rather than facing each other, since the absence of visual cues may cut down on their need to interact with each other. In contrast to this, shy members may profit through the visual support offered by sensitive group members or by the leader.

Length of Group Life—Fixed and Continuous Groups. The length of a group's life is partially a function of whether the group initially is conceived as a fixed or continuous group. Fixed groups are composed of a defined membership and are organized for a definite purpose. When the purpose has been achieved the group either disintegrates or develops a new goal around which to unite. An example of such a fixed group might be a citizen's committee organized to elect someone to office.

Continuous groups are not dependent upon a specific membership for existence. Their goal tends to include societal needs which are ongoing in nature. Fraternal organizations like the Masons or Elks would fit this definition.

Admitting New Members

In both types of groups the admission of a newcomer to the group after initial organization involves considerable group concern and attention. Each group develops its unique atmosphere. The flavor of the group comes from the rituals, limits, permitted behaviors, and interpersonal relationships they develop. When admitting a new person, the group basically is faced with two alternatives. They can indoctrinate him into the mores of the group so he does not change the status quo or they can allow him to examine present traditions and make recommendations for modifications which would increase his security in the group. The way any group handles this question provides a rapid clue to the security of the membership. The more rigid groups will tend to find their security in form and content rather than personal relationships. Groups that are secure about themselves and the value of their ideas do not feel threatened by competing ideas.

The basic thesis of this book has been that groups serve as a tool to meet individual needs. The termination, continuation, or modification of the group, therefore, becomes an issue that the group itself needs to face, examine, and resolve.

When, because of the setting, a group's purpose and way of functioning have been predetermined by an outside agency, it is the responsibility of that agency to interpret for any prospective member what group membership will demand of him.

In schools, the teacher has the responsibility of interpreting for the student the defined goals of a class, the way the class operates, and the demands that will be made on the student. Similarly, any referral of a client to a group setting carries with it the responsibility of helping the client face and evaluate what potential group membership could mean to him.

It is not wise to place a person in a group at the time of a specific crisis in his life. He will feel the need for immediate help, which the group will share, but which realistically cannot be offered by the group. Feeling inadequate to help in a crisis will precipitate considerable hostility against the referring agency which put them in this spot.

The Silent Member

In previous protocols the concern of the group over members' participation is made quite clear. Although group members accept nonverbal signs of participation, a time is reached when the highly verbal members feel guilty and exposed by all they have said. At this time they begin to pressure silent members to talk. Their motivation is complex. Not only do they desire a feedback and reaction to their ideas, but also they wish to make all members equally vulnerable since everyone is treated the same. This pressure, coming from the group, is far preferable to leader-based techniques designed to pull silent members into the group. Not only would action by the leader reinforce his authority role, but it would also threaten the group, since each member would wonder when he would be forced into a role he might find uncomfortable.

The protocol which follows demonstrates how a group, while applying pressure, provides support by identifying verbally with *Ir*. This protocol also demonstrates a typical reaction of a silent member. Frequently the silent person says little because she feels inferior to her peers. As the silent person talks, and as others identify with her and accept her feelings, she feels more worthwhile.

Do: I would like to, ah, change the subject a little because I have a little need—I would like to know something about Ir. Ah, we all had our say about our background . . . I don't know anything about her except that she's sitting there. (*Laughter*) I know her name is Ir ———, and I would like a run down on your background (*to Ir ———*). I think we should give her the same treatment all of us had.

E: May I pose one thing now? I don't know if anybody else is doing this, but I was upset because Ir hadn't said anything. And I think maybe, I don't know whether . . . I was trying to think up some way that I could get Ir in. I didn't know this was your need too (*to Do*), but this is what you felt too . . . is it that you want to know about *her*, or is it that you want to bring her into the group?

Do: Well . . . well, I think that's up to her—I just wanted to know about her so I could feel more comfortable, and I think we should give her the same treatment in terms of the group. This is one of the ways I feel we could bring her into the group—I mean pretty much the same thing. We are all talking about *our* needs while Ir is sitting there. (*Laughter*)

Ir: I am, ah, getting all my needs satisfied . . . I'm more or less trying to find out where I am 'cause I came in late and, ah, the class had already started . . . but, ah, my background is very slim—I got out of school in June last year and I started last summer doing graduate work and when E. said something about being scared about these people, I had an experience in the summer 'cause I was the only person in any of my classes who had done no work at all—I had no experience and everything was done in terms of experience.

Do: What kind of experience have you had? You were an Illinois grad?

Ir: No, I got my undergraduate degree in Mississippi.

Do: Uh huh.

Ir: And I came to Illinois last summer and started my graduate work.

Do: What did you do your undergraduate work in?

Ir: Social Sciences.

Di: Teaching of Social Sciences or . . .

Ir: Yeah, social science education.

E: And now you are going into guidance work.

Ir: Uh huh—so there. (*General laughter*)

Do: Are you married?

Ir: Yeah.

Ro: She was telling, before class, that she has her husband in the hospital ever since the first of January and she is kept rather busy running back and forth between here and Chicago.

Ir: Oh. Right now he has pneumonia. On the first of January he had a punctured gall bladder.

Do: Got any children?

Ir: I just got married. (*Laughter*)

Do: Well, the only way to find out is to stumble into it.

Ir: I just got married. (*Laughter*)

Do: Oh! I see.

Do: Ir, you and B have a lot in common.

As suggested before, silence usually reflects fear on the part of the silent member. Silence may indicate a desire not to reveal too much or to expose feelings. Sometimes silence represents a fear that no one would listen if he did talk, coupled with anxiety over testing the hypothesis out. It is not unusual for the quiet person to desire strongly to speak but to be genuinely unable to break through his own resistance.[34] Since, basically, these people fear that speaking will cause them to be looked down on by the group, there are two avenues open to help the quiet ones. The first and most preferable approach is to help the person feel wanted and secure in the setting so that his fears lose force. The second and less usual approach is to allow the person the security of knowing that he can enter the group when and in the manner he finds most comfortable.

An illustration may help demonstrate this second approach. All patients in the author's battalion at Welch Convalescent Hospital were informed that at a set time all men were expected to attend group therapy sessions. The men would gather around the center of the long barracks and arrange their foot lockers in a circle.

One of the men chose a bed at the far end of the barracks, and to all appearances went to sleep. A few days passed, and instead of sleeping he now read comic books. After a few more days he began to move from bed to bed, getting closer to the circle. The day finally came when he arranged a foot locker in a concentric circle to the group. He listened intently to the men discussing their fears in combat and freely admitting their reactions. He would nod his head in agreement. The next day he further identified with speakers by saying "Me, too," or "I'll say!" Finally the day arrived when, listening to the men, he broke in saying, "You think you guys had it tough, well . . . .," and at last he was a full-fledged participating member.

This man's feelings of inadequacy were such that any pressure from the leader or the group would have forced him to defend himself by building a higher wall so others could not penetrate or reach him. This illustration may sound extreme, but have you ever watched a small timid child in a play area? He may choose a toy which he appears to be using, but which actually permits him to observe others freely. Slowly he moves into the group choosing the children who threaten him least. The shy adolescent at the party who gets busy fixing punch to avoid being forced to cope with the total group is not too different.

Talk as an Avoidance Technique

The way in which group members persist in discussing a specific topic or introduce apparent irrelevancies can, in and of itself, tell a group leader something about the security level and cohesiveness of the group: As Bradford[35] points out:

When individuals are feeling their own anxieties and fears most keenly, they seem to conspire to keep the discussion centered on group action or on events unrelated to the present anxiety. Later, when some predictability has developed, some norms for sharing feelings and perceptions have been constructed, and greater understanding of one another has been established, concern centers on the group and its developmental problems. But now there is much more discussion of individual feelings, perceptions, and needs. Indeed, group problems are resolved through open discussion of individual reactions. A problem of group movement is examined not only in terms of suggestions for group action, but also in terms of individual perceptions and individual needs.

The Army expression of doing a "snow job" reflects the way in which a mass of words can cover up feelings or behaviors that the speaker isn't ready to reveal to others. In addition to achieving camouflage through a flurry of words, actively holding the attention of the group by forcing them to listen rather than react enables the speaker to hold off from others comments he would rather not hear or face. Generally, the less a person feels accepted in a group, the more he may feel pushed toward introducing safe and irrelevant material.

Silence in the Group

Just as with the individual, silence in the group can be a sign of resistance, but to interpret it this way all the time would be an error. Silence can also represent the fact that all members need time to digest the ideas that preceded the silence.

In so-called leaderless groups, the start of a session frequently is marked by silence. Group members chat with one another waiting for all to arrive. When everyone is present, the chatter dies down, and the group prepares to shift gears. One sign of the security of a group is their ability to tolerate silence when it represents the need of the members to gather steam or face a block.

Regardless of the cause of the silence, just as in individual counseling, the group learns that the ideas expressed immediately after a silent period tend to be ones loaded with meaning for the speaker.

For many groups in which social convention is strong, lack of talk is felt at first to be rude. Along with this is the feeling that people must constantly interact verbally to be productive. Ultimately the group learns that you can't think and talk at the same time. Neither can you think your own thoughts and listen at the same time. At that stage, silence becomes something precious. It provides a chance to think without pressure from others, but with the security of knowing the group is there if you need them.

The Missing Member

In the preceding section it was stated that cohesive groups feel a strong kinship to each other. In a sense every member is essential to the total group. This feeling is expressed by the group's reluctance to start until every member is accounted for. Members experience this sense of being important to the group. Early in a group's life it is not unusual for members to react with hostility toward people who are late or who are absent without letting the group know ahead of time. The hostility, when explored by the group, quickly is traced to the feeling of loss among the people present. There is a real feeling of being incomplete and of missing a part the group needs to function well. This attitude becomes so strong a part of group life that members rarely miss sessions unless physically unable to attend. This group practice is particularly helpful for members who have been chronically late in the past or negligent in their responsibilities. The reconditioning process for them is immediate and consistently maintained by the group. While receiving the support that comes from realizing how important a person the group feels the missing person to be, the missing person receives the full blast of their hostility. In the group, unlike in polite society, the absent member learns the price he is paying for his behavior.

The Missing Leader

Particularly in groups where the leader has been initially active in trying to help the group learn how to use the group setting, there may be a residual dependence on him. Despite the fact that group members may have served as temporary leaders for topics of concern to them, the group has difficulty in forgetting the status of the initial leader. The group seems to experience security in feeling that if any situation that they cannot handle should arise, the leader is present and will bail them out.

If for unavoidable reasons the leader cannot attend a session, the group is faced with proceeding on their own. As was demonstrated in Chapter 4, typically the more active aggressive member tries to step into the status leader role. If, by this time, the group has learned to use its own resources, any attempt by the new leader to direct the action as he thinks it ought to go will precipitate rapid censure of him by the group. With the second leader deposed, another mem-

ber may try his hand.   In this fashion member after member seeking
status recognition learns that in this group status comes from helping
others, not from controlling them.

The Monopolist

Many authors have stated that the monopolist inhibits group
growth.   Although no one can take exception to this idea, the question certainly is raised as to how groups can learn to cope with people
like the monopolist if they are not given a chance to learn to do so.
In many ways the monopolist resembles the member who seized group
leadership described in the preceding section.   He tends to be a person with strong status needs and frequently is a rather basically insecure person despite his overt behavior.   The monopolist has learned
that as long as he controls topics and direction, people cannot raise
issues that will threaten him.   It is this last dynamic that spells out
how a group can both control and help the monopolist.

The monopolist's behavior causes hostility in the group.   When the
group has learned to express its feelings, these hostile reactions will
be verbalized and directed toward the monopolist.   When this happens, the monopolist is confused.   Why, he wonders, are people acting this way?   "I'm trying to help them and they don't appreciate
me."   As his anxiety grows, he reaches a point where, since he is dependent on group approval, he asks the group to help him understand
their reactions.   In a way he has learned that the group's attack
on him demonstrates that they really care about him (supportive) but that he isn't getting the relationship with them he desires.
Since the monopolist tends to have used his aggressive tactics for a
long period of time before the group started, these crises in the group
may have to occur repeatedly until the monopolist has learned a new
mode of relating which will be equally effective as his unwanted
controlling tactics.

At all points of hostility between group members, it is the role of
the person serving as leader to remain objective and help the participants examine their behavior.

Resistance

Looking at one's behavior or feelings creates anxiety.   Every member of the group has established some way of coping with his environment.   His present method is working sufficiently well for him to get

some rewards. Although each person dimly suspects that life could be more rewarding, he is not sure he has the ability to change or that changed behavior will be an improvement. Feeling this way, there is a strong effort on the part of group members to maintain the status quo.[36]

Resistance takes many forms. As with the monopolist it could represent an attempt to control the environment. With the silent person it can be achieved by remaining beyond the reach of the group. These are both direct and clearly observable methods. However, group members employ more devious techniques that are not always easily recognized. One person in a group the author worked with kept his mouth full of chewing gum until the group observed the repetitious nature of this act. For another person, taking voluminous notes provided a "legitimate" excuse for lack of verbal participation.

Catharsis

At the opposite extreme from the nonparticipating member is the person who, while under pressure, bubbles out ideas and feelings to the point that he feels empty and exposed.[37] All of us know that being able to blow off steam from time to time makes us feel better. The problem is that a certain amount of steam (anxiety) is needed to motivate a person to solve a problem. Just like the steam engine with a hot fire underneath, letting out steam may relieve the pressure, but as long as the fire is lit pressure will build up again. Letting out the steam, then, is symptom treatment but it doesn't get to the heart of the trouble.

Because losing symptoms gives a feeling of relief, and since the experience of catharsis is part of group members' societal tools, a group needs to learn how to deal with this device to achieve more therapeutic results. The person who is permitted to cathart without group intervention may discover that, while reacting to the pressure, he has verbalized feelings or ideas he is not ready to face. Feeling threatened by what he has exposed, the person grows hostile toward the group. His hostility reflects a feeling that they have no right to know things about him even *he* does not wish to face. His hostility is also defensive, because he anticipates rejection as a result of what he has said or done.

Some authors would feel it was more important that the ideas the member expressed be verbalized and available for inspection, than to be concerned over the period of hostility which may result.

This author believes that ultimately the person and the group grow faster if the group setting can maximize rather than minimize security. Accordingly, when a person catharts under pressure, every effort is made to continually reflect to the catharter the feelings he is expressing. By helping the member hear what he is saying as he says it, the group enables the person under pressure to decide if he wants to continue to reveal himself. At the same time, by continuously reflecting feelings, the group provides the person with evidence of their support. They also demonstrate that the ideas being expressed are not effecting the person's acceptability to the group.

The Role of Stereotypes

The word stereotype has developed an unpleasant meaning in our society. It tends to indicate a tendency to think of others in terms of characteristics that are assumed to be universal for a certain type of person. We resent a person's tendency to stereotype because by so doing he robs people of their individuality and overlooks worthwhile characteristics and personal feelings.[38,39]

In any interpersonal situation, and certainly in a group setting, people try to relate to each other in terms of things they share in common. Initially, knowing nothing about the other person, we tend to predict, based upon our past experiences, what a person like the one to whom we are talking might be interested in. Failing that, we tend to assume that the other person is not too different from ourselves, and, assuming similarity, we use our interests as a model.

Neither of these two bases for stereotyping is inherently bad. As a matter of fact, we couldn't function without using bases like these. The problem of stereotyping others becomes "bad" when, after having put forth ideas we think others might like, we fail to hear in the person's response anything that would prove our initial diagnosis incorrect. In other words, being able to perceive the uniqueness of another person's response is an essential second step needed after the initial stereotype.

People do not correct their misperceptions when to do so might prove threatening. For some, just the fact that they misperceived initially would cause them to feel that others would reject them. It is easier to defend their stand than to admit error. For many, perceiving the uniqueness of another is threatening because they feel they have no existing way of dealing with this new and strange kind of person. In either case, willingness to admit failure and ability to get support to meet new situations certainly are characteristics of group members who have found security and acceptance within their group.

Although, in this description, stereotyping has been presented as an initial response, this attempt to find security in the familiar can occur at any time in a group's life. The protocol which follows is an example of this.

R₁: That's why I'm so mad at you all saying, "Let's do that damn sociogram."
D₁: I was going to say, was anybody mad at me yesterday, Do? I was doing this to a certain extent.
Do: It was because I could look at what you were doing and I seemed to feel that you purposively put it down in your notes—I happened to read a note he wrote—"I do not feel like I am a group member" —period. And, ah, this was early in the meeting I felt that he didn't want to be a group member—for a good reason, ah, I didn't know what it was exactly, but I sort of felt on the pan, because I was opening myself up and he was sort of sitting back and saying that he was not going to be a group member. Although some of the other people who do not speak I don't mind, because I feel that they are a group member, but I . . . there are certain groups that you find people that just sit but you can see that they actively are participating in a sense and this is tolerable in terms of the group.
W: You are saying that as a person you are secure in a group where the individual is consistent with your perception of what his behavior in the group ought to be.
Do: Uh huh. That's right—in a way.
W: Suppose that your perceptions of Ro and A's perception are different.
Do: I hope so. . . .

Helping the group perceive the accuracy of their perceptions and of the cues they are using to interpret their perceptions is a basic part of the group's work.

Decision Making—To Vote or Not to Vote

From the very beginning each group faces the problem of which method to use to achieve group decision. Partially because it is the most familiar technique and partially because it seems most expedient, groups use voting to make decisions.

Similar to the experiences reported by Gordon,[40] the author found that voting brought with it problems the group was not sure how to solve. Desiring to provide all the needed time for discussion, the group could not decide when to vote. When several members of the group were ready to vote, but the others were not, they found themselves voting about whether to vote. The group perceived how ridiculous this was, but initially knew no other way of solving the dilemma. Robert's *Rules of Order* provides a method, but does not recognize individual needs.

When because of individual pressure a group votes prematurely, they frequently ignore the decision and act out their unmet needs. In one group, based upon discussion by group members it was decided to end each session earlier than originally planned to enable one group member time to get to her next activity. During the following several sessions, the group found itself in animated discussion at the new closing time. Despite the fact that the young lady got up and left, the group continued until their initial time limit. When the young lady pointed out how the group was failing to respect its own limits, the group was forced to examine its behavior. In so doing they discovered that although they desired to help the young lady, they resented losing time they originally had. Seeking ways to solve the problem, they explored with the girl ways she could solve *her* time problem. Several members provided solutions that would involve their help. This they did willingly, in order that the total group could meet as originally planned.

This sensitivity to the needs and rights of the individual makes it difficult for a group to accept the concept of a minority subgroup within the total group. In one group with which the author worked, this concept of the rights of the individual met the supreme test. A young man, whom we will call Mr. X, joined a group knowing its purpose and typical method of operating. He reasoned to himself that if this group was truly democratic he had the right, as an individual, to participate or not as he chose, and to vote or not when he chose. Participating or voting when he didn't want to represented coercion of a minority member by the majority.

The total group, desiring to respect his needs, found themselves immobilized because they:

1. Did not want to set up limits he would not respect (confidentiality, time, etc.)

2. Were threatened by his perception of them when the absence of feedback made them unable to know his true thoughts.

3. Felt cheated by not getting a contribution from him that would enrich the group.

In trying to solve this problem the group developed the following concepts:

1. Groups have a responsibility to be aware of minority group needs and the effect of a majority group decision upon the minority.

2. Minority group members have the right, following a group decision, to continue to work toward changing the beliefs of others so that their values might someday represent majority opinion.

3. Minority group members need to be helped to evaluate the price they are paying for their decision *and* to discover other needs the group *is* meeting that makes giving up a specific need worthwhile.

4. The majority group recognized that if it has met the previous criteria by providing opportunity and support to minority members, then when a group decision is being made silence must be construed as consent.

*5. In a democracy people not only have a right to vote but beyond that also have a responsibility to do so. Failure to vote involves more than individual rights; it involves taking from others something they need to be successful. Being interdependent, no man has the right to receive group benefits without accepting his share of responsibility.

It is this last concept that our schools and citizenry have failed to comprehend. Unless youngsters are helped early in group life to learn the lesson of their voting responsibilities, no government that uses votes as a method of group decision can succeed.

As a sidelight to the illustration above, the reactions of the author to this situation might be of interest. Like the group, he was threatened by the man's behavior. Feeling responsibility as the initial leader, it became important to try to understand the needs behind Mr. X's behavior. Because he felt that it might be difficult to be objective about the situation, he asked an outside person to provide answers to his questions. The questions and answers received were:

1. Is Mr. X a psychopath?   No.
2. Is Mr. X a monopolist?   No.
3. Is Mr. X a cultural deviant?   No.
4. Is Mr. X deeply neurotic?   No.
5. Does the group appear to be accepting and supporting Mr. X? Partially accepted by three people. Acceptance of his ideas but not his emotions.
6. At what point do you feel this group's demands on the individual are going beyond the rights of the group?   Felt group had no right to insist on verbal participation.
7. Is Mr. X a person who cannot be helped in a group?   Why? Mr. X has a real need for help, but at present seems unable to face receiving help from this group.

* Major rule in group's eyes.

As the reader can see, the answers suggested a lack of real support for Mr. X and an impatience by the group at the rate of his ability to participate.

There is an interesting sequel to this incident. Approximately seven years later the author met Mr. X at a professional convention. After being greeted warmly, the author was brought up to date on Mr. X's life. With surprise he learned that not only was Mr. X working with groups but that he felt his early experiences in class had been meaningful and helpful. Once again the lesson was brought home that the true meaning of any situation can only be evaluated subjectively. It also demonstrated how time can affect the way an experience is evaluated.

Within these examples, it is felt, lies the whole crux of the democratic philosophy. At some point, a truly democratic group needs to accept the limitation that it can move only as fast as the slowest member. With this concept comes the corollary that the speed of movement of the individual is a function of his security in the group, security which the group has the responsibility of facilitating. Last but not least, the contribution of each individual makes for total group strength, and therefore no person is truly expendable.

In the last analysis then, voting is meaningful and helpful only when the needs of all the members have been evaluated and only when the group is able to accept loss of some freedoms as a price for having others.

Responsibility in a Group

One of the fundamental assumptions behind the philosophy presented in this book is that individuals, given the freedom to grow *and* the help to perceive what they are doing, will accept responsibility for themselves and others. They also will choose healthy and societally acceptable solutions to problems.[41]

This philosophy is one many people find difficult to accept. Not infrequently people respond with the feeling that the idea is all right in the abstract but would not work in their concrete situation. At times, the author himself has wondered if he was in an ivory tower. When such moments have happened typically he has tried to put himself in these "impossible" settings and see what happens. The following illustrations represent some such experiences.

When the author worked with a teacher group concerned with discipline, he found that several of the teachers felt that greater controls were necessary because children were not old enough to handle responsibility for their behavior. The author suggested that people learn to be responsible only by handling responsibility (along with support to face the anxiety it raises) and that children not only could handle responsibility but that they also might have good solutions to the discipline problems that were worried about.[42-44] To test this hypothesis it was decided to secure a group of youngsters and see what happened. One fifth-grade youngster from each of six different schools was purposely chosen to differ as to his race, socio-economic status, intelligence, school adjustment, and verbal ability. None of these youngsters knew each other.

As planned, the author met these youngsters for one hour before going with them to a teacher's meeting where they were to conduct a panel discussion. It was explained to the children that the teachers were concerned about discipline and that they felt that the students might have some good ideas which would help.

The youngsters' initial reaction was one of concern. They raised questions like:

"I would like to tell about the troubles in our class, but I wouldn't want to hurt my teacher."

"If I tell about something they will think it's my problem I'm talking about. What will they think of me?"

"How can we say things so they will not laugh at us?"

To summarize, the group was concerned about defining limits and protecting their security and the rights of others, while trying to find ways to be helpful and communicate clearly. The group was helped to see the problems it was raising. It developed several ways of coping with these problems. The author was instructed to tell the audience that the things the children said were to represent the thoughts of others who were not present, that they had swapped problems so that the source could not be identified, and that they were interested in solutions rather than criticisms of the status quo. The youngsters did a particularly fine job of proving how able and ready they were to handle responsibility. One problem faced in the panel session might demonstrate this:

One youngster complained about the slow learner in his class who was monopolizing the teacher's attention. Although the youngster did not say so, this was a good example of possible sibling rivalry in a class where a teacher gives different or favored treatment to those she feels may require it. Faced with this problem, the group decided that the brighter youngsters who finished earlier should help the slower ones. They felt that students could explain in a way another student could understand, and that by this help the total group would be speeded up. In other words, they solved the problem by accepting more responsibility themselves.

In a completely different setting, the author was asked to help a high school-age church group plan a regional conference.[45,46] The group came to the planning session loaded with suggestions from adults as to what they thought it would be good for these youngsters to discuss. Idea after idea was rejected. Finally, one boy said "everyone tells us what to do and think, why can't we be free to do as we please?" Because this feeling seemed to be highly popular in the group, the author asked the group if this feeling itself might not serve as a theme for their sessions. Rather quickly things fell into place. The group decided that their theme would be "If I could do anything I wanted, as long as the people with me agreed to it, what would I do?" Since they did not want to be told answers to their question, they organized the conference around work groups. Each group had the same problem of answering the idea raised in the theme. Being curious about other groups' decisions, they planned on a general session where ideas from each group could be reported and where they could see what they had in common.

Given the freedom to organize society to meet their needs, the groups happily tackled what they considered failures of our society. The role of the family, sex, money, government, politics, freedom to think, and problems of minority groups all were areas for decision making. The members of some groups, with tongue in cheek (and partially to test adult reaction), suggested organized prostitution, no family life, etc. It was particularly interesting to see the total group reaction to such proposals. They asked which of the girls were willing themselves to serve in degraded roles. They also asked if anyone really did not feel he wanted someone special to share life with. In other words, when faced with living out the ideas that initially seemed to represent freedom, time after time the total group decided on a way of life which was closer to existing society than ideas that meant overthrowing the past. The major result of the sessions was that the youngsters now had reasons that made sense to them for the rules and limits of society. These limits were now seen as desirable rather than as something being imposed on them by others.

As a last example there is the case of the group of residence hall workers who were up in arms over the behavior of their superior They came to the author seeking help in finding ways of coping with the situation.

Each of the women recited grievances and problems she experienced. The author clarified feelings, pointed up areas of similarity and disagreement in the perceptions of group members, and helped them feel free to express their negative and hostile feelings. After releasing these feelings, the group began to examine how they might deal more effectively with their superior. Feeling accepted themselves, they began to try to perceive the feelings or needs the superior was having. In the process they found many needs she was expressing to be ones they could meet. They also began to realize that just as they were threatened by her, so too the group was a source of threat to the superior. Ultimately the group began to accept responsibility for their own behavior, for their obligation to provide support to the superior so she could be able better to perceive their needs, and to help her see how she could relate to them in ways that would be mutually more satisfying.

These cases are but a few demonstrations of the fact that groups given the security needed to face themselves react with increased responsibility for themselves and others.

Other Tools and Techniques

Beyond the ways discussed thus far in this chapter, groups employ a vast array of devices to help group members express, practice, and facilitate interpersonal skills.

Probably most common is the use of role playing.[47-50] Some groups employ available scripts depicting scenes representing areas of common concern to the group. Others have the individuals in the group describe situations they desire to work out. The leader selects the other roles needed to develop the setting and he instructs group members in the kind of person they are to play. The way people are introduced into this acting situation very readily reflects the concept the leader has of the group's role and purpose. Some groups[51,52] have developed groups within larger groups, with the outer group serving primarily in a spectator role. Groups or leaders needing[53] a more structured setting have worked from textbooks, where the text serves as the common denominator toward which all members relate feelings and experiences.

At the other extreme there is a wide range of projective methods[54,55] using art, puppetry, adult play therapy, music, etc., to help provide members with a means of expressing feelings they cannot or are not ready to put into words.

Common to many groups is the use of food as a basis for making the setting more comfortable and informal. Psychoanalytically oriented leaders see food as meeting the succorance needs in the group as they are met in family life. In the author's groups the ritual of deciding on coffee, making it, and cleaning up becomes a vital part of group growth. Through this area the less verbal members typically make an active effort to take their share of responsibility. In this way they demonstrate their concern without having to expose their needs to the group. The group also discovers that coffee served in the middle of the session has a disrupting influence, and eventually groups make and serve food at the beginning, both to facilitate communication and to avoid later confusion.

All of the techniques mentioned in this section have as their ultimate purpose the improvement of communication and of the relationship skills of group members. They are basically only a means toward an end, and their continued use may reflect the lack of maturity ultimately needed in groups. Truly secure and mature groups require no subterfuges to permit them to express their real problems and feelings.

Summary

This chapter has included a description of a number of problems and practices typically found in groups. At best it can represent just a few of the more critical situations in group life. In the chapters that follow, the reader will find descriptions of the application of group techniques in working with several groups. The problems raised in this chapter will fall into perspective when viewed from the significance of their effect on group growth and maturation. The reader will find the appendix specifically helpful in obtaining a longitudinal view of a group.

BIBLIOGRAPHY

1. Jennings, Helen. *Leadership and Isolation.* New York: Longmans, Green, 1950.
2. Haiman, Franklyn S. *Group Leadership and Democratic Action.* Boston: Houghton Mifflin, 1951.
3. Hare, P., Borgatta, E. and Bales, R. *Small Groups.* New York: Knopf, 1955.
4. Bettelheim, Bruno, and Sylvester, Emmy. "Therapeutic Influence in the Group on the Individual," *American Journal of Orthopsychiatry,* 17, 684–692, 1947.
5. Bradford, Leland P., Gibb, Jack R., Benne, Kenneth D., (Editors). *T-Group Theory and Laboratory Method,* Ch. 8 "From Polarization to Paradox" by Kenneth D. Benne, p. 247. New York: Wiley, 1964.

6. Gordon, Thomas. "The Functioning of the Group Leader." *Perspectives on The Group Process,* p. 240, Gratton Kemp. Boston: Houghton Mifflin, 1964.
7. Thibaut, John W. and Coules, John. "The Role of Communication in the Reduction of Interpersonal Hostility." *Journal of Abnormal and Social Psychology,* 47, 770–777, October 1952.
8. Winder, Alvin, and Stieper, Donald. "A Prepracticum Seminar in Group Psychotherapy." *International Journal of Group Psychotherapy,* VI, 410–417, October 1956.
9. Hadden, Samuel, "Countertransference in the Group Psychotherapist." *International Journal of Group Psychotherapy,* III, 417–430, October 1953.
10. Kotkov, Benjamin. "Vicissitudes of Student Group Psychotherapists." *International Journal of Group Psychotherapy,* VI, 48–52, January 1956.
11. Knopka, Gisela. "Knowledge and Skill of the Group Therapist." *American Journal of Orthopsychiatry,* 19, 56–60, 1949.
12. Slavson, S. R. "Qualifications and Training of Group Therapists." *Mental Hygiene,* 31, 386–396, 1947.
13. Blocksma, Douglas D. "Leader Flexibility in Group Guidance Situations." *Educational and Psychological Measurement,* 9, 531–535, 1949.
14. Gorlow, Leon. *Nondirective Group Psychotherapy: An Analysis of the Behavior of Members as Therapist;* 1950, Columbia University, Microfilm Abstract #2109. Also in *The Nature of Nondirective Group Psychotherapy,* Leon Gorlow, Erasmus L. Hoch, and Earl Telschow. New York: Teachers College Press, 1952.
15. Gordon, Thomas. *Group Centered Leadership,* pp. 197–200. Boston: Houghton Mifflin, 1955.
16. Gibbs, J. R., Platts, Grace and Miller, Lorraine. *Dynamics of Participation Groups.* St. Louis: J. Swift, 1951.
17. Beck, Dorothy Fahs. "The Dynamics of Group Psychotherapy as Seen by a Sociologist." *Sociometry,* 21, 98–128, June 1958.
18. Bach, George R. "Observations on Transference and Object Relations in the Light of Group Dynamics." *International Journal of Group Psychotherapy,* 7, 64–76, January 1957.
19. Glatzner, H. T. "Transference in Group Therapy." *American Journal of Orthopsychiatry,* 22, 499–509, July 1952.
20. Tropp, Emanuel. "The Military Social Worker as a Discussion Leader." *J. soc. Case Work,* XXVI, 377–383, February 1946.
21. Cotton, John M. "The Psychiatric Treatment Program at Welch Convalescent Hospital." *Research Publications of the Association for Nervous Mental Disease,* 25, 316–321, 1946.
22. Slavson, S. R. "Criteria for Selection and Rejection of Patients for Various Types of Group Psychotherapy." *International Journal of Group Psychotherapy,* VI, 13–30, January 1955.
23. Bach, George. *Intensive Group Psychotherapy,* pp. 18–27. New York: Ronald, 1954.
24. Powdermaker, Florence, Powdermaker, Frank J. et al. *Group Psychotherapy—Studies in Methodology of Research and Therapy.* Cambridge: Harvard University Press, 1953.
25. Ash, P. "The Reliability of Psychiatric Diagnoses." *Journal of Abnormal Social Psychology,* 44, 272–276, 1949.

26. Cartwright, D. "Achieving Change in People: Some Applications of Group Dynamics Theory." *Human Relations,* 4, 381–392, 1951.

27. Thelen, Herbert. *Dynamics of Groups at Work,* p. 62. Chicago: University of Chicago Press, 1954.

28. Little, Harry M., and Konopka, Gisela. "Group Therapy in a Child Guidance Center." *American Journal of Orthopsychiatry,* 17, 303–311, 1947.

29. Konopka, Gisela. *Therapeutic Group Work with Children.* Minneapolis: University of Minnesota Press, 1949.

30. Axelrod, P. L., Cameron, M. S., Solomon, J. C. "An Experiment in Group Therapy with Shy Adolescent Girls." *American Journal of Orthopsychiatry,* 14, 616–627, October 1944.

31. Spotnitz, Hyman. "Observations on Emotional Currents in Interview Group Therapy with Adolescent Girls." *Journal of Nervous Mental Disease,* 106, 565–582, 1947.

32. Thelen, Herbert. *Dynamics of Groups at Work,* p. 44. Chicago: University of Chicago Press, 1954.

33. Barnes, M. J. "The Educational and Therapeutic Implications of Working with Parent Study Groups around Problems of the Normal School Child." *American Journal of Orthopsychiatry,* 22, 268, April 1952.

34. Slavson, S. R. "A Contribution to a Systematic Theory of Group Psychotherapy." *International Journal of Group Psychotherapy,* IV, 3–29, January 1954.

35. Bradford, Leland P., Gibb, Jack R., Benne, Kenneth D. (Editors). *T-Group Theory and Laboratory Method;* Ch. 7 "Membership and the Learning Process" by Leland P. Bradford, p. 198. New York: Wiley, 1964.

36. Redl, Fritz. "Resistance in Therapy Groups." *Human Relations,* 1, 307–313, 1948.

37. Slavson, S. R. "Catharsis in Group Psychotherapy." *Psychoanalytic Review,* 38, 39–52, January 1951.

38. Thelen, Herbert, and Dickerman, Watson. "Stereotypes and the Growth of Groups." *Educational Leadership,* 6, 309–316, February 1949.

39. Gage, N. L. "Understanding and Helping Your Group." *Adult Leadership,* V, No. 2, 57–59, June 1956.

40. Gordon, Thomas. *Group Centered Leadership,* p. 269. Boston: Houghton Mifflin, 1955.

41. Turner, Marion E. *The Child within the Group: An Experiment in Self-Government.* Palo Alto, California: Stanford University Press, 1957.

42. Hymes, James L. *Discipline.* New York: Teachers College Press, 1949.

43. Stendler, Celia. "Climates for Self-Discipline." *Childhood Education,* 27, 209–211, January 1951.

44. Sheviakov, George V., and Redl, Fritz. *Discipline for Today's Children and Youth.* Washington, D. C.: Department of Supervision and Curriculum Development, National Education Association, 1944.

45. Cope, J. Raymond. "The Church Studies its Emerging Function." *Journal of Social Issues,* 6(1), 5–13, 1950.

46. Coffey, H. S., Freedman, M., Leary, T., and Ossorio, A. "Community Service and Social Research—Group Psychotherapy in a Church Program." *Journal of Social Issues,* 6(2), 1950.

47. Schwebel, Milton. "Role Playing in Counselor Training." *Personnel and Guidance Journal,* XXXII, No. 4, 196–201, December 1953.

48. Boring, R. O., and Deabler, H. L. "Simplified Psychodramatic Approach in Group Therapy." *Journal of Clinical Psychology,* 7, 371–375, October 1951.

49. Horwitz, Selma. "The Spontaneous Drama as a Technique in Group Therapy." *Nervous Child,* 4, 136–205, April 1945.

50. Haas, Robert Bartlett (Editor). *Psychodrama and Sociodrama in American Education.* Beacon, New York: Beacon Press, 1949.

51. McCann, Willis H., and Almada, Albert A. "Round Table Psychotherapy: A Technique in Group Psychotherapy." *Journal of Consulting Psychology,* 14, 421–435, 1950.

52. Moreno, J. L. "Psychodramatic Production Techniques; The Technique of Role Reversal, the Mirror Technique, the Double Technique, and the Dream Technique Transcript of a Didactic Session." *Group Psychotherapy,* 4, 243–273, March 1952.

53. Samler, Joseph. *Vocational Guidance Through Groups.* Washington D. C.: The B'nai B'rith Vocational Service Bureau, 1943.

54. Bach, George. "Dramatic Play Therapy with Adult Groups." *Journal of Psychology,* 29, 225–246, 1950.

55. Moreno, J. L. *Psychodrama.* New York: Beacon Press, 1946.

6

Group Procedures
in Educational Settings

No discussion of school-related groups makes any sense unless we examine first the needs of students as they mature, the existing skills and attitudes of teachers and other group workers, and the relationship of the curriculum and school organization to the goals to be achieved.

Writing this chapter involves a paradox. The school as an institution exhibits one of the most vivid examples of cultural lag to be found anywhere. Since people in school settings want help that is useful for their current working conditions, an author finds himself forced to provide material suitable for the status quo. In so doing, he must, however, encourage a flexible approach to this material so that schools will not be prevented from catching up to the other reality—a school which reflects the changing needs of our society and recognizes new methods and instructional techniques. These changes also introduce new and different problems. Kvaraceus states:[1]

> There is a growing threat of impersonality and isolation in many crowded classrooms today. In solving the problems of over-crowded classrooms and teacher shortages, innovations involving the more frequent use of self-teaching machines and devices have been widely recommended. There is the danger that these self-teaching devices will greatly reduce teacher-pupil interactions. Increased dependency on the TV screen, language tapes, teaching machines, movie and film projectors and recordings should be justified not only in terms of learning increment but also in terms of the time saved for an increase rather than decrease of opportunities for more and deeper human relationships in the classroom. Otherwise, teaching machines, robot-like human teaching, as well as

automation, can become a major threat to the mental health of pupils who need the security of a warm and reassuring human relationship in a big and impersonal world.

Social Forces and Education*

The current movement from the self-contained classroom to a departmentalized approach in the elementary grades not only depersonalizes the student-teacher relationship but also puts a heavy premium on a child's ability to adjust to rapidly changing limits, personalities, and group climate. The more diverse elements a youngster needs to cope with, the more likely it will be that the motivation for achievement will have to be rooted in discrete subject areas rather than the desire for teacher approval or the enjoyment of a comfortable learning situation.

The organizational structure of the school thus may be demanding greater student flexibility at the same time that it demands that he make critical decisions at ever lower grade levels. If the student takes foreign languages in the sixth grade, will they improve his chances of getting into college? Is Latin better than French? This emphasis on the need for flexibility and intrinsic security, along with restrictive decision making, can also be seen in another significant sector of the environment.

How many of you can remember the numberless times you were asked by aunts, uncles, and other assorted adults what you wanted to be when you grew up? This adult concern was consistent with a society worried about square pegs in round holes. A man's job title represented his status in the community, his daily satisfactions, and his claim to economic security. We are now, however, in an economy where John Diebold[2] among others, tell us that each youngster will have between three and five careers in a lifetime. Security in an era of automation will not depend on a specific job title but will depend on the ability of the youngster to assess his skills realistically, his awareness of current occupational possibilities, and his skill in translating past experiences to meet current needs. As he chooses adult models he also frequently accepts their job title as desirable. So it develops that youngsters in the elementary schools need two conflicting kinds of help. On the one hand, they need significant

* Parts of this section appeared in a paper, "Social Forces and Guidance in the Elementary School" written by W. Lifton in *The Vocational Guidance Quarterly*, **12**, No. 2, Winter 1963–1964, pp. 89–92.

adult models to emulate; concurrently, they need to develop an acceptance of the job family concept, required for adjusting to a rapidly changing society.

At this point, one might well inquire about the heroes who serve as role models today. As in the other areas examined, here, too, change is evident. If one were to read just the results of the research by Deeg and Patterson,[3] Welch,[4] and others who use a forced ranking of occupational titles, little change in rankings would be noticeable. If, however, one examines data from studies like Stefflre's,[5] Dipboye's,[6] or Project Talent,[7] a different picture emerges. Although in the ninth grade engineering is the field chosen most frequently, a college population reveals that business, formerly ranked low on the scale, has usurped engineering as a major career interest. So too with girls. In the ninth grade girls select nursing as first choice. In college they switch to education with nearly half of all women's degrees awarded in that field.

In a *Saturday Evening Post* youth survey, 85 per cent of all entering high school students wanted to go to college. About 58 per cent really planned on going, but most of them underestimated the cost. About 50 per cent planned on working their way through college, in whole or in part. (Actually some 40 per cent of all high school students drop out of school without a diploma.) The Roper polls document that 18 per cent of those questioned had preferences toward one of the professions, but only 6 per cent actually reached their goal. Conversely, 15 per cent became factory workers, whereas only 1 per cent had expressed such a choice when young. Why this drastic shift in careers? Is it, as some suggest, just a function of maturation and reality testing? This author thinks not, and he has some evidence to back up his opinion. As reported in *Introducing the World of Work to Children*,[8] studies tapping teacher occupational knowledge and jobs mentioned in elementary texts and fiction books provide youngsters with the most information about the jobs they are least likely to get. In other words, from teachers, text books, and society, youngsters learn most about professions and least about the skilled trades. It is not surprising, therefore, that adult-inspired career goals of youngsters need to give way to reality factors as the day for job selection approaches.

Role Models

A close inspection of the problem of the role model used by present-day youngsters reveals some interesting facts. Horatio Alger's heroes now tend to be replaced by the most noticeable person with whom the youngster can most easily identify. It is not surprising to discover that adolescents turn to personalities made famous through their activities in space flight, television broadcasts, or because of their unique racial or national characteristics.

One basic requirement of a hero is that he be discoverable. The slum children, the suburban children, the Negro children, the orphan children, the city and rural children will find him in a dozen different places; for as they grow up they are confronted with slices of society so varied as to be almost from different pies. The same heroes simply are not visible to all groups. If this is a cause for concern, it immediately suggests that guidance people need to take an active role in publicizing desirable role models in populations now using antisocial models. Obviously, teacher bias and unrepresentative treatment of minority groups in published textbooks are all objects of concern if we seek to have societal influences maximize guidance objectives.

Let us examine typical pressures exerted by parents on their children. It is truly difficult to find parents who do not want their children to move up the socio-economic ladder. Even if parental strivings were not enough, the rash of articles on the importance of a college education would create pressure toward high-level occupational goals. Lacking information about the world of work or education beyond his own level, the parent tries to motivate his child by painting the status quo as undesirable. "Do you want to slave like me?" "Don't you want to amount to something?" Unwittingly, by deprecating his own status, the parent is sowing the seeds for later trouble. Youngsters whose motivation is based on an escape from something rather than on an attraction toward a desirable goal tend to use large portions of their potential energy coping with their anxiety about the future. Feeling that they and their parents are worthless in our society, they react with frustration and sometimes with aggression. Ultimately, in order to reach adult status they are forced to dissociate themselves from their parents before they can be free to be themselves. Clearly parents need help in learning new ways to motivate youngsters. Without doubt, they are unaware of the way they are currently laying the foundation for their later rejection by their children.

Giving recognition to the jobs held by parents of students not only helps children learn that all people are important and worthwhile, but at the same time helps parents feel accepted by society. The parent is therefore free to let the youngster consider his future career without the hampering effects of parental demands. Parents need help too in understanding current employment patterns and training levels required. Parents need to realize that, although post high school training is desirable, attendance at college is not mandatory for securing a job.

Some Educational Problems That Need to Be Faced

Riessman,[9] and many others have recently tried to explain and explore that segment of our society which is variously called culturally deprived, alienated, or disadvantaged. They have eloquently demonstrated that these people are not culturally deprived at all; their culture is a rich one. There is ample evidence of tremendous ability to cope with a hostile environment. Current emphasis seems to be on utilizing the existing skills of this "different" group to lead them into our societal pattern. Then, theoretically, they and we will be happy. It is at this point that Lindner's[10] struggle to dignify nonconformity comes to mind. Remember his hypothesis in *Prescription for Rebellion*, that, since society can now control the environment, we may be filtering out the mutant who represents a superior adaptation to our environment. Even if one questions the role of therapy as a societal tool toward conformity, the recent work by Getzels and Jackson[11] demonstrates how, in a different setting, creative people are taught early in life that deviant responses are not rewarded by society.

Milton Hahn,[12] in an article entitled "Forgotten People," tells about the normal individual in our society and about the psychologist's confusion over the balance needed by a normal person between adaptation, adjustment, and distribution.

Faced with problems of assessing educational potential and realistic vocational goals, counselors have for many years assumed the existence of a broad spectrum of intellectual potentials in the population. As a contrast to this point of view, it is interesting to note the following reports.

Chauncey,[13] reporting on his evaluation of Soviet education, states:

> . . . Soviet leaders have decreed that all students—except the 1% who are defective—must take the rigorous academic program through the tenth grade. Every educational official with whom I talked assured me that 99% of the students who entered the ten-year school were capable of completing the academic program successfully.

He then goes on to say:

> In this country we assume that only 30% or 40% of our high school students can satisfactorily complete a rigorous college preparatory program and perhaps only half as many with profit to themselves.

Although Chauncey does not share the Soviet rejection of hereditary influences, he does believe that the superior performance of Soviet students is a function of higher academic motivation. Once again, the question of the dominance of environment over heredity is coming to the fore.

A report presented by Schwebel,[14] describing the work of Pasamanich and Knoblock, certainly implies that intelligence, like most other biological functions, *may not be* normally distributed. The startling idea is presented that at conception individuals are quite alike in intellectual endowment, and that it is the life experiences and socio-cultural environment which influence the actual functioning potential of the person. It is these environmental influences which are cited as the cause of individual differences.

With this stress on the role of the environment, it becomes very relevant for counselors to examine the influences in our society which impinge upon clients and may lead to distortions in the way they perceive and cope with reality. Without this understanding, attempts to evaluate and diagnose become a meaningless activity. Although counselors have long been aware that early childhood experiences have a crucial role in determining adult values and behaviors, we have only recently begun to consider the counselor's role in working with family constellations.

Fullmer,[15] reporting on the development of family group counseling at the University of Oregon, indicates that this approach appears singularly successful in breaking the linkage of behaviors passed down from parent to child. He also indicates that this approach to counseling may succeed because it combines actual confrontation of clients with real situations at the same time that it offers alternate possible behaviors for consideration.

Barbe and Chambers,[16] in *The Vocational Guidance Quarterly*, point out that the training of guidance counselors for the elementary school has often neglected to make clear the differences which appear to exist between the children and their parents with respect to requirements for an ideal job.

Group Guidance as a Maturational Process

Traditionally, when textbooks have described programs designed for group guidance, they have geared their approach to the concept that guidance groups are most effective at the point where the student perceives the greatest need—at points of transition to another school level or where academic decisions need to be made.

This approach implies that the major job to be done at these crisis points is to help youngsters gather data and assess their meaning. Theoretically, the job is one of synthesis rather than of development of new concepts. Unfortunately, the approach frequently fails because it does not recognize that the significant factors affecting a youngster's decision were experienced many years before, and by the sixth, ninth, or twelfth grade they operate as unconscious determiners of choice.

It should be obvious that the school must have a role in helping youngsters secure and understand experiences which form the building blocks for later decisions. Basically, the experiences in school must facilitate helping a student answer two questions: "Who am I?" and "What could I be?" It must also recognize that children start getting their answers to these questions from infancy on. Deutsch[17] and Goodman[18] have documented the early effects of race awareness on four-year-olds' feelings about themselves and others. Studying a different dimension, Cowen et al.[19] have found it possible to "red tag" children in primary grades. The holders of the "red tag" are prime candidates for future mental difficulty, which probably will reflect itself through poor school adjustment. In their studies they found that almost one-third of the children needed preventive help to avoid future difficulties.

Many people experience confusion about what guidance is and what it ought to be. Part of this confusion reflects the fact that the guidance movement has felt the impact of many disciplines as it grew. In turn, the emphasis has shifted from education to economics, from mental hygiene to social case work, and now at last from clinical psychology to a synthesizing approach which focuses on guidance as a maturational process.

The past years have provided us with rich insights about how people experience vocational maturity. Anne Roe[20] has focused our attention on the role of the parent-child relationship in terms of its effect on personality. She has postulated that the warmth of this relationship affects a person's later desire to work either with people or with things.

Leona Tyler[21-23] has been conducting a longitudinal study of the ways in which children's interests grow and change. Her results to date are fascinating because, unlike most other people, she has tended to focus on what people dislike, seeing the rejections as more critical than the preferences. Her findings suggest that, at least for children in grade school, interest development is primarily a matter of learning to rule out clusters of things and activities one once liked. Her study is based on the premise that children have a chance to experience. For the culturally deprived child, providing broadening experiences may have to precede the selection process of likes and dislikes.

In almost parallel fashion, Cottle[24] found that people's interests really represent pairings. Each liking has associated with it the rejection of something else.

Each of these people has focused on at least one element affecting vocational maturity. Equal interest has been expressed through research studies which focus on the developmental stages through which a person passes as he matures. Some of these findings are provocative because they appear to be placing increasing emphasis on the crystallizing and important impact of experiences that occur up to grades 3 or 4. Many studies, like Bennett's,[25] suggest that broad areas of interest begin to appear as early as eight years of age. From the fourth through the eighth grade, up to 40 per cent of students tested expressed concern over what they would be when they grew up. At this early stage the child begins to show preferences for words versus numbers, people versus things, concrete versus abstract experiences.

One of the most prominent theories about the stages involved in career choice is that of Ginzberg[26] and his associates. They postulate at least three periods of development. In sequence they involve the making of fantasy, tentative, and realistic choices.

The contribution of Super and his associates has been reserved for major discussion. It was this group that in 1953 crystallized the concept of vocational maturity through defining its attributes. Many of the concepts to be discussed come from their work. Super listed five components of vocational maturity:

a. Readiness to choose
b. Consistency of preference or choice
c. Crystallization of traits
d. Information and planning
e. Wisdom of choice

Let us now examine each of these.

Readiness to Choose. Teachers and counselors have a direct impact on a child's readiness to choose. This readiness is basically dependent on a child's awareness of the eventual need for making a choice. Associated with this is the child's growing ability to accept responsibility for making decisions and to consider factors which will influence his decision. Parental attitude, peer group mores, and socio-economic pressures all are relevant factors.

We can well ask ourselves how effective we are in opening a child's eyes to the world of work and to the choices which confront him. Equally relevant are the pressures we put on him for special kinds of achievement, which, although intrinsically worthwhile, may create a greater dependence upon authority figures who manipulate rather than create a capacity for self-direction. Knowing that people under threat narrow their range of vision, teachers need to ask themselves about the way in which the classroom fosters or retards a child's feelings of security. Bany and Johnson[27] have listed a series of classroom conditions which may cause individuals to deviate from the norms of their class groups.

> 1. *Lack of communication prevents the child from perceiving the regions of behavior that are approved or disapproved.* The system of communication in the class group may be weak with respect to this individual, so that he has little opportunity to know what the group expects in the way of behavior from him, or he is unable to communicate effectively with others and thereby receives an inaccurate perception of the norms.
> 2. *The class group is unattractive to the child.* Needs for friendship and group affiliation may be satisfied by membership in outside play groups or gangs. He has few positive feelings toward the group and very little desire to be like its model members.
> 3. *Deviating from group norms is rewarding in itself.* The child receives praise and approval from the teacher, parents, or others for *not* following the group norms, and this may be more rewarding than group acceptance and approval.
> 4. *The group norm runs counter to a highly prized conviction concerning right and wrong.* Certain attitudes and beliefs acquired from the family or other sources are valued more highly by the child than those that the group expects him to accept.

Consistency of Preference. Many people have the mistaken notion that consistency of vocational choice is in and of itself a sign of vocational maturity. Consider the case of the young boy who is asked at age eight, "What do you want to be when you grow up?" At the moment he is intrigued by the idea of being a criminal lawyer like Perry Mason on television. Accordingly, he tells all who question him that he wants to be a lawyer. Since this is a nice, impressive occupation, all his questioners respond to his choice with approval. Year after year he discovers that his answer keeps people from bothering him, and after a while he begins to believe in his fantasy goal himself. Suddenly he is confronted with information about the real job demands of his chosen career and with the many ways his interests and abilities make this goal unrealistic. Until he can discover an alternative goal, he will continue to hold on to his earlier unrealistic goal. He is consistent, but how mature is his decision? Consistency can be demonstrated, as in the above example, by holding to only one occupation, by holding to the same general level of ability or education, or by seeing relationships between jobs in the same field and level. This last example of consistency can provide security since it helps the person see a variety of possibilities where his interests and abilities can find fulfillment. To assist in the process of helping children to clarify their goals, both teachers and counselors need to examine the degree to which they are forcing youngsters to choose job titles instead of areas, fields, or levels of achievement as career goals. School people also need to discover how effective they are in helping children learn about the ways in which jobs are related to one another. Senesh,[28] with his focus on economic education, is teaching first and second graders about producers and consumers. Lifton[29,30] has provided a series of materials designed to facilitate the development of self-concept and the concept of job families.

Now, let us explore how crystallization of traits affects vocational maturity.

The Crystallization of Traits. Much of our counseling takes the form of helping youngsters assess their interests or abilities by comparing their own ability with the ability of people presently successful in the field. As noted earlier, the existence of available role models is critical. Within this context, then, vocational maturity might be defined as the degree to which a person's measured abilities approximate adult norms. Although this yardstick can be ultimately helpful, it does not present an on-going picture of the crystallization of the child's traits, nor does it provide a comparison of how well the child stacks up against other children who hold similar career choices, come from similar cultural backgrounds, are the same age, and are at the same level of schooling. One oblique way of perceiving a child's vocational independence can be inferred from the kinds of part-time experiences a child has had, the way he responded to job demands, and the way he secured these exploratory job experiences. Certainly, the youngster who seeks a job on his own shows a maturity not shared by the youngster working for his dad, at his father's suggestion. We also need to recognize, however, that it will be increasingly difficult for young people to find any work. The school may need to consider providing vicarious job experiences. For those youngsters in the poverty strata of our society, we now provide experiences through the Job Corps or the Youth Employment Corps. Where will the rest of the young people get a chance to learn what it feels like to have a job?

Attitudes toward work are of considerable interest. Tyler's study suggests that young boys are allergic to anything that smacks of work, but change their attitudes as they mature. Correlated with this is an interesting shift in the way jobs are ranked according to prestige levels. Knowing how differing age levels rank jobs in terms of status can provide the teacher with an index of the relative vocational maturity of the child.

Let us now turn to an area typically considered as basic to the school's role. How has the child secured vocational information? How has he been helped in planning his career?

Information and Planning. The amount of information a person has about the world of work and about the demands of his chosen area represents another index of vocational maturity. Here more than in most places the school and teachers have been indicted for failing to provide youngsters with adequate and accurate information.

As stated earlier, recent studies[31-34] have documented the ways in which teacher background, existing textbooks, and parental pressures all are operating to provide youngsters with the most information about the jobs they are least likely to get. As a result, large segments of our school population either see no relevance between school and the real world as they know it or feel that going to college is the only sure road to security.

Wisdom of Vocational Preference. This index of maturity, more than any other, is a basis for controversy. Many of the yardsticks one could employ here would reflect the values, attitudes, and biases of the teacher or society. For example, see how you react to the following sample situations:

Susy has been an "A" student. She has chosen to go to college to study mathematics. All tests and grades support her ability to do so. In her high school senior year, Suzy falls in love. Her boy friend is going to college in a distant town. She is considering getting married and working to help put her boy friend through school. Should she marry?

Jim is a boy with many abilities. Beyond his skills in the science area, he is also an accomplished musician. Jim is torn between society's pressure on him to become a scientist and his own preference for music. Where does his responsibility to society begin and end?

Bob is a Negro. His family is poor and is unable to help him through school. He is strongly interested in banking. Few Negroes have obtained jobs in this field. Should he be encouraged to take the risk of training in an area where he may not be able to get a job?

Mary and her parents have always seemed to measure the value of any project in terms of its material rewards. Suddenly, Mary states quite definitely that she wants to be a foreign missionary for a religious order. How do we decide if her choice really represents her goals in life? How do we help her assess the reality of her decision?

Each of these cases, beyond the psychological factors involved, also contain problems based upon differences in values in our society. The school has been defined as the transmitter of our culture to the next generation. Increasingly, we find ourselves being asked, "Are the values you are transmitting broad enough to reflect the full spectrum of our society?"

*Planning the Content for Group Guidance**

VOCATIONAL MATURITY: A PYRAMID OF DECISIONS AND EXPERIENCES

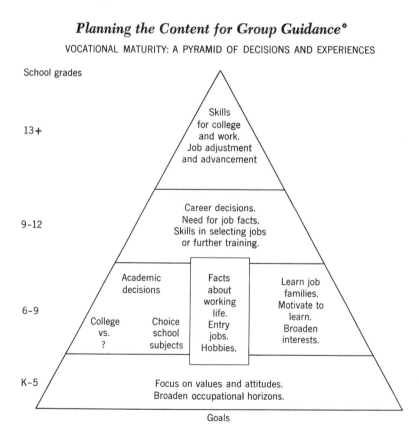

* Parts of this section appeared in a paper, "Where Is the Guidance Movement Heading? The Publisher's Role in Determining Direction" written by W. Lifton in *The SRA Newsletter,* February, 1961.

The development of an individual's self-concept is critically related to the occupational role he hopes to play in society. Materials created to help the child go through the process of vocational maturation must be in keeping with the stages through which he will pass and the kinds of decisions that he will face. The accompanying diagram embodies the idea that at each level of schooling there is a narrowing of the range within which decisions are made.

The diagram represents the broad objectives. We have assumed that the following specific guidance goals exist for each school level.

The Elementary School. Materials and class discussions in the elementary school should strive to:

a. Enlarge the child's conception and awareness of the world of work.

b. Help the child realize the many values that provide job satisfaction.

c. Develop the child's awareness of the relation between school, his family, the community, and the world of work. Here again, class discussions help provide the needed bridge.

d. Provide the child with a chance to recognize his social and cultural heritage and to relate its effect on occupational attitudes to the mores of his group—for example, by helping minority groups see that their parents' attitudes may be based upon past experiences that they themselves may never encounter.

e. Help the child isolate and face anxieties that may constitute blocks to learning.

f. Help the child develop an acceptance of individual differences and an awareness of the need for many kinds of people in our society.

g. Introduce the idea that jobs are related to each other within family groups, with each job family having a different common denominator—skill, interest, industry, and so on.

h. Help the child realize that changes in his interests and goals are to be expected and are a natural part of the maturational process.

i. Help integrate guidance into the existing curriculum or free periods. To maximize interest at the elementary level, the use of games, activities, and puns is appropriate. Pictures are a vital part of the text. To gain students' acceptance, use of bright colors and concrete examples should be considered. Maximum use of the students' own experiences should be the goal.

The Junior High School. The development of the junior high school reflected an awareness of the need to ease the transition from elementary to high school for students.

Junior high school is the first major fork in the road where those who drop out of school are separated from those who continue on. Taking into consideration all of the above factors, material for the junior high school should:

a. Be designed to meet the needs of two separate populations. For school leavers there needs to be developed information about *entry* jobs that are available for people with limited schooling. Since the dropout may tend to be the poor reader and the less academically oriented student, the material should more closely resemble that prepared for the elementary school (in terms of reading level and simplicity of concepts presented). The remainder of the school population need materials that will help them in planning courses and in crystallizing potential goals.

b. Focus, as in the elementary school, on enlarging occupational horizons rather than on encouraging youngsters to concentrate on one specific occupation. In recognition of the student's growing awareness of his interests and abilities, he ought to be helped to discover the many jobs available that will be compatible with his emerging self-concept.

c. Recognize the adolescent's need for fantasy or his tendency to select an occupation based upon current prestige or status needs. The guidance person need not worry because the occupation being explored does not represent the real goal of the student. What is of more relevant concern is that the material be so designed that a student, as he explores his unrealistic choices, is helped to realize the factors that make these choices of a career inappropriate. The major goal should be to capitalize on the motivation arising from a student's needs, and to help him discover how the securing of information is part of the problem-solving process.

d. Evaluate the kinds of information to be included in occupational materials for the junior high school group. For many students actual employment is four to eight years away. Current statistics on salary and job opportunities do not give an accurate picture of the job as it will be in years to come. There is also a real question whether occupational material should reinforce typical student bases for evaluating career plans. (How much will I make? How easy will it be for me to get a job?) Instead, occupational materials for this level might more properly emphasize the concepts that job security stems from the way in which the individual compares with others seeking the same job, and that security is a function of the degree to which an occupation provides the individual with meaningful rewards.

e. Emphasize students' motivation toward a goal. A basic goal at this level ought to be to help students develop security by discovering the many jobs and job families that they could consider.

f. Accept the idea that students at this level are not usually willing to read a detailed job description. Anecdotal material, use of illustrations, and limitation of length all ought to be considered as means of increasing the readability of materials. The more mature youngsters at this level ought to have available references to more sophisticated presentations. This listing of allied readings can also be used to develop research and reference skills as part of the school program.

g. Acknowledge that students in junior high are at an age where they are vigorously trying to discover their abilities and interests. Occupational materials and class discussions ought to help them find a wide range of activities, hobbies, and part-time job experiences that could provide clues to areas of real competence and interest.

h. Use a method of presentation that is appropriate for junior high. Occupational materials may require a semifictional approach to motivate students to read beyond their immediate needs for information. The use of a glossary to facilitate an increased knowledge of new terms may be helpful. At this level it is vital that students be given support to face their anxiety over the choices they need to make. At the same time the approach should reflect the students' desire to be considered young adults. Emphasis ought to be on the psychological rewards of work. (What does it feel like to be a _____?)

The High School. As in junior high, guidance materials ought to meet the needs of two separate populations—those for whom high school is terminal education, and those who will go on for further training. Since approximately 80 per cent do not go on to college, material for this level must be as accurate as possible in describing actual job demands and working conditions. Present criteria reflected in material developed for the *Occupational Outlook Handbook* and in current National Vocational Guidance Association standards are quite appropriate. There is, however, a real question whether these standards need to apply to all material prepared for high school youth. For many there is still a need to broaden occupational horizons through exposure to material that focuses on the relations between jobs rather than on the specific requirements of a single occupation. With the increased departmentalization of schools into subject-matter groups, occupational materials need to be diversified in format so that they are suitable for use under different conditions and in different school settings. The criteria to apply in evaluating materials therefore should vary with the goal and use of the materials.

High school materials should:

a. Provide comprehensive and complete information about specific jobs. Although the content and format may not lend themselves to pleasure reading, attention must be paid to the reading level of the material. To insure maximum comprehension, the reading level ought to be approximately eighth grade. References for more extended reading can include more challenging material.

b. Be useful for exploration purposes, broadening students' awareness of the range of potential jobs that could be considered. To accomplish different goals, these approaches need to vary in format. For example, for a student with a keen interest in medicine but with minimum ability, material presenting the many jobs involving similar interests but requiring different levels of skills—male nurse, X-ray technician, and so on—would be helpful. In similar fashion, helping students see the job implications of subject-matter areas increases the motivation to learn.

c. Consider the effect on students (as in *b*) of the format and way the material is made available for use. For example, current acceptance of the Dictionary of Occupational Titles system is based on good historical reasons. New materials grouped in different ways to facilitate the movement of people between closely related jobs need to be encouraged. For example, the Fine system of ideas, people, and things provides one way of avoiding the status implications of a D.O.T. system. Evaluation of each system ought to be based on the defined purpose of that system rather than on an arbitrary statement of facts that all materials must include and emphasize.

d. Emphasize, as in junior high, the presentation of facts needed for good decision making instead of attempting to sell jobs or to indoctrinate certain values.

e. Develop the awareness of the need for objective reporting, whether for educational or vocational purposes. Wherever possible primary sources of information should be cited to insure accuracy. Although job descriptions are factual, the direction in which the field is moving and the ideas of the people in the field about the role the worker ought to have represent value judgments students need to know about. Wherever possible, all viewpoints ought to be reported.

f. Help the student understand job demands by equating job characteristics with common situations where the skills needed are comparable. Facts like those found in Part IV of the DOT, relating hobbies, extracurricular activities, and personality characteristics to jobs, provide a good example.

g. Emphasize the job skills and rewards rather than projected estimates of future demands. Technological change, world situations, aging, and other factors modify estimates in unpredictable ways. To increase feelings of security, materials ought to cover jobs that are on a horizontal plane and that could be obtained with a minimum of retraining.

h. Provide help for the college-bound youngster both in selection of courses required in high school for admission to college and in selection of the most appropriate colleges for training in the desired field. The same approach is needed for students seeking advanced technical training.

The College. Although theoretically college students are expected to have solved their problems of career choice, realistically many students in college are undecided about their goal. Even where areas for study have been selected, the choice of a specialty needs to be made. For example, a person might want to be a psychologist but may not have decided what kind of psychologist—clinical, experimental, industrial, etc.—he wants to become. Monographs providing detailed information on training requirements and day-to-day tasks are very important. Students should also have information on current developments in the field.

The Relationship of Different Educational Media to Group Guidance and Teaching*

Traditionally, major attention has been given to the counselor's role as a provider of information, and as an agent who helps others improve their understanding of themselves and the world in which they live. Because counselors have seen words as their method of communicating with others, inadequate attention has been given to the ways in which other educational media fit into the developing role which counselors are establishing for themselves. This section is devoted to an exploration of the relationship between some of the major assumptions underlying counseling process and the criteria counselors might employ as they try to determine if a specific educational media will facilitate the type of communication desired.

* Parts of this section appeared in a paper, "Counseling Theory and the Use of Educational Media" written by W. Lifton in *The Vocational Guidance Quarterly,* 13, No. 2, 77–82, Winter 1964–1965.

The Use of Information

It is fairly well accepted that clients will incorporate information when:

a. The information is presented in a way which enables them to use the facts with a minimum of transfer.

b. They are secure enough to allow themselves to perceive the situation broadly, rather than using tunnel vision to protect themselves from seeing potentially threatening situations.

c. They have perceived that this information is necessary to achieve a goal important to themselves.

Let us examine the ways in which these concepts relate to the use of various educational media. Some time ago, Joseph Samler,[35] in an article evaluating the use of occupational briefs, pointed out that printed material available at that time failed to deal with the psychosocial rewards of a job. He demonstrated effectively how youngsters were seeking to learn what it feels like to be a machinist or a butcher. Since his article, many printed materials have attempted to meet the goals of emotionally involving youngsters in the data being presented. Typically, the approach has involved a fictional situation in which, it was hoped, the youngsters would identify with a major character and become aware of their reactions to the situations they faced.

Other Educational Media. It is time for educators to become equally discriminating in their use of other educational media. Although films, tapes, slides, and other media are being used with increasing frequency, few educators have stopped to examine whether the approach used accomplishes its purpose. There are many films available on the market put out by commercial publishers and business organizations, describing the jobs in our country. The photography is excellent, the voices of the announcers appealing, and the general development of the story theme is sufficiently exciting to maintain our attention; but when we are through watching the films, we might readily ask "What has the viewer learned? Has he learned anything about the way he would feel if he were part of the situation?" The use of role playing and similar devices in counseling is not new; yet somehow when we use audio-visual aids, we do not attempt to see how we can involve the listener actively in the experience.

Involving the Learner. The question of how to involve the viewer in a manner which helps him learn in new and different ways should not remain pedantic. Let us see if we can increase our learning by involving ourselves, right now, in solving a specific problem. Suppose you and I were faced with the task of helping one of our clients learn to tie a bow tie. Let us also suppose that we had available to us a motion picture camera with a sound track. How would we go about attempting the task? Most of us would tend to take a picture of someone tying his tie and we would have an accompanying sound track describing the motions the person was going through.

If we think about the problem for a moment, we will readily recognize that a camera facing the subject is not presenting the same picture which the subject himself experiences as he tries to go through the motions. As a matter of fact, one way to photograph the process we are trying to teach in this particular operation would be to take a photograph of the subject in a mirror, since this is the image our learner sees as he tries to check himself in his learning experience. Similarly, the counselor serves as a mirror for the client's feelings.

Let us try another problem. Suppose we are trying to help a child learn to tie a shoe. Many of us became familiar in our education courses with the Montessori techniques. We all can remember the mock shoes designed to help youngsters learn to lace and tie. Sometimes we wonder why, as the youngster develops proficiency in lacing and tying these toy shoes, he still has difficulty in tying his own. Again, we have failed to look at the problem involved from the point of view of the learner. If one were making a motion picture of what we are trying to teach, the perception of the learner of the shoe-tying process would demand that we put the camera over his shoulder and face it down toward his shoe, tilted in the position that the learner is in when he tries to manipulate his shoe laces.

Thus far we have been examining communication in terms of our initial assumption that the more closely and concretely the learning experience relates to future tasks, the more rapid and efficient the learning will be.

Learning and Security Needs. Let us now examine our second counseling assumption: that learning is related to the security needs of the viewer. To explore this concept, let us consider the problem of developing industrial filmstrips for junior high school youngsters. We are fairly clear about the kinds of experiences and information that we believe youngsters at this age need. We are also aware of another problem. One characteristic of adolescents is the tendency to reject adult figures. In striving to achieve adulthood, the adolescent tends to be fearful of accepting adult instruction on faith, since, if he does, he will never know if he would have come to the same conclusions himself. To the degree that this is true, and to the degree that any media employed seems to be lecturing or telling these youngsters what they ought to do, it is quite reasonable to expect that they will reject the facts being presented, in the same way that they would reject adult advice.

Similarly, we know that adolescents are quite responsive to peer group pressures. In developing educational materials for this population, therefore, the characters portrayed ought to be people with whom adolescents can identify. Certainly, in the area of racial characteristics we have become sensitive to the fact that we need to include a wide variety of role models to accommodate the equally wide range of characteristics of our viewers. Since some viewers' past experiences may be limited, we need to also introduce new concepts, so that each viewer will have as much information as possible from which to make decisions. To the degree that these new experiences are alien to the viewer, we are obligated to present a comparable familiar situation so that he can have a basis for understanding the new concept we are presenting. In so doing, we are following the well-known dictum of moving from the known to the unknown. For example, when introducing the concept of job families to youngsters, the author helped the viewers explore the many ways in which family groups develop in our society. These familiar ways of grouping people were then applied to jobs and job families.[36]

The author is suggesting that we present a variety of stimuli from which viewers can draw conclusions. There is less motivation to reject one's own answer to a problem than answers which are presented as the result of an adult's experience. Again, a concrete example might be helpful. In developing a training film to teach study skills, we all know things we typically teach youngsters to improve their study skills. We stress the importance of adequate lightning, comfortable temperature, availability of material, etc. How can we communicate this message to youngsters in a way that might be meaningful to them, and yet recognize the ways in which their age level might affect their perception because of the approach being employed. One technique is to provide youngsters with a series of visual problems requiring a decision on the part of the viewer. For example, in a split frame a picture could be shown on one side of a youngster in a very hot room, sweating and uncomfortable; on the other side, a picture of a youngster in another room where he is relatively cool. The observers would be asked to decide which of these two people they felt would find studying easier.[37]

In the same way, each of the other conditions necessary for a good study situation is presented to youngsters. In each case, viewers are provided wih a variety of answers on which they can make their decisions. Having come up with these answers, based upon an experience in which they were actively involved, hopefully they would then incorporate these insights as part of the fabric of their being, rather than as facts to be learned for a test and rapidly forgotten.

Establishing a Readiness. Let us now proceed to the last assumption presented; that there needs to be established a readiness for information before it will be either sought, used, or incorporated. This readiness, of course, stems from the ease with which the client can see his need for information. He must see why he requires certain tools to achieve objectives of importance to him.

Typically, for reasons of expedience, counselors tend initially to think of their group guidance responsibilities in terms of providing information through lesson plans. Films, tapes, and other devices are planned for and scheduled far in advance. Like other educators, they have allowed current practice or administrative convenience to determine teaching or counseling methodology.

In the current process of redefining counseling role, it is certainly timely for us to recognize the ways in which the structure of the school is shifting. The concept of the learning center is not new; but few counselors have considered how the counseling office might utilize this approach. Schools currently being built include private study cubicles for students[38] (see Figure 1). They are equipped with closed-circuit television and a dial phone hooked into a computer center which will feed via the television screen any type of information available that can be transmitted over a visual and sound system. How many of us have begun to prepare for this shift in information retrieval? No longer will our clients need to come to us for facts. Instead, they will utilize mechanical sources to secure information. The counselor may no longer have to feel guilty because he hasn't an adequate or up-to-date supply of facts. His role will be to help clients learn to use these educational resources. His responsibility will also be to insure that the facts or materials stored for retrieval by clients are adequate and appropriate.

It is indeed unfortunate that few counselors realize how rapidly new techniques of data processing, branched learning systems tied to computers, and transmission of photographic material over long distance wires, are effecting a revolution which will enable their client to secure information at the moment when the client perceives his greatest need. Certainly, current group guidance classes designed to disseminate information to large groups may no longer be either effi-

Figure 1. Source: The School Library—Facilities for Independent Study in the Secondary School. Study carrels. Part of a complex communications system, these carrels to be installed at Grand Valley State College contain fixed mechanical equipment. Student uses dial to signal control room for program of his choice.

cient or desirable. They have long been inappropriate from a counseling point of view.

The Counselor's Future Role

The simple fact is that counselors of tomorrow will basically be concerned with counseling. They will continue to be concerned with providing experiences which broaden perception. New and different areas requiring emphasis are already appearing on the scene. How will counselors develop vicarious experiences to help youngsters learn job adjustment skills to replace the experiences obtained by earlier generations through part-time jobs or summer employment, but now not available for the young worker. Figure 2 pictures a device used

Figure 2. Source: *AV Communication Reviews.* Student teacher stands facing large rear-projection screen upon which life-size image is projected. Supervising teacher (seated) operates equipment by remote controls. Motion picture and slide projectors and other components of electronic data processing equipment are located behind the screen.

to provide student teachers with a vicarious classroom experience. One answer may be to develop a similar device to simulate work experience.[39,40]

Discussion

This chapter has presented the concept that the content of group guidance courses must reflect the changing needs of students, the limitations of the educational setting, and the impact of new technologies on the educational process.

Both the textbook edited by Gage[41] and the textbook edited by Henry[42] provide a comprehensive overview of the relationship between teaching effectively and the dynamics of the classroom group.

Readers unaware of the scope of educational or vocational information to be imparted will find Baer and Roeber's[43] textbook, *Occupational Information,* helpful.

Specific techniques useful in the school setting can be found in Mahler and Caldwell's *Group Counseling in Secondary Schools*,[44] Caldwell's *Group Techniques for the Classroom Teacher*,[45] and Glanz's *Groups in Guidance*.[46]

Chapter 7 deals with applying the group techniques explored so far.

BIBLIOGRAPHY

1. Kvaraceus, William C. "Helping the Socially Inadapted Pupil in the Large City Schools." *Exceptional Children*, 28, 402, April 1962.
2. Diebold, John. "Automation: Its Implications for Counseling." *The Vocational Guidance Quarterly*, 11, No. 1, Autumn 1963.
3. Deeg, Maethel E., and Patterson, Donald G. "Changes in Social Status of Occupations." *Occupations*, January 1947.
4. Welch, Maryon K. "Ranking of Occupations on the Basis of Social Status." *Occupations*, January 1949.
5. Stefflre, Buford. "Analysis of the Inter-Relationships of Ranking of Occupations." *Personnel and Guidance Journal*, February 1959.
6. Dipboye, W. J., and Anderson, W. F. "The Ordering of Occupational Values, by High School Freshmen and Seniors." *Personnel and Guidance Journal*, October 1959.
7. Flanagan, John C. "Project Talent Preliminary Findings." *Guidance Newsletter*. Chicago: Science Research Associates, November 1959.
8. Lifton, Walter. *Introducing the World of Work to Children*. Chicago: Science Research Associates, 1960.
9. Riessman, Frank. *The Culturally Deprived Child*. New York: Harper, 1962.
10. Lindner, Robert. *Prescription for Rebellion*. New York: Rinehart, p. 172, 1952.
11. Getzels, Jacob W., and Jackson, Philip W. *Creativity and Intelligence: Exploration with Gifted Students*. New York: Wiley, 1962.
12. Hahn, Milton. "Forgotten People." *American Psychologist*, 17, No. 10, 700–705, October 1962.
13. Chauncey, Henry. "Some Notes on Education and Psychology in the Soviet Union." *The American Psychologist*, 14, No. 6, 307–312, June 1959.
14. Schwebel, Milton. "Some Missing Links in Counseling Theory and Research." *The Personnel and Guidance Journal*, 325–331, December 1962.
15. Fullmer, Daniel, and Bernard, Harold. *Counseling: Content and Process*. Chicago: Science Research Associates, 1963.
16. Barbe, Walter, and Chambers, Norman. "Career Requirements of Gifted Elementary Children and Their Parents." *Vocational Guidance Quarterly*, 11, No. 2, 137–140, Winter 1963.
17. Deutsch, Martin. "Minority Group and Class Status as Related to Social and Personality Factors in Scholastic Achievement." *Monograph 2, Society for Applied Anthropology*, pp. 10, 11, 19, 1960.
18. Goodman, Mary Ellen. *Race Awareness in Young Children*. New York: Crowell-Collier, 1964.

19. Cowen, E. L., Izzo, L. D., Miles, H., Telschow, E. F., Trost, M. A., and Zax, M. "A Mental Health Program in the School Setting: Description and Evaluation." *Journal of Psychology,* 56, (Part 2), 307–356, 1963.

20. Roe, Anne and Siegelman, Marvin. *The Origin of Interests.* Washington D. C.: American Personnel and Guidance Assn., 1965.

21. Tyler, Leona. "Toward a Workable Psychology of Individuality." *American Psychologist,* 14, 75–81, February 1959.

22. Tyler, Leona. "The Measured Interests of Adolescent Girls." *The Journal of Educational Psychology,* 561–572, November 1941.

23. Tyler, Leona. "The Development of Vocational Interests: I. The Organization of Likes and Dislikes in Ten-Year-Old Children." *The Journal of Genetic Psychology,* 88, 33–44, 1955.

24. Cottle, William C. *A Factual Study of the Multiphasic, Strong, Kuder, and Bell Inventories Using a Population of Adult Males* as cited in *Estimates of Worker Trait Requirements for 4,000 Jobs,* U. S. Department of Labor.

25. Bennett, Margaret. *Guidance in Groups,* pp. 54, 246. New York: McGraw-Hill, 1955.

26. Ginzberg, Eli. "Toward a Theory of Occupational Choice." *Occupations,* 30, 491–494, 1952.

27. Bany, Mary A., and Johnson, Lois V. *Classroom Group Behavior,* pp. 143–144. New York: Macmillan, 1964.

28. Senesh, Lawrence. *Our Working World.* Chicago: Science Research Associates, 1964.

29. Lifton, Walter. *What Could I Be?* Chicago: Science Research Associates, 1960.

30. Lifton, Walter. *Widening Occupational Roles Kit.* Chicago: Science Research Associates, 1962.

31. Arbuckle, Dugald. "Occupational Information in the Elementary School." *The Vocational Guidance Quarterly,* 12, No. 2, 77–84, Winter 1963–1964.

32. Tennyson, Wesley W., and Monnens, Lawrence P. "The World of Work through Elementary Readers." *The Vocational Guidance Quarterly,* 12, No. 2, 85–88, Winter 1963–1964.

33. Lifton, Walter M. "Social Forces and Guidance in the Elementary School." *The Vocational Guidance Quarterly,* 12, No. 2, 89–92, Winter 1963–1964.

34. Lifton, Walter M. *Introducing the World of Work to Children.* Chicago: Science Research Associates, 1960.

35. Samler, Joseph. Psycho-Social Aspects of Work: A Critique of Occupational Information." *Personnel and Guidance Journal,* 39, 458–465, 1961.

36. Lifton, Walter M. *Guide to the Use of the Widening Occupational Roles Kit.* Chicago: Science Research Associates, 1962.

37. Lifton, Walter M. *The Successful Student-School Skills for Today and Tomorrow* (Series of 6 Filmstrips). Chicago: Society for Visual Education, 1963.

38. Ellsworth, Ralph E., and Wagener, Hobart D. "A New Concept for a School Library." *The School Library-Facilities for Independent Study in the Secondary School.* New York: Educational Facilities Laboratories, 1963 (Picture 1).

39. Bushnell, Donald D. "Computor-Based Simulation." *AV Communication Review,* 2, 1963, Figures 23, 53 (Picture 2 plus legend).

40. Magoon, Thomas. "Innovations in Counseling." *Journal of Counseling Psychology,* **11,** No. 4, 342–347, 1964.
41. Gage, N. L. (Editor). *Handbook on Research on Teaching.* Chicago: Rand McNally, 1963.
42. Henry, N. B. (Editor). *The Dynamics of Instructional Groups.* Fifty-Ninth Yearbook, Part II, National Society for the Study of Education. Chicago: University of Chicago Press, 1960.
43. Baer, Max, and Roeber, Edward. *Occupational Information: The Dynamics of Its Nature and Use.* Chicago: Science Research Associates, 1964.
44. Mahler, Clarence, and Caldwell, Edson. *Group Counseling in Secondary Schools,* Chicago: Science Research Associates, 1961.
45. Caldwell, Edson. *Group Techniques for the Classroom Teacher.* Chicago: Science Research Associates, 1960.
46. Glanz, Edward. *Groups in Guidance.* Boston: Allyn and Bacon, 1962.

7

Group Techniques Applied

The material in Chapter 6 focused on goals and types of materials. Little was said about where these insights or experiences are to occur. In this chapter we will explore the use of classrooms, homerooms, guidance courses, career days, community agencies, as well as other group settings designed to help people get significant answers to their problems.

Although most teachers have had training in relating to students and in recognizing the needs of individuals, the classroom atmosphere typically revolves around the teacher and the curriculum. There are authors who, when talking about the group dynamics of the classroom, really are describing teacher-centered groups where movement, direction, and rewards are all determined by the teacher.

Harris,[1] Maas,[2] Perkins,[3] Laycock,[4] the A.S.C.D.,[5] Cantor,[6] Prescot,[7] and Trow[8] are but a few authors who have tried to focus on the group-centered climate needed for optimal assimilation of social and content learnings in the classroom. The article by DeBoer[9] relating group dynamics to instruction in English may serve as a basis for seeing group process in a subject matter setting.

Gillies,[10] Metcalf,[11] Cole,[12] Elkins,[13] and Jenkins[14] have described how, within the school framework, it is possible to develop groups that have a therapeutic goal as their major objective.

There is little question in the author's mind that the objectives stated for the elementary school must take place in the classroom, usually under the supervision of the teacher. In schools where specialists are available, it may be possible for them to come in and handle specific discussions where the teacher feels uncomfortable. The most effective programs will occur, however, where the teacher can relate the guidance objectives to subject matter content. Students will be most strongly motivated to study academic subjects if the teacher can relate their current concerns to the material to be learned.

Group Techniques in the Subject Matter Classroom

The defined goal of the public school and many other agencies in our society is to transmit the culture and heritage handed down to us from our forefathers. A typical question that teachers hear is, "Why do we have to study math—or English—or?" The question implies two major concerns of the students. First of all, they are challenging the meaningfulness of the experience. Second, they are reacting to having the limits of a specific situation predetermined.

When the leader can accept the feelings of hostility that arise from youthful rebellion to societal limits, the group is free to use its energies toward discovering ways in which the course involved can be made personally meaningful to them. At this point it is most helpful for the group to be given responsibility for getting answers to the question of the value of the material.[15-18]

One example of this comes to mind. A chemistry teacher who was accustomed to having students groan on the first day as he outlined the concepts to be learned decided to reverse his approach and ask the group about the ways in which chemistry was affecting their lives. After giving a few socially approved schoolbook answers, the children went off on a more personal basis. "I'd like to know what makes lipstick kissproof." "I want to know if detergents really make washing easier." "I want to know what makes high octane gas better for cars."

At this point the instructor indicated on the blackboard what he expected them to know at the end of the semester. (Limit of the course.) He then asked the group to see if they could see any relationship between the questions they wanted answered and the skills they needed to learn. Together they mapped out projects that would answer their questions while involving school skills needed to get answers.

This first illustration represented an area in which the focus is typically subject matter knowledge. Certainly, as the group became motivated to learn, and as they discovered ways to make their experience meaningful, their whole attitude toward the classroom situation changed. In areas like social studies, English, and guidance, helping children relate their needs to the course content becomes less tenuous and difficult. Ojemann[19] has completed a series of studies designed to discover why, despite the relevance of courses like English and social studies to the development of human relations skills, people still grow up with a surface approach to behavior. He found that typically textbooks and teachers who treat human behavior fail to focus on the dynamics which cause typical human reactions. It is his finding, and that of Stiles,[20] that to develop causally oriented children we need teachers who both teach in a causal approach *and* who practice causal approaches in their daily relations with pupils. Where teachers do not possess these skills, it becomes the responsibility of the school system to use human relations specialists to provide in-service training for staff.

As Seeley[21] has pointed out, even when class time is used to discuss human relations at the expense of time spent on subject matter, the classes achieve well in subject matter learnings.

One interesting way of combining subject matter and human relation goals has been developed by the Illinois Curriculum Program.[22] In their *Reading for Living* bulletin they have developed an index of fiction reading materials that have been grouped according to the way they might provide answers to problems that students checked on the Mooney Problem Check List. The concept here was that as youngsters could empathize with fictional characters having problems similar to their own, they might be provided with cathartic experiences along with alternative solutions to their problems. Coincidentally, it provided students with the motivation to read, since the content of the books had very personal importance to the reader. A comparable reading list has been developed by the American Council on Education.[23]

As cited earlier, Stiles found it important that teachers practice causal approaches in their teaching. It should be obvious that the degree to which the classroom incorporates the therapeutic atmosphere described in preceding chapters will determine the degree to which class members will be able to verbalize needs they wish to be related to the course. Similarly, a person can accept individual difference only when he feels that his uniqueness is valuable.

Group Guidance

At the junior high school level it may be possible to set up separate groups to explore questions of a personal, social, or vocational nature.

The leader of these groups should be a person who can accept the passive role needed to allow group members to find their own answers.

Teachers or counselors who seek cook-book guidance units are missing the boat completely. Thelen[24] has described the nonlearning concerns of children, concerns which must be recognized as the drive for classroom interaction. Such factors as the need to conform, sex identifications, reactions to authority, and relations with peers tend to be more motivating for children than their concern for the academic tasks prescribed by the school. It might be helpful for educators to realize that school subjects may be seen by students primarily as vehicles for getting answers to their social, emotional and sexual needs. Any book which sets forth the way to organize a group guidance class can do so only to promote a pet belief rather than to suggest the most appropriate techniques to employ.

On a pragmatic basis, however, teacher reports and discussions at professional conferences, concur about approaches that secure better student and staff acceptance. Agreement seems to be high that:

1. *Any group program, to be successful, must consider the interests of potential group members.* An established curriculum of topics routinely covered in grades 7, 8, 9, or in a boy's club, etc., fails to recognize that groups of comparable chronological age may differ markedly in their social sophistication and concerns. There is as much individual difference between groups as there is between group members.

2. *To insure that all members of a group share common concerns, it is helpful to involve members in locating areas of concern and in establishing the limits of the group.* An institution's concern that members receive the information they need at critical choice points frequently overlooks the fact that if these really are points of common concern, group after group on their own volition will choose to cover the same ground. The major difference will be their attitude and motivation to participate, not necessarily the areas discussed. Some agencies have found that instruments like the Mooney Problem Check List or SRA Youth Inventory[25] provide youngsters with two kinds of help. Since both of these inventories list common problems all youngsters face, they help structure potential common sources of anxiety. For the youngster, learning that these are inventories of *common* concerns frees him of feelings of anxiety and enables him to consider these topics for group discussion. Comparable instruments are available for adult groups.

Career Days

It is this need to secure common understanding that should underlie the development of courses in "Ethics for Living," "Problems of Everyday Living," "Careers and Occupations," and schoolwide activities like career days and college days. In the development of any of these programs an initiating agency should ask itself the following questions:

a. Has the group had a chance to define clearly the information they desire? Within the defined purpose of the group, have they explored the concerns most group members wish to face first?

b. Has the group developed a setting in which its members will feel secure? For example, what is the effect of college day programs on noncollege-going youth?

c. Has the group developed skills in evaluating the accuracy of the information they receive from resource people? For example, do the guests at a Career Day Conference provide an objective picture of their areas of interest?

d. Has the group secured sufficient prior information so that it has a basis for evaluating the current program? For example, prior to a Career Day have the members considered what they need to know about their interests and abilities so that they see the way in which occupations being presented match up with their pattern of similar skills and interests?

e. Has the group had a chance to develop skills they need to achieve their goals? Have devices like role-playing and socio-dramas been used to help the group see how they are coping with present situations—and at the same time have they provided the group with a chance to learn and practice new skills?

Each of the questions above should point up one major factor. No group guidance activity can be successful unless it is considered in terms of the total context of the agency within which it takes place. The meaningfulness of any group experience is definitely related to the things that both precede and follow the group activity. Local research into the effectiveness of any program highlights the areas needing additional study.

Consider Table I. It reflects data gathered by Harley Neal (Rockford, Illinois) in a study of the vocational preferences of junior high students. These youngsters were going to attend a career conference sponsored by the Chamber of Commerce. Although the job distribu-

TABLE I

DISTRIBUTION OF CHOICES FOR TEN MAJOR OCCUPATIONAL FIELDS
COMPARED WITH WORKERS ACTUALLY FOLLOWING THESE
OCCUPATIONS IN THE JEFFERSON JUNIOR
HIGH SCHOOL AREA

Major Occupational Fields	Student* Vocational Preferences (1959)	Locally† Employed Parents (1956)
Professional, technical, and kindred workers	66.4%	7.4%
Managers, officials, and proprietors, except farm	0.0%	10.5%
Farmers, farm managers, foremen, and laborers	0.8%	1.4%
Clerical and kindred workers	12.5%	3.2%
Sales workers	1.1%	3.7%
Craftsmen, foremen, and kindred workers	8.7%	42.8%
Operatives and kindred workers	0.0%	9.7%
Service workers, except private household	9.6%	7.6%
Private household workers	0.6%	1.4%
Laborers, except farm and mine	0.3%	12.3%
Total per cent of distribution	100.0%	100.0%

* Information was obtained through Ninth Grade Vocational Questionnaires.

† Information was obtained through the cumulative records of ninth-grade students.

tion of their parents approximates the national job picture, clearly the student-expressed job preferences suggest an inadequate understanding on the students' part of the jobs they reasonably might hope to get in their community. Such data certainly not only raise questions about the role the school must play prior to the conference but also about the nature and purpose of a career conference designed to help youngsters make realistic plans.

3. *The atmosphere must stress security and freedom to explore ideas, along with the responsibility of the group to its members.* This is one point where the administrator frequently becomes unhappy. For example, the use of the homeroom for group guidance activities simplifies school programming and organization of on-going programs. When the home room includes youngsters with widely different needs or values, or when the relationship of the teacher to the group involves contradictory roles (disciplinarian versus permissive leader), it is difficult for all the people involved to feel secure in the setting. It

is important to realize that even if the teacher or counselor can effectively live and serve in two roles, it is not always possible for group members to perceive or accept him in both roles.

Since the home room[26] is so well established as one way of meeting guidance needs, it is worth reviewing typical reasons as uncovered in studies by McFarland[27] and McCorkle and O'Dea[28] as to why home rooms fail. The five major causes, as found in these studies, were:

a. Lack of time for groups to explore adequately areas of concern.

b. Failure to use home room appropriately. Use of time for announcements, roll call, etc., all distort the atmosphere and meaning of the hour.

c. Indifference of leaders (teachers). Many are uncomfortable discussing areas they would rather not face in themselves.

d. Tied in to cause *c*, there is an adequate number of trained personnel.

e. Inadequate program planning. Programs are either not planned at all or reflect overstructuring by leaders to meet their needs.

All of the above comments could be applied with equal accuracy to typical Sunday School programs.

4. *Teachers or leaders of the group need to be comfortable in their role.* As has been explored in earlier chapters, the behavior and needs of the leader have a real effect on the way a group can establish the controls they need to feel secure. Helping teachers or other group leaders express their feelings can be achieved as they are helped to participate in groups themselves, where they can discover what such experiences can mean.[29] In this fashion, too, they can learn how to serve as a leader from within the group. Such experiences also help potential group leaders become sensitive to group interaction.[30]

The concept that the leader needs to feel secure is clearly related to perceiving his role and knowing how to live out that role. The basis for this security comes from having clearly worked out his responsibility to the agency in which he works. Ethically, the leader's first responsibility is to the agency that employs him. It is only when a leader knows the limits of freedom within agency policy that he can help a group determine those decisions it has the freedom to make for itself, and those that it is not permitted to make while continuing to derive benefits from the institution.

An example here might help. One common goal in activity groups is to help youngsters find socially approved ways of expressing hostility. One leader may tolerate curse words but ban destruction of the building, whereas another will allow wrestling and jostling but ban fights where the battlers use weapons other than their bare hands. The limits of the situation really become defined at three levels. First there is the limit set by the agency. Second there are the limits developed through the structuring by the initial group leader. These limits frequently reflect the biases and needs of the initial leader. The third and operating level develops as a group establishes mores designed to reconcile their needs with those of the agency and initial leader.

Orientation Programs

The problem of helping new people adjust to the mores and practices of an organization is one shared by groups with widely disparate goals. Although social work agencies have long used in-take interviewers to partially serve this function, few have tried group methods for orienting new clients. One of the primary sources of confusion in this area comes from the difficulty in separating informational needs of clients from their anxieties over facing unfamiliar demands and threats. Lectures, handbooks, and movies all have served to provide background information about an agency; but as counselors and teachers subsequently discover, they have failed to help the clients accept their role as it relates to the agency. They also fail in providing the client the support he needs in facing his feelings of inadequacy in a new situation.

In the School Setting. Orientation, to be effective, ought to occur *before* the student is moved into the new setting. In some cases students may need help to develop new skills. Nowhere is this seen more sharply than in the adjustment problems of the youngster from cultures which lack an emphasis on academic experience. It is partially because of the size of the adjustment required that we now find a major emphasis on preschool education designed to overcome the cultural deficiency.

Prior to discussions or experiences designed to help students adjust to the next level of schooling, it is vital that the demands required of students at the next level first be made meaningful to them. This can best be achieved by extended visits to the next level of school to be entered and by reports to the youngsters by prior graduates who are still seen as peers.[31]

In a Community Agency. The threat of the unknown is equally apparent when one sees the shock experienced by clients trying to use community agencies. The following is an approach developed to facilitate clients' ability to use and relate to an agency.

When the Hunter College Veterans Guidance Center was organized, the staff explored all the steps a veteran had to complete prior to his working with a counselor. Beyond an initial screening by a Veterans Administration representative, to insure his rights to the service, a new client was asked to fill out a series of forms that provided background information about himself, his family, and his goals. Over a period of time it became apparent that the clients' attitudes toward the agency were being structured by their reactions to the forms they were being asked to fill out. As indicated by their questions, clients seemed to be asking themselves: Why does anyone else need to know these personal things about me? What will they do with this information? How is this helping me achieve my goals? Where is all this leading?

To meet these kinds of concerns, the Center tried another procedure. All new clients were asked to come to the Center at a time set for a group meeting. After being seated informally, a member of staff started the session by indicating that people had many different reasons for seeking counseling and many questions about how a counseling center functioned. This meeting then was called to provide a chance for people to ask questions about anything that they wanted to know. The more courageous people started the ball rolling by expressing their concern over the seriousness of the vocational choice that they felt a need to make. Others in the group felt reassured when they discovered they were not alone in their confusion and feelings of guilt over their prior inability to make a decision. As their anxiety about seeking help began to diminish, the group slowly moved toward a more positive orientation. They became interested in how they and the counselors could solve their problems. As a response to their questions, it was possible to tell them everything about forms, procedures, etc., but *this time* it reflected information for which they had already perceived a need and which could now be seen as something in which they were sharing rather than as operations being used on them.

This illustration was chosen deliberately because it demonstrates how group procedures can be used in community settings and also points up a major concept.[32–35] *Although a major role of orientation is to provide information, it falls on deaf ears if the hearers have not been helped first to perceive the need for the information and then to face the anxieties the new situations may provoke.*

For readers desiring more information about similar programs,

Chapter 5 and Appendix B in Shostrom and Brammer[36] will be of interest.

The Value of Orientation Materials and Lectures

For some time, schools have been concerned about improving the articulation between the different levels of schooling. Studies like White's[37] which discusses the value of orientation handbooks, have pointed out that for a handbook to be successful its immediate objective must be to make students feel welcome, important, and secure in their environment. White found many handbooks presenting a tone that was authoritarian, prescriptive, and dictatorial in nature. One handbook devoted more than 50 per cent of the book to rules of the school and the penalties for infractions. It brought to mind the reactions of soldiers in the service who were forced to listen to the articles of war, and who responded either by tuning out the speaker or by showing open hostility.

Failure of handbooks and other inanimate devices to complete the orientation process represents a lack of awareness that receptivity and acceptance of any information given through impersonal devices is based upon several prior assumptions:

1. That all people want to know the facts available through the booklet, film, etc.
2. That the words used in these devices are understood by the recipient in the same fashion as the author intended.
3. That the recipient is able to transfer the meaning of an answer from one situation to another.
4. That the material not only reflects the needs of the agency but also meets needs of the recipients.

The use of group guidance orientation lectures, like handbooks or devices, can result in the economical transmission of a body of information, but unless these group settings allow for a two-way exchange of ideas and feelings, the devices are likely to be no more effective than the written word.

The problems involved in the *process* of orienting students to a new level of schooling are not different for the various levels of schooling, although topics explored may differ. Basically the purpose in all cases is to help the new person relate his goals and needs to the structure of a new setting. An exploration of college orientation problems can therefore provide clues for other levels as well.

Surveys like those of Bookman,[38] Copeland,[39] Fitts and Swift,[40] and Kamm and Wrenn[41] have documented the wide range of procedures used in the orientation process. Bookman's study, although somewhat dated, suggests that orientation is given more lip service than real, thoughtful planning. For example, at the Twelfth Annual Conference of Orientation Directors held at Southern Illinois University, it appeared evident that although schools were increasingly concerned about their orientation role, there was evidence of marked disparity over the goals and techniques to be employed in orientation programs. Cleavage still exists between the group that holds "Students are too immature; you've got to tell them what to do and think" and the group that states "We want to help students get answers to their questions because giving information too early is a waste of time."

Increasingly, handbooks are becoming the products of upper classmen rather than faculty members. These students try to recall their earlier concerns as freshmen and bring to these books a more accurate survey of real student concerns. They also tend to phrase their thoughts in a way that reflects current student jargon and thus facilitates communication.

More and more schools are selecting a group of freshmen to come to school before the school year and receive training as leaders so that they can help orient their peers. Although this has typically been true on the college level, some high schools have tried this technique successfully. More frequently schools use upperclassmen as freshmen advisors, on a big brother or sister basis. Although these devices overcome many of the problems that arise when an adult tries to offer information and advice, the programs often fall short of their goal because schools have not adequately trained their students to be competent in these group leadership roles. Hopefully, this book has demonstrated that the skills involved include more than a knowledge of *Robert's Rules of Order* and the material the administration wants all new people to know and accept. If schools wish to increase their effective use of peer group leaders, prior systematic training of these people must be planned.

Studies by Goodrich[42] and by Lowenstein and Hoppock[43] suggest that moving college orientation down into the high school or into precollege clinics is effective in improving student grades and adjustment to school. Equally effective results could be expected at the elementary and junior high school level if comparable programs were instituted. But like the studies reported, these orientation programs cannot be appendages to other programs with differing climates and goals. A homeroom program where much of the time is spent in announcements or school-controlled activities does not lend itself to free-flowing discussions.

The emphasis on orientation has been on helping people get information needed immediately, and in helping them understand and accept the procedures and demands of the institution. Rogers[44] has pointed out, however, that orientation needs are an ongoing thing.

> Suppose that instead (of the usual college orientation program) students met once a week during the first semester in groups of not over 20, to talk out their confusions, their fears, their resentments, their feelings of inadequacy, and their sense of growth. The group could be conducted in such a way as to make it their group, and an opportunity to develop a clear and realistic orientation to their own situation.

Some colleges are achieving this goal through residence hall programs. The topics such groups discuss are interesting because they provide one clue as to the kinds of concerns people have with which typical orientation programs do not deal. One group of girls discussed: "How do you handle yourself on a blind date?" "Now that we made college, what's the value of getting good grades?" "Is college the place to get a man or prepare for a career?"

Although high schools frequently do not have groups that are unstructured enough to allow equal concerns to be voiced, some high schools have used club activities as one way of developing comparable group settings.[45]

In one high school, a group of senior boys met in a series of bull sessions. Their concerns are of interest since they demonstrate the unusual and unexpected anxieties which typical structured programs fail to deal with. These boys wondered: "Is it true that on the first day you enter the Army they inject you with a four-inch square needle?" "Why should I listen to all that jazz about college, I can make more than my old man right now?" "Why bother to take scholarship exams? Even if you pass, if you aren't top dog it doesn't matter anyway—also, if I make the grade, my folks will really ride me."

Successful orientation programs need to allow enough time for real concerns to be explored and faced. They must offer information when the group has discovered its need for the information. The structure of the group should permit group members to express feelings and to introduce topics that represent their concerns. The leader needs to be skilled, and, if effective, he will help the group reduce its anxiety as the individuals discover they are not alone in their feelings of inadequacy. Also, as groups explore the mores and rules of the institution they have a chance to discover personal reasons that enable them either to accept the status quo or to uncover socially approved ways of obtaining change. No orientation program can ever really end, since adjustment is a continual process. Planning, therefore, on continued sources of support and release in a group setting may facilitate the continued integration of people into the framework of the institution.

Throughout this chapter there has been a repeated emphasis on the need for the leader to be comfortable with his leadership role. Many agencies thrust responsibilities on people without giving them adequate help in learning the skills that go with the role. Whether he be a teacher forced to handle a club or group guidance program, or a parent recruited to teach Sunday School, we have an obligation to prepare the person so he can be effective.

To plan most intelligently we would help these potential group leaders learn skills in a nonthreatening environment until they themselves felt ready to handle their group assignment.

The Case Conference Approach

How, then, can we help leaders learn these skills? One helpful technique involves the case conference method. If group members are given a problem outside themselves to focus their attention on, the desire to be helpful to others becomes one of the group mores. As person after person presents his perception of the problem and how he would deal with it, the group members inevitably are helped to see ways of coping with the problem that they had not considered before. This approach is particularly helpful in settings where many old timers who may be threatened by new approaches are present. Being free to listen to others' ideas, they do not need to publicly profess their own ignorance. At the same time, they can learn about new ideas without having to admit that new ways may be superior to their existing approach. If the threat to the group is really great, the leader can help them by preparing a fictitious case that embodies problems they will face later, to free participants from the fear of doing something wrong because of their own ineptness.

One of the commonly accepted concepts in education is that one works from the known to the unknown. The speed with which a group develops programs or new skills needs to be paced by the security of the group. When a group is truly group-centered, they speed up or slow down to account for the needs of all the members. As their insights grow, directions will shift.

Developing a Club Program

Consider, for example, the case of a junior high that was seeking to initiate a guidance program. While planning meetings, for which they called in a consultant, they became painfully aware of the many activities that needed to be started. They also became sharply aware of their own reluctance to take on these responsibilities. As they explored the problem, they discovered that the one area where all the faculty felt there was an immediate need for action and where they were willing to be involved was an extracurricular program after school. The teachers were concerned about keeping children off the streets after school; they also saw a way in which they could indulge in their favorite hobbies. A science teacher wanted to sponsor a knitting club. A mathematics teacher was interested in teaching children chess. As plans began to form, the suggestion was made to have students on the planning committee. The addition of students introduced a new and interesting element. The children raised questions as to the students' interests in the clubs that were being proposed and suggested alternate clubs representing current student interests. This experience gave the school an awareness of the concept that any guidance program, beyond considering the needs of the school, has to incorporate the needs of the children as the children perceived them.[46] This learning was truly major, despite the fact that the total guidance program for the junior high school was limited at that stage to adding clubs to the school.

Student Councils*

Student councils, to be effective, must insure that the students are actively involved and given real responsibility. The following illustration may demonstrate these concepts.

In 1952, the Illinois Association of Student Councils was faced with the problem of planning its convention for the following year. Desiring to use the initials of the organization as the basis of their theme,

* Parts of this section appeared in a paper, "Counseling the Student Council," written by W. Lifton in *Educational Administration and Supervision*, 41, No. 2, 103–108, February, 1955.

they decided to focus the convention on the idea that "Intelligent Action Stimulates Cooperation." It was a motto that rang true, offended no one, and was not limited in meaning. The group then selected a guest speaker and a student panel to discuss the implications of the slogan for student councils. It was at this point that the author, as guest speaker, became involved in the plans.

It seemed to me appropriate to employ the concepts of the field of guidance on the job to be done. A check list containing the following questions was developed.

1. How can the slogan be made meaningful?

2. What are the needs of the group and how can we meet them?

3. How can the setting of the panel at the convention be arranged to provide maximum security for all, so that all will be free to think and participate?

4. How can the planning and action of the panel be used to illustrate dynamically the ideas being expressed?

Having been given a free hand in organizing the panel, the author corresponded with the panel members to get their ideas as to how we could best work as a group. Every letter written had copies made so that each of us received all of the letters we were writing to one another. This facilitated communication and made all feel a constant sharing in the group's planning. We all agreed that for the panel to be interesting we should talk about the issues that the membership was most concerned about.

To meet objectives 1 and 2 (making the slogan meaningful by tying it to the needs of the group) we went to the student body to discover what needs they had. The following letter was sent by the students to secure the information we wanted.

ILLINOIS ASSOCIATION OF STUDENT COUNCILS

Peoria, Illinois
April 9, 1953

Dear Member of I.A.S.C.:

In order to have the planned panel discussion on "Intelligence Action Stimulates Cooperation" at the I.A.S.C. convention be one that really makes sense and is worth while, we need your help.

We would like the representatives of each school to determine those problems in their school which the students see as ones where cooperation from the student body or from the faculty has been slow in coming. We plan to summarize these difficulties and use them as a basis for our panel discussion.

The more specifically you feed to us the issues and stumbling blocks you are facing, the better the pay-off will be when the panel tries to help you with your concerns.

The panel discussion will become real and interesting to you if you will participate by sending us your problems. This must be done immediately, for the convention is close at hand.

Please send the information to:

> Dr. Walter M. Lifton
> College of Education
> University of Illinois
> Urbana, Illinois

We need your cooperation! Don't let this be a stumbling block to the panel. Respond as quickly as possible.

> Yours for Stronger Student Councils,
> Michael Lipkin
> 1st Vice Pres. I.A.S.C.

The returns from this letter not only helped us plan our convention program, but also clarified for us why many of the student councils were not succeeding. The returns were grouped, and the final tabulation was reproduced so that we could distribute this material at the convention. This duplication of material was done to accomplish objective 2—to help contributors feel that their contribution was recognized and to facilitate the cohesion of the group as they discovered the many problems they shared in common.

Summary of Problems Submitted

(After the general problem area appears the number of problems in that area which were submitted.)

I. Definition of council's role and duties: (24)
1. Should there be student government in high school? (3)
2. How much power do councils have and how much should they have? (6)
3. How much say should the students have in making their own constitution? (3)
4. Need better leaders: elections not a popularity contest. (7)
5. Better communication needed between council, faculty, administration and student body. (9)

II. Administration and faculty: (18)
1. Lack of respect and confidence from either of those groups; neither group very interested or cooperative in many schools. (11)
2. Lack of clear definition of power the above groups will allow council. (2)
3. Detention, assignments, class and library situation. (5)

III. Student body: (66)
    1. Development of school spirit and interest in council, all school activities, etc., for better care of building and grounds and better participation in all phases of school life.   (43)
    2. Traffic: in the building and out.   (8)
    3. Cliques and other selfish individuals and groups.   (2)
    4. Detention, assignments, and class atmosphere.   (5)
    5. Manners: courtesy and respect for one another and faculty.   (8)
One school wrote that they have no problems to submit.

The forum panel was composed of six students representing high schools from different parts of the state. Although as a group we had been successful in gathering data for our use, we felt we needed to get together and discuss how best we could present the material so that our audience would be interested and become involved in the subsequent discussion. The group spent several hours together informally getting to know each other and swapping ideas on how to best do our job. As alternatives were being considered, one student said he felt if the convention could be in the room with us then, relaxed as we were, they surely would get as interested as our own group. Another member of the group volunteered the idea that the thing he hated about meetings and conventions was the boring lectures, and he surely did not want to have to be one of the speakers people listened to.

Rather suddenly we hit on our solution. Instead of lecturing panel fashion about the data we had available, why not recreate on the convention floor just what we were doing then? Each member of the panel scanned the letters we had received and picked out those ideas and attitudes he felt most strongly about. In order to find a theoretical setting where we could express these ideas, we planned our role-playing scene in a family living room where friends from different high schools were rehashing the doings at the convention and the problems of student councils. In this fashion we achieved our third objective—a setting where participants and observers could be relaxed and feel more secure. Through our mouths the audience could hear and react to the ideas of their peers. By identifying with or reacting to one of the members of the panel group the larger group could share and become involved in the ideas being explored.

During the presentation of the program, panel members were seated in a semicircle so we could see and talk to each other. Microphones were placed so our audience could hear us, but at no time (after the panel program had been explained) did the panel talk directly to the audience. Each of us in our own way expressed ideas obtained from the original letters of the members. We tried to express ideas like the following:

> The most tremendous problem we have is putting over the idea to the student body and faculty that the student council is a government body instead of just another school club or organization. Since our council is relatively young, this problem confronts us the most.

> We have trouble in rousing interest in the student body toward various campaigns and activities that we sponsor throughout the year, such as clean-up campaigns, dances, and fire drills. Another outstanding problem that hinders us is lack of respect from the faculty. Some of our elderly teachers refuse to accept the up-to-date thinking of the student council. They do not respect our meeting time and fail to give their cooperation in council sponsored activities.

> How can we overcome too much rivalry and not enough cooperation between the classes?

> How can we promote better understanding between teachers and students?

> Everyone wants more and better parties but won't help to get them. What can be done?

> How can we get the parents and students together to form a Teen-Age Recreation Club?

> What methods are used most widely in choosing class advisors?

> I would appreciate a discussion by the panel on the area of student council authority. My students have a mistaken idea that the council is all powerful. Needless to say I have discouraged the idea by explanations, but the idea doesn't get across. (This idea came from a faculty sponsor.)

> In our school my council members feel that too much is expected of the council. We are very active. Any good idea presented by the students is acted upon. If the council meets defeat, then the students feel that the council has failed. This is our big problem.

> The members elected are not always the best of the school. (Students sometimes elect those they like instead of those who can serve best.)

> Some older teachers resent certain student rulings, such as checking the rooms for cleanness and so forth.

After about fifteen minutes of role-playing we opened the discussion so that the audience could participate. Questions and ideas came rapidly and were directed not only to the panel members but also to other members of the audience who expressed ideas.

In closing the session we achieved our fourth objective—using the actual content of our planning and panel session to point up the ideas being explored.

Basically we decided that each of the following points was necessary for a successful student council.

1. The rights, responsibilities, and authority of the group should be clearly defined from the start. Once defined they must be consistently maintained. (We had checked with the officers of the IASC as to our freedom in planning the session.)

2. The purpose of the focus of the student council must reflect the interests and needs of the students rather than serve as extensions of the administration. (We sent a letter to the grass roots to tap their interests.)

3. The student council must serve as a means of feeding responsibility back to the grass roots rather than of relieving them of responsibility by acting for them. (We did not lecture on what ought to be done by members but considered the problems and solutions available.)

4. Communication about all activities must be designed to reach and involve the entire student body. (Both our mimeographed material and use of microphones were designed to involve the total group.)

5. Faculty and administration can best develop the student council by vesting in the council rights, responsibilities and authority which are indicative of faith in students as mature and interested citizens of the school. (This arose from the discussion period, where the security of the council representatives appeared to reflect their awareness of their rights and responsibilities to their school.)

Moral and Spiritual Values

It would be difficult indeed to describe any group in which questions of values or ethics were completely absent. There are many problems in our society where the major issue is predominantly moral in character. The question of which agency in our society—the school, church, or community—can most appropriately handle these problems is obviously one on which consensus in our society is absent. Begging that issue for the moment, society has certainly failed to utilize group settings adequately to solve some of its concerns. The following illustrations may demonstrate ways in which groups have been used effectively.

One school was greatly troubled by the high incidence of illegitimate pregnancies among the girls in the student body. Lectures in school and at church seemed to have no effect. Courses in sex education also seemed not to be getting the desired result. Finally, somewhat in desperation, the school got the students together and said to them that they believed the students were also concerned about the situation. They asked the students to suggest remedies. After the students formed permissive discussion groups, the problem was given over to them. After setting up limits and testing peer acceptance of ideas, the boys and girls began to open up. Rather quickly it became apparent that most of the group members assumed that acceptance by their peers demanded promiscuous behavior. On an individual basis, though, each member, as he described his picture of the mate he desired to marry, tended to adhere to the societal values of the moral person. The group discovered, as person after person talked, that there was an unverbalized but common acceptance of values that were the opposite of the ones popularly voiced. A new standard became the basis for group acceptance. "Will this behavior get me the mate I desire?" This value did not ignore sex drives but rather helped put them into perspective with other needs.

Another school had a major problem with youngsters recklessly driving hot rods. Following a precedure like the group described previously, the boys and girls again found that instead of only one value system being in operation, a second unverbalized one was equally present. Up to the time the group met, they had assumed that peer group acceptance was based upon proving one's courage by the speed with which one drove. Demonstrating one's physical control by fast driving also seemed a way of proving adulthood. After several group sessions, members began to express some of their hidden feelings. Many had a real fear of being hurt in a car accident and felt guilt over the potential injury to others. As person after person demonstrated his feeling that fast driving also implied a lack of concern for others, a new group value began to form.

One school, in developing its guidance program, called in students to become part of the planning group. As the students felt free to express their concerns, they raised question after question about the cheating that was going on in the school. Although the teachers had been aware of the problem, they had failed to realize the depth of student concern about it. With the help of the students on the committee a plan was developed to permit students in the school to explore the problem. Beyond providing students with a chance to face the situation, the discussion provided the faculty with new insights into the reasons behind the cheating. Both faculty and parents were putting extremely high pressure on students to achieve scholastically.

Rewards for A students were large, and rejection of others was great. Because a curve system was used in grading, only the very top people could get recognition. As one student after another cheated in order to achieve the desired grades the person who did not cheat could not survive. Although the non-cheaters were hostile toward their classmates, they knew no acceptable way of correcting the situation. In this case, not only the students but also the faculty and the parents needed group sessions to discover the factors that precipitated the situation.

In an elementary school, a classroom teacher became aware of snobbery in the attitudes of the students. Using a phantasy situation she suggested to the class that it might be fun to build an imaginary city in which each student could have any job he wanted. Keeping track of the students' choices, the group discovered they had several doctors, lawyers, and engineers. One individualist wanted to be a bum. The group was then asked to see if the proposed city could survive. The need for farmers, toolmakers, and garbage collectors became clear. In the ensuing discussion the children became aware, for the first time, not only of the inherent importance of every job in our society but also of the yardsticks they were using in determining the value of any job or person. The values in our society that placed premium on monetary rewards, status, social service, etc., moved from the unconscious to the conscious concern of all group members.

For a last example, consider the experiences of a Baptist minister concerned with preparing a group for their confirmation. He was disturbed by their apathy in group discussions and the rote manner in which they were learning their creed. Restructuring the group, he tried to help them raise their concerns, fears, and anxieties as they related to their religious beliefs. Once they saw him as not sitting in judgment, they were able to voice their doubts and confusion. Having expressed these feelings, they were interested in using the minister as a resource person to see what the denomination had to offer as ways of facing or solving their concerns.

Using Groups with Failing and Underachieving Students

Three illustrations of the use of therapeutically oriented groups to achieve better academic adjustment may help demonstrate these concepts.[47]

At Sullivan, Illinois, all youngsters who were failing in school were seen by the school counselor. In the counseling sessions, each child was given the chance to join a group that would meet after school and would be composed of students who were doing poorly at school. Over a period of several sessions there was developed an in-group feeling which provided members with feelings of worth to replace their former feelings of social rejection. Guilt over not having measured up to parental standards was alleviated and replaced by group support in learning new ways of adjusting to school and themselves. Grades improved and antisocial acts decreased.

A major study involving several groups of gifted underachievers was conducted at Evanston Township High School (Evanston, Illinois). Youngsters who were getting acceptable grades but were not achieving up to their potential were given a chance to join counseling groups and to see if they could discover why they were not doing as well as they could. During group sessions many dynamics for desiring to fail became clear to the group. As reported by Dr. Broedel,*

> Although underachievement was the identifying trait of the sample of gifted adolescents involved in the study, the evaluative instruments and the clinical assessment of the research team showed them also to be characterized as hostile persons. Prior to group counseling they rejected themselves, including their giftedness, and they were rejecting of others. The administration of a projective instrument, the Picture Story Test, before and after an eight week period during which two experimental groups participated in group counseling, demonstrated that the fourteen experimental subjects made significantly greater gains in acceptance of self and others than did a similar number of non-counseled control subjects.

One reason for desiring to fail became graphically clear in a group of college women who were meeting in a dormitory to explore their feelings about the grades they had received that quarter. An attractive young lady asked the group the following question. "I wonder why I don't study. I get B's without cracking a book while other kids work hard for the same grade. If I even tried a little I know I could get A's, but I never do. I wonder why?"

The group continued in its discussion only to be interrupted by the girl a little later on. She said, "I know why I don't study! If I got A's my mother would say, 'Why don't you do better!'" For this young lady the insight was followed by questions she needed to think through. Why was pleasing her parents her goal in college? What did she need to do to feel she had really achieved something? Were her goals and standards realistic?

* John Broedel, Merle Ohlsen, and Fred Proff. *The Effects of Group Counseling on Gifted Adolescent Underachievers.* (Paper read at the American Psychological Association meetings in Washington, D. C. on August 29, 1958.)

Clubs and extracurricular activities offer a vehicle for group counseling and serve in that way frequently without prior planning. The writings of Coyle,[48] Driver,[49] Haas,[50] Fedder,[51] and Hoppock[52] will be helpful in exploring ways in which agencies have used these group settings to meet counseling goals.

The Workshop

One other example of the use of group process skills in an educational setting will be presented. The example chosen involves a workshop setting where the goal of the group involved learning skills, members feared, and where some of the membership was of an involuntary nature. This example was chosen because it involves mature teachers, not young children. But, as is indicated, the problems of group development are very similar.

For some time the Illinois Curriculum Program under the direction of Dr. Fred Barnes had been concerned about ways to interest classroom teachers in doing research.[53] In evaluating the problem, Dr. Barnes and his associates felt that they needed to achieve several objectives.

1. Doing research had to be seen as desirable by teachers. In other words, they had to see value in it for them.

2. Teachers had to feel secure in doing research, since people do not voluntarily choose activities which are unpleasant or threatening to them.

3. In line with number 2, teachers had to have a chance to develop skills in this area in a setting where failure would not cause them to lose either peer or self-respect.

4. During the learning period, information had to be available. Consultants and textbooks were on hand to supply data on techniques or design.

5. A group atmosphere rewarding research-focused activities needed to be developed to provide support to the individual and to reinforce the desire to learn a skill that met group approval.

To achieve these objectives, several experimental workshops were held where ways of developing subgroups interested in common problems were devised and techniques for giving these groups responsibility for their achievement were perfected.

Dr. Barnes and his associates recognized that one of the major problems associated with securing total group participation was the underlying fear of failure felt by workshop members. Accordingly, it was decided that in a subsequent workshop the sessions would start with a period devoted to helping people feel free to express negative feelings and to exploring their motivation to participate in this type of activity.

A socio-drama was planned that represented a faculty meeting where the school superintendent was to describe a forthcoming workshop and a member of the faculty was to be selected (drafted?) to attend. The workshop members were encouraged to represent their own teaching levels and specialties at this mock session. Rather quickly the group expressed common resentments, fears, and needs. At this point the role-playing was stopped and the group was asked to evaluate what they thought was happening and why the needs which had been expressed were present. As the group evaluated the role-playing, the focus shifted from the "characters" to the ways in which the workshop participants identified or perceived the situations.

One effect of this session was that the workshop members soon discovered that they were not alone in their anxieties and fears. At the same time they were discovering that it was permissible in this setting to express feelings that were blocking their ability to examine content and relate it to themselves.

In typical counseling fashion, after the group members had catharted their negative feelings, they were free to discover and accept the positive possibilities of the setting they were in. Achieving this positive attitude, the group then became aware of its desire to develop skills to meet its own needs and not to meet external demands. Later, in the subgroup work sessions, the groups periodically took stock of their feelings and the way the group was proceeding. At stated time intervals the groups were given a chance to rate the preceding session. In this fashion the groups had objective evidence of their reactions to different activities, and could, through this form, express both positive and negative feelings. These illustrations indicate that to improve group atmosphere in the classroom we need to think about many factors and values.

Reference Sources for Developing Guidance Units

Traditional guidance units will soon disappear, as emphasis on providing maturational experience become a more significant part of early childhood education.

The educator faced with the need for materials to fit into an existing structure may care to evaluate the following materials to see if they meet the needs of his school. Because no materials can provide the support and understanding available through human relationships, all materials ought to be seen as spring-boards for facilitating group interaction.

Elementary Grades
A comprehensive summary of books, films, records, and other media is to be found in:

Norris, Willa. *Occupational Information in the Elementary School.* Chicago: Science Research Associates, 1963.

Specific help for the classroom teacher is provided in:

Caldwell, Edson. *Group Techniques for the Classroom Teacher.* Chicago: Science Research Associates, 1959.

Also helpful to teachers are:

Cunningham, Ruth, and associates. *Understanding Group Behavior of Boys and Girls.* New York: Bureau of Publications, Teachers College, Columbia University, 1951.

Flanders, Ned. *Teaching with Groups.* Minneapolis: Burgess Publishing Co., 1954.

Lifton, Walter M. *Introducing the World of Work to Children.* Chicago: Science Research Associates, 1960. (Contains suggestions as to ways of relating guidance concepts to typical subject matter units of study.)

Junior High and High School
Allen, Richard D. *The Inor Group Guidance Series,* Volumes I-III. New York: Inor Publishing Company, 1952.

Engle, T. L. *Psychology,* 3rd ed. Tarrytown, New York: World Book Company, 1957.

Katz, Martin. *You Today and Tomorrow.* Princeton, New Jersey: Educational Testing Service, 1959.

Lifton, Walter. *Widening Occupational Roles Kit.* Chicago: Science Research Associates, 1962.

Lifton, Walter (Editor). *Keys to Vocational Decisions.* Chicago: Science Research Associates, 1964.

Lifton, Walter and Belanger, L. *Occupational Exploration Kit.* Chicago: Science Research Associates, 1961.

Mahoney, H. J., and Engle, T. L. *Points for Decision,* rev. ed. Tarrytown, N. Y.: World Book Company, 1961.

Science Research Associates, Inc. *Directory of Sources for Higher Education Planning.* Chicago: Science Research Associates, 1965.

College
Bernard, H. W. *Toward Better Personal Adjustment,* 2nd edition. New York: McGraw-Hill, 1957.

Borow, Henry, and Lindsey, R. V. *Vocational Planning for College Students.* Englewood Cliffs, New Jersey: Prentice-Hall 1959.

Glanz, E. C., and Walston, E. B. *An Introduction to Personal Adjustment.* Boston: Allyn and Bacon, 1958.

Martinson, W. D. *Educational and Vocational Planning.* Chicago: Scott, Fores-
man, 1959.

Discussion

Each of the examples presented has differed both in the amount
of freedom available to the groups and the degree of task orientation
initially present.

Cartwright,[54] in summing up research on techniques of achieving
change in people, has developed eight principles that provide a good
summary of the goals to be considered in working with groups. The
principles are:

1. If the group is to be used effectively as a medium of change, those
   people who are to be changed and those who are to exert influence for
   change must have a strong sense of belonging to the same group.
2. The more attractive the group is to its members, the greater is the
   influence that the group can exert on its members.
3. In attempts to change attitudes, values, or behavior, the more relevant
   they are to the basis of attraction to the group, the greater will be the
   influence that the group can exert upon them.
4. The greater the prestige of a group member in the eyes of the other
   members, the greater the influence he can exert.
5. Efforts to change individuals or subparts of a group which, if successful, would have the result of making them deviate from the norms of
   the group, will encounter strong resistance.
6. Strong pressure for changes in the group can be established by creating
   a shared perception by members of the need for change, thus making
   the source of pressure for change lie within the group.
7. Information relating to the need for change, plans for change, and
   consequences of change must be shared by all relevant people in the
   group.
8. Changes in one part of a group produce strain in other related parts
   which can be reduced only by eliminating the change or by bringing
   about readjustments in the related parts.

To the degree that a group accepts responsibility, they will become
increasingly concerned over problems of evaluation. The chapter
which follows presents a discussion of the problem of evaluation and
how some groups have solved this issue.

BIBLIOGRAPHY

1. Harris, F. E. "Techniques for Guiding Group Experiences in the Classroom."
   Elementary School Journal, 49, 5, 32–36, 1958.
2. Maas, H. "Applying Group Therapy to Classroom Practice." *Mental
   Hygiene,* 35, 250–259, April 1951.

3. Perkins, Hugh V. "Effect of Climate and Curriculum on Group Learning." *Journal of Educational Research*, 44, 269–286, 1951.
4. Laycock, S. R. "The Mental Hygiene of Classroom Teaching." *Understanding the Child*, XVI, 39–43, April 1947.
5. Association for Supervision and Curriculum Development. *Group Planning in Education*. Washington, D. C.: ASCD, 1945.
6. Cantor, Nathaniel. *The Dynamics of Learning*, Third Edition. Buffalo, New York: Henry Stewart, 1957.
7. Prescot, Daniel. *The Child in the Educative Process*. Chapter 9. New York: McGraw-Hill, 1957.
8. Trow, William Clark, et al. "Psychology of Group Behavior: The Class as a Group." *Journal of Educational Psychology*, XLV, 322–338, October 1950.
9. DeBoer, John J. "Implications of Group Dynamics for English." *English Journal*, XVI, 239–244, May 1952.
10. Gillies, Emily P. "Therapy Dramatics for the Public School Room." *New Child*, 7, 328–336, 1948.
11. Metcalf, H. H. "Group Counseling at the Eleventh Grade Level." *School Review*, 54, 401–405, 1946.
12. Cole, Natalie R. "Exploring Psychodrama at the Fifth Grade Level." *Sociatry*, 2, 243–245, 1948.
13. Elkins, Deborah. "How the Classroom Teacher Can Help the Emotionally Disturbed Child." *Understanding the Child*, 20, 66–73, 1951.
14. Jenkins, David. "Counseling through Group Activities." *The Clearing House*, 23, 8, 488–493, 1949.
15. Zeleny, Leslie D. "The Sociodrama as an Aid in Teaching International Relations and World History." *International Journal of Sociometry*, 1, 29–33, 1956.
16. Stripling, Robert O. "Role Playing in Guidance Training Programs." *Teachers College Record*, 55, 425–429, 1954.
17. Hanszen, Myra, W., and Hollister, W. G. "Teaching Human Relations through Spontaneous Pupil Play Writing and Play Acting." *Understanding the Child*, 25:103–110, 1956.
18. Warters, Jane. *Group Guidance: Principles and Practices*, Chapter 7. New York: McGraw-Hill, 1960.
19. Ojemann, Ralph H. "The Human Relations Program at the State University of Iowa." *Personnel and Guidance Journal*, 37, 198–206, 1958.
20. Stiles, Frances A. *A Study of Materials and Programs for Developing an Understanding of Behavior at the Elementary School Level*. Doctoral Dissertation, University of Iowa, 1947.
21. Seeley, John R. "The Forest Hill Village Human Relations Classes." *Personnel and Guidance Journal*, 37, 424–434, 1959.
22. DeBoer, John, Hale, Paul and Landin, Esther. *Reading for Living*. Springfield, Illinois: Superintendent of Public Instruction, Circular Series A No. 51, *Illinois Curriculum Program Bull.* No. 18, 1953.
23. Crosby, Muriel (Editor). *Reading Ladders for Human Relations*. Washington, D.C.: American Council on Education, Fourth Edition, 1963.
24. Thelen, Herbert A. *Education and the Human Quest*, p. 24. New York: Harper, 1960.
25. Singer, Stanley L., and Stefflre, B. "Concurrent Validity of the Mooney Problem Check List." *Personnel and Guidance Journal*, 35, 298–301, 1957.

26. McKown, Harry C. *Home Room Guidance,* Second edition, New York: McGraw-Hill, 1946.

27. McFarland, John W. "Developing Effective Home Rooms." *School Review,* 61, 400–405, 1953.

28. McCorkle, David B., and O'Dea, David J. "Some Problems of Homeroom Teachers." *Personnel and Guidance Journal,* 32, 206–208, 1953.

29. Moustakis, Clark. "A Human Relations Seminar at the Merrill-Palmer School." *Personnel and Guidance Journal,* 37, 342–349, 1959.

30. Wright, Wayne E. "Multiple Counseling: Why? When? How?" *Personnel and Guidance Journal,* 37, 551–557, 1959.

31. Hoffman, R. W., and Plutchik, R. *Small Group Discussion in Orientation and Teaching.* New York: Putnam's, 1959.

32. Grunwald, Hanna. "Group Counseling in a Case Work Agency." *International Journal of Group Psychotherapy,* 4, 183–192, 1954.

33. Harlow, George. "A Group Guidance Inter-Faith Project." *Personnel and Guidance Journal,* 35, 34–36, 1956.

34. Rosenberg, Bernard. "Group Vocational Counseling in a Rehabilitation Center." *Journal of Rehabilitation,* 4–6, Jan.-Feb. 1956.

35. Harlow, George. "A Group Guidance Summer Project." *Personnel and Guidance Journal,* 34, 441–442, 1956.

36. Shostram, Everett L. and Brammer, Lawrence M. *The Dynamic of the Counseling Process,* Chapter 5 and Appendix B. New York: McGraw-Hill, 1952.

37. White, Robert, M. "Student Handbooks: Observations and Recommendations." *Personnel and Guidance Journal,* 37, 43–46, 1958.

38. Bookman, G. "Freshman Orientation Techniques in Colleges and Universities." *Occupations,* 27, 163–166, 1948.

39. Copeland, Theodore. *Freshman Orientations Programs.* Doctor's Thesis. Temple University, 1954.

40. Fitts, Charles T., and Swift, Fletcher H. *The Construction of Orientation Courses for College Freshmen.* Public Education Monograph 3, University of California, 1930.

41. Kamm, Robert, and Wrenn, C. Gilbert. "Current Developments in Student Personnel Programs and the Needs of the Veteran." *School Society,* 65, 89–92, 1947.

42. Goodrich, Thomas A. "Gains in Self Understanding Through Pre-College Clinics." *Personnel and Guidance Journal,* 31, 433–438, 1953.

43. Lowenstein, Norman, and Hoppock, Robert. "High School Occupations Course Helps Students Adjust to College." *Personnel and Guidance Journal,* 34, 21–23, 1955.

44. Rogers, Carl. R. "Some Implications of Client-Centered Therapy for College Personnel Work." *Educational and Psychological Measurement,* 8, 545, 1948.

45. Driver, Helen. *Multiple Counseling.* Madison, Wisconsin: Monona Press, 1954.

46. Trueblood, Dennis L. "The Counseling Role in a Group Advisory Context." *Journal of College Student Personnel,* 1, 13–17, 1960.

47. Cohen, B., et al. Reports on Project (D-040) sponsored by U.S. Office of Education. *The Effects of Group Counseling on School Adjustment of Underachieving Junior High School Boys Who Demonstrate Acting-Out Behavior,* 1963.

48. Coyle, Grace L. *Group Experience and Democratic Values.* New York: The Woman's Press, 1947.
49. Driver, H. "Small Group Discussion as an Aid in Counseling." *School Review*, 59, 525–530, December 1951.
50. Haas, Robert (Ed). *Psychodrama and Socio-Drama in American Education.* Beacon, New York: Beacon Press, 1949.
51. Fedder, Ruth. *Guiding Homeroom and Club Activities.* New York: McGraw-Hill, 1949.
52. Hoppock, Robert. *Occupational Information.* New York: McGraw-Hill, 1957.
53. Barnes, Fred. *Practical Research Processes.* Springfield, Illinois: Superintendent of Public Instruction, 1958.
54. Cartwright, Dorwin. "Achieving Change in People: Some Applications of Group Dynamics Theory." *Human Relations*, IV, 381–392, 1951.

8

*Evaluation and Research**

EVALUATION

In the preceding chapters it has been pointed out that an effective group climate[1] produces an atmosphere where group members are continually trying to clarify their ideas and behavior. The protocols in the preceding chapters demonstrated how, as a group matures, they become increasingly concerned about the yardstick to use in measuring their growth and present status. As the question is explored by the group it becomes apparent that there are at least three aspects of the problem of evaluation worth looking at. These aspects include the growth of the group as a group, the growth of an individual from the beginning session to the present, and a comparison of an individual's present functioning with "norms" described from society's expectations.

Group Growth

Although authors differ in the areas they emphasize, almost all authors would agree that the following characteristics are typical of mature groups.

1. An increasing ability to be self-directed (not dependent on leader).
2. An increased tolerance in accepting that progress takes time.
3. An increasing sensitivity to their own feelings and the feelings of others.

* Parts of this chapter originally appeared in Lifton's "Group Therapy in Educational Institutions," *Review of Educational Research,* **XXIV**, No. 2, 156–158, April 1954. I wish to acknowledge the help received from Dr. David Zimpfer, University of Rochester, in locating current relevant research.

4. Marked improvement in the ability to withstand tension, frustration, and disagreement.

5. A perception of the common denominators which bind the group as well as areas of individual difference.

6. A better ability to anticipate realistic results of behavior and to channel emotions into more socially acceptable ways of expressing these emotions.

7. An increased ability to change plans and methods as new situations develop.

8. A decrease in time needed to recover from threatening group situations. Peaks and valleys of emotional group crises become less pronounced.

9. Increased efficiency in locating problems, engaging in problem solving, and providing help to individuals as needed.

10. A willingness to face one's own responsibilities and to assist others when help is needed.

11. An acceptance of the right of the other person to be different.

12. An acceptance of the idea that people are different.

It seems odd that there are still people who insist that there can be no such thing as group counseling or therapy and who claim that what is being observed is actually counseling of individuals in a group. This point of view conveniently overlooks some of the characteristics of the group setting which cannot be equated with a one-to-one relationship. The growth that comes about by identifying with another person who is working out a similar problem, the attempt to define reality by testing how many peers need to see something the same way for it to be real, and the learning involved in assuming a leadership role are all samples of phenomena that are based on group life. No equivalent experience can be presented in the individual therapy session.

Despite the many problems in research design discussed in this chapter, the frequency with which studies demonstrate significant findings must make the objective individual wonder if all this smoke cannot help but suggest a fire underneath.

Individual Growth

In previous chapters there have been check lists that a leader can use to determine if his behavior reflects a helping relationship or is a function of his own personal needs.

The personal logs of each group member provide data that can be objectified and quantified.[2] Plotting these data over time indicates the direction in which the person is moving and gives him a basis to use in looking at himself. Log data can be analyzed in some of the following ways. The logs provide:

1. A comparison of the frequency with which the log deals with content versus feeling areas.
2. A comparison of the locus of attention on self versus others.
3. A record of the changing attitudes toward specific group members and the reason for this change.
4. A record associating specific content areas with the type of emotional reaction they precipitate.
5. A record of goals set and those finally achieved.

In many ways, logs can serve a unique function. Just as a mother is shocked into realizing how much her child has grown, when the child tries on last year's dress, so, too, the logs help demonstrate changes that have occurred so slowly that they fail to evoke notice. Probably the greatest virtue of this device is that it provides the reader with a tool for self-evaluation when supervision or the group itself cannot share in the process. As teachers and other group workers learn to keep a record of their daily activities and impressions, they develop the habit of introspection which is the basis for growth.

A Comparison of Self with Others

One of the most threatening moments in a group's life occurs when the group members realize that the true measure of their capacity will be realized only insofar as others perceive and accept them at that level. This concept occurs most clearly when students have a chance to explore their feelings about course grades and the manner in which the grades reflect their level of achievement.

Because grades are labels that most students have had no share in deciding, the initial reaction to the grading problem is that grades represent the views of others and that therefore the individual need feel no responsibility for the yardstick employed. When, however, as in some of the courses described in this book, students share in the grading process, it is no longer possible to avoid looking at grades and what they mean.

Typically groups go through the following stages:

1. "Let's dichotomize between individual growth and course grade." "People entered the group at different levels. It is unfair to not reward the person who has grown most." The idea here is that grades are rewards for efforts and not for the level of achievement.

2. "Let's give everyone an 'A' so no one need be hurt." Since it is painful to accept that some people are better than others, the group tries to make all members equal. When this idea is explored with the group, hostile feelings are expressed rather quickly. Although people wish to help each other, they do not wish to do so at the expense of losing their own identity. It is soon realized that a common label for all makes the label meaningless and another means of differentiating between people will arise.

3. "Since the true measure of our value to society and to ourselves is in terms of what we offer in the way of skills, how can we determine the skills society anticipates from us? How can we develop ways of recognizing the differences between people while using the same basis for comparison?"

Although the concept of evaluation has been demonstrated in a course setting where there is need for precise labels, a similar path is followed by groups who are seeking to assess whether they have achieved the goals they have set for themselves.

It is in this last stage of maturation that a group begins to examine the bases by which they can determine if they have reached their goal. As the criteria involved are put into words, the associated discussion provides a synthesis of all that has gone before. Criteria labels become associated with specific group experiences and are remembered long after the group dissolves. This association also causes the criteria and the subsequent label to have personal meaning for each group member.

Because the group has learned that it is easier to face threat when others help, and that the perceptions of others are meaningful, it is not surprising that final evaluations typically take the form of sociometric ratings. Sociometric ratings are tools that have been developed to measure the relative standing or distance between people on a given dimension. The data are gathered in the following way. Members of a group are asked to indicate the names of other people in the group with whom they would prefer to be closely associated in a defined activity. By tallying the number of times each person is chosen, and by examining the way a person both chooses and is chosen by others, one gets a clear picture of the intended relationships between group members. Group sociometric ratings differ from the typical classroom use of sociometric ratings in several important ways. Typically, sociometrics are used as a basis for objectifying group structure so that the teacher or leader can locate individuals who need help and people who are in positions of leadership.[3] They often provide the basis for a diagnosis which is then followed by a manipulation of the environment to promote change in the direction the manipulator thinks is best. One rather forceful reaction to this type of activity is the concern now being expressed in our gregarious society whether the individual diagnosed by this device as an "isolate" needs to be socialized. Increasingly we are concerned over the need for "isolates" in our society who represent the well-adjusted person who feels better able to create by himself rather than with others. To put it differently, we are becoming concerned over the meaning of the behavior to the person himself, and we are recognizing that society requires many different kinds of people. Of equal concern with this diagnostic use of sociometric data is the effect on the people completing the instrument. Since people typically are asked to rank others in terms of a specified characteristic, the effect of this action is to focus the perception of people on each other in terms of the status derived from their acceptance (or rejection) by their peers. Since studies tend to focus on one dimension rather than on the differing strengths of different people, they tend to create a status hierarchy in the group. Smucker[4] raises an interesting and provocative question when he points out that negative sociometric data is equally diagnostically useful in revealing the tension and disruptive potentials in a group.

In contrast to the foregoing description, groups have frequently used sociometric ratings to give the person being rated an objective picture of how others see him. It not only provides a basis for helping a person compare one of his characteristics with other traits he possesses, but also, if the group shares the total group data it allows each person to see how he compares with all others on each characteristic. Since the pooled data can be kept anonymous, no person need feel threatened by others knowing how the total group perceived him. The major threat comes, instead, from facing the differences between his own self-concept and the opinions of others. To provide this help, groups typically insist that sessions be held after ratings are made available, so that anyone who desires can ask the group for help. At that time, not only is support given, but also, where confusion exists in the mind of a group member about the reasons for the disparity between his own perception and those of the group, the group tries to help by providing examples of behavior which caused their perception to develop.

Probably the most threatening aspect of this approach is the unexpectedly high (in the group's eyes) agreement between group members in the way they perceive specific characteristics in the person being rated. The ratings also demonstrate to the group that even when all attributes are considered, some people are more effective than others. At this point, if the group can examine the pattern of total ratings for the entire group, it is relatively easy to assign labels or grades. Since this is done without awareness of the scores of specific individuals it carries no implication of group rejection of an individual.

Presented here are two instruments developed by different groups. In both cases the groups were concerned with developing skills in group process. Although derived independently, it is interesting to see the characteristics that both deemed important.

Group A

	(Less)					(More)	
	1	2	3	4	5	6	7

How much did   Joe

(a) solve his problems through identification with others' problems	1	2	3	4	5	6	7
(b) solve problem by accepting responsibility for his actions	1	2	3	4	5	6	7
(c) understand (empathy) others' feelings	1	2	3	4	5	6	7
(d) understand (diagnosis) others' actions	1	2	3	4	5	6	7
(e) help others feel accepted	1	2	3	4	5	6	7
(f) show concern with others' problems	1	2	3	4	5	6	7
(g) show preoccupation with own problems	1	2	3	4	5	6	7
(h) use others to gain information	1	2	3	4	5	6	7
(i) offer help to others on request	1	2	3	4	5	6	7
(j) show consistency between what he says and does (judge from classroom situation)	1	2	3	4	5	6	7
(k) effectively make himself understood	1	2	3	4	5	6	7
(l) efficiently make himself understood	1	2	3	4	5	6	7
(m) change within this group	1	2	3	4	5	6	7
(n) How competent would this person be as a group leader?	1	2	3	4	5	6	7

Group B

(Rating scales available with each factor)

1. Awareness of group process   Helps structure limits, helps group solve problems)

(a) Observer (doing nothing)   (b) Participant (cohesiveness)

2. Does he use others to get answers for himself (parasite)?
3. Does he let others know when he feels the same way?
4. Does he express feelings?

(a) Positive   (b) Negative

5. When he serves as a therapist can he understand another's feelings without getting emotionally involved himself the same way? (Does he cry when you do?)
6. Does he try out new ideas (new behavior, new ways)?
7. Listening—does he respond:

(a) Verbally   (b) Physically

8. Is he a conformist?
9. Is he getting through audibly and clearly
10. Does he dig you? (Do you feel understood?)
11. Does he focus on others' needs?
12. Does he focus on my needs?
13. Does he contribute when he has something to contribute?
14. Does he assume a client role?
15. Does he assume a therapist role?

Obviously, not all of these qualities were rated in the same way. The group had to make value judgments, for example, as to their attitude toward the person who always conformed as compared to the one who never conformed. The result of the rating process in Group B was a sharper perception of the specific areas needing attention by the group members who wanted to improve their over-all effectiveness.

RESEARCH*

Research Design. The preciding section was labeled "evaluation" to distinguish between data used for descriptive purposes and data secured, under controlled conditions, to provide answers to predetermined questions.

It would be nice, in discussing methods of research in this area, if it were possible to provide precise, clear-cut instructions. Unfortunately, available research designs and tools are not truly adequate for the task to be done.

The person planning research on group process is faced with a choice of possibilities for establishing a control group against which to measure the effects of the experimental variable. One method in-

---

* This section reflects a summary of research problems. For a detailed exploration of research on group counseling, readers should refer to *Guidelines for Future Research on Group Counseling in the Public School Setting*. Benjamin Cohn (Editor): a report of Cooperative Research Project No. F-029, New York: Board of Cooperative Educational Services, 1965.

volves one group only, with data gathered during a period where the variable is not operating, then an equal period involving the experimental variable, and then another equal period where the experimental variable is again absent. This approach avoids the major problem of matching groups on the basis of the atmosphere that characterizes each group as unique. It has the weakness of not being able to assess the effects of uncontrolled variables, maturation, or the effect of the second phase on the third. Although maturation would appear to be controlled, the assumption is being made that the growth due to maturation during all three phases is constant.

An alternative and traditional method of control is to try to establish a control group that matches the experimental group on the significant variables in the research. Many studies have dodged the issue involved here by assuming that if characteristics like age, diagnosis, personality type, I.Q., etc., were comparable, the groups could be considered matched. Although this is a convenient escape hatch, it ignores the fact that the major variable in most studies of groups is the group climate itself. Admittedly this is a difficult variable to quantify, but the author believes that it is this problem which most needs our present attention.

The literature does suggest some promising approaches that deserve further inspection. Bach[5] has compared the quality, quantity, and verbal interactions of the same members of a psychotherapy group when they faced reality (discussion) versus fantasy (play-drama) conditions. Martin, Darley, and Gross[6,7] have developed an "Index of Cohesiveness" and an "Index of Mutuality," which attempt through sociometric choices to equate groups in terms of group atmosphere. Canter[8] has developed a multiple-control group technique as a means of factoring out unwanted variables. Statistically, it is possible to establish control. To accomplish this purpose one needs a large enough population so that members can be assigned to groups on a random basis. If the number of people and groups is large enough one can assume comparability between groups. Unfortunately, few studies can capture a large enough sample to use this approach with a real sense of confidence.

Bonney and Foley[9] have traced the evolution of a group from a social atmosphere to a therapeutic one and have developed indices of movement toward a therapeutic goal. Volsky and Hewer[10] have experimented with groups involving constant versus shifting membership. McWhinney[11] has developed an analytical tool to isolate the behavior of the group as a group from the behavior of the members of the group as individuals. Zimpfer,[12] through the use of a large number of groups and group leaders, has tried to solve the problems related to the small sample typically necessary in research with groups, but found that mere increase in the total N did not solve methodological problems.

Zlatchin[13] used two groups of subjects, his experimental group and another composed of all boys in the same grade level. The initial and final test results of the untreated group were intercorrelated and treated by correlational-profile analysis and multiple correlation to obtain two independent, weighted, composite measures. On the basis of *each* measure, control groups were matched with the experimental population to form two control groups, one for each major measure. In other words, using a large pool of subjects, matched experimental and control groups were developed independently for each variable studied.

One of the other sources of difficulty in research on groups comes from the role of the leader or therapist. The literature has amply illustrated the effect of the leader's personality and value system on his behavior and relationships with the group.[14-16] Control groups using different leaders certainly have introduced a major variable that will effect the results. Unfortunately, using the same leader in both experimental and control groups does not solve the problem either. Since group composition, in and of itself, will effect the reaction of the leader, it is impossible for any one person to relate equally to two groups. Differences here are compounded when the leader employs different methods in each group, since few people are equally adept at alternate methods of working with others.

The measures the investigator employs will very readily reflect his concept of group process as being individual learning in a group or a group which represents something different than the sum of individual reactions.

The range of techniques developed to quantify group process is both varied and long. It includes sociometric techniques,[4,17-20] interaction-process analysis,[18,21-26] group dimension scales,[27] genatypical dimensions (reactions of warmth, hostility or flight recorded in terms of direction and intensity),[28-30] client reports and observer reports.[31-36]

The years between the original edition of this book and the current revision have contributed toward a change in preference in tools used in research studies. The earlier edition reported[39] a slight preference for the Minnesota Multiphasic Personality Inventory, the Thematic Apperception Test, and the Rorschach.[40] Beyond these, all other devices seemed equally chosen. This survey also revealed considerable concern over whether the typical absence of significant changes in test scores reflected the lack of sensitivity of the instruments chosen or were in fact evidence of no change in the variable being studied.

There now appears to be an increasing emphasis on the use of on-the-spot observers. Because the use of tape recordings has ruled out vital visual cues of the members' identification with each other and also has blurred the intended meaning of the words expressed, there has been a real growth in studies using television monitors and kinescopes.[36-38,41]

Because of the problems involved in doing research in this area, no clear-cut answer about the effectiveness of group counseling exists. Evidence does suggest that people exposed to group counseling report the process as helpful, even when the instruments used in measurement do not provide data which demonstrates statistically significant change. Studies supporting the value of group counseling indicate its value in different settings and with different populations. Research evidence is available involving underachieving students,[42-45] anxious college freshmen,[46] gifted adolescents,[47] prospective counselors,[48] citizenship training,[49,50] placement counseling,[51] and test interpretation.[52]

The papers by Burchard, Michaels, and Kotkov,[53] as well as those by Frank[54] and Heyns and Zander,[55] provide excellent summaries of problems of research in the area. The most comprehensive summary of all the dimensions of research in group counseling is to be found in the report on group counseling by a research seminar sponsored by the U. S. Office of Education.[56]

It is not realistically possible within a brief chapter to review the results achieved by all the research conducted to date. Several recent texts[57-59] have been specifically designed to serve that purpose.

There appears to be little agreement among these books over the meaning of the results. For example, studies like those conducted by Fiedler[60] that relate interpersonal relationships in a group with the group's effectiveness, seem to suggest that good leaders interpose greater psychological distance between themselves and their co-workers than do poor leaders.

How can readers of this text reconcile these conclusions with the thesis presented in this book that group effectiveness is related to strong empathic relationships between group members? A close examination of these studies reveals several major defects that may make possible a different interpretation of the results obtained.

The primary source in many studies comes from the use of a Q technique to derive measures of assumed similarity. Cronbach[61] has clearly demonstrated some of the mathematical and psychological fallacies involved in the concept of assumed similarity. At the very least, there is experimental evidence involving sociometric data[62] that demonstrates little correspondence between whom a child in a study said he liked to be with and with whom he was observed to spend time.

Even if there were no question about the validity of the measurement technique, there still remains confusion if truly effective democratic groups are to be equated with friendship relationships based on identification and sympathy, rather than on empathy and acceptance of individual difference. There can be no quarrel that most existing groups tend to function on a friendship basis that equates acceptance of the person with accepting and meeting his needs. The entire purpose of this book has been to demonstrate that it is possible to structure groups so that they retain the warmth and support available in friendship but are modified to develop relationships that are more conducive to growth. Given that type of group, the author believes that the leader no longer need be distant to help members of the group use each other effectively.

Stock[63] presents evidence suggesting that group productivity and group cohesiveness are intimately related:

> . . . a relationship could be observed between group productivity and group cohesiveness. The T Group which displayed the greatest cohesiveness was also the most productive. Also, groups in which the participants showed greater "membership orientation" (defined as moving away from a concern about liking and disliking and toward a concern with intermember influence) also showed less distractibility from the task. Groups with greater membership orientation also showed greater awareness of group structure. Groups displaying a good deal of interpersonal hostility were more defensive and more likely to respond to social inductions with positive or negative emotionality.

One of the definitions of leadership is that the person who is chosen as leader supplies or meets the needs of the group. Part of the security group members have comes through identifying with the leader. Group members also seek to be accepted by the leader and their peers. To the degree that the leader epitomizes an ideal, real identification is impossible because members recognize considerable distance between their capabilities and those they have projected onto their leader image. Feeling unworthy, they then tend to desire a leader who can make decisions for them. As presented in the section on evaluation, groups have ambivalent feelings about their desire for equal status of all group members and their need to recognize true differences in ability. This ambivalence is resolved as personal security grows. One common result of studies on therapeutic groups is the observed positive relationship between a person's security and his ability to accept individual difference.

In some ways Army tradition epitomizes the concept that effective groups demand social distance between leaders and members. Recruits are taught that they are saluting the uniform and not the man (overlooking, of course, that the uniform can give no support or understanding). There is, however, at least one illustration in the service that completely refutes this hypothesis. Carlson's raiders functioned as a total group; before any operation, every man was given the chance to contribute his ideas and all men understood and accepted the goal of the group. Because they felt worthwhile as people, this rugged group was able to function in isolation from others. They also were able not only to delegate responsibility, but also to assume leadership roles with no previous definition of status or preserved psychological distance.

The studies cited and illustrations presented all seem to suggest a need for renewed attention to our definition of what constitutes a democratic group and a need to redefine the kinds of affect which relate to effectiveness in groups.

Summary

One measure of the sophistication of a discipline is the extent and quality of the research that has been performed. There is little doubt that many questions in the area of group process need investigation. Equally obvious should be the need for any researcher to have defined for himself, prior to starting on his research, the assumptions and hypotheses he cares to make. The traditional starting place for any study is a review of what others have done so far. To assist the reader in taking that first step, this chapter has presented a summary of studies and textbooks which may provide the research-oriented person with clues as to how to plan his study. There is little question that, at this point, there are more questions than answers.

BIBLIOGRAPHY

1. Perkins, Hugh V. "Climate Influences Group Behavior." *Journal of Educational Research*, 45, 115–117, October 1951.
2. Allport, G. W. *The Use of Personal Documents in Psychological Science.* New York: Social Science Research Council, *Bulletin 49*, 1947.
3. Jennings, Helen H. "Sociometric Grouping in Relation to Child Development." In Caroline Tryon (Ed.), *Fostering Mental Health in Our Schools.* Washington, D. C.: ASCD, National Education Association, 1950.

4. Smucker, Orden. "Measurement of Group Tension through the Use of Negative Sociometric Data." *Sociometry*, 10, 376–383, November 1947.
5. Bach, George R. "Dramatic Play Therapy with Adult Groups." *Journal of Psychology*, 29, 225–246, April 1950.
6. Martin, William E., Darley, John G., and Gross, Neal. "Studies of Group Behavior: II. Methodological Problems in the Study of Inter-Relationships of Group Members." *Educational and Psychological Measurement*, 12, 533–553, Winter 1952.
7. Gross, Neal, and Martin, William E. "On Group Cohesiveness." *American Journal of Sociology*, 57, 546–563, May 1952.
8. Canter, Ralph R., Jr. "The Use of Extended Control-Group Designs in Human Relations Studies." *Psychological Bulletin*, 48, 340–347, July 1951.
9. Bonney, Walter C., and Foley, Walter J. "The Transition Stage in Group Counseling in Terms of Congruence Theory." *Journal of Counseling Psychology*, 10, 136, 1963.
10. Volsky, Theodore, and Hewer, Vivian. "A Program of Group Counseling." *Journal of Counseling Psychology*, 7, 71–73, 1960.
11. McWhinney, W. H. "Isolating Organizational Dynamics In A Small Group Experiment." *Sociometry*, 26 (3), 354–372, 1963.
12. Zimpfer, David George. "The Relationship of Self Concept to Certain Affective Dimensions in Multiple Counseling." Doctoral Thesis, State University of New York at Buffalo, School of Education, 1964.
13. Zlatchin, Philip J. *The Effects of Group Therapy Upon Some Aspects of Behavior, Social Relationships, and Personal Attitudes of Adolescent Problem Boys.* New York: New York University, 1950.
14. Tollard, George A. "Role and Status Structure in Therapy Groups." *Journal of Clinical Psychology*, 13, 27–33, 1957.
15. Daniel, Marvin. "The Influence of the Sex of the Therapist and of the Cotherapist Technique in Group Psychotherapy with Boys," *Dissertation Abstracts*, 18, 1489, 1958.
16. Grater, Harry. "Changes in Self and Other Attitudes in a Leadership Training Group." Personnel and Guidance Journal, 37, 493, 1959.
17. Davis, Ruth G. "Group Therapy and Social Acceptance in a First-Second Grade." *Elementary School Journal*, 49, 219–223, December 1948.
18. Evans, John T. *Objective Measurement of the Therapeutic Group Process.* Cambridge: Harvard University, 1950.
19. Nelson, Alice D. *The Effect of Group Self Study on Sociometric Ratings.* East Lansing: Michigan State College, 1951. Abstract. *Microfilm Abstracts* 12, No. 6, 852–853, 1952.
20. Pepinsky, Harold B. "Measuring Outcomes of Classroom Therapy." *Educational and Psychological Measurement*, 7, 713–724. Winter 1947.
21. Psathas, George. "Interaction Process Analysis of Two Psychotherapy Groups." *International Journal of Group Psychotherapy*, 10, 430–445, 1960.
22. Munzer, Jean, and Greenwald, Harold. "Interaction Process Analysis of a Therapy Group." *International Journal of Group Psychotherapy*, 7, 175–190, 1957.
23. Bales, Robert F. *Interaction Process Analysis: A Method for the Study of Small Groups.* Cambridge: Addison-Wesley, 1950.
24. Noble, Frank, Ohlsen, Merle, and Proff, Fred. "A Method for the Quantification of Psychotherapeutic Interaction in Counseling Groups." *Journal of*

Counseling Psychology, **8**, 54–61, 1961.

25. Bales, Robert F., and Borgatta, E. F. "Size of Group as a Factor in the Interaction Profile," in Borgatta, E. F., Hare, P., and Bales, R. F. (Eds.), *Small Groups: Studies in Social Interaction,* 396–413. New York: Knopf, 1955.

26. Fine, Harold J., and Zimet, Carl N. "A Quantitative Method of Scaling Communication and Interaction Process." *Journal of Clinical Psychology,* **12**, 268–271, 1956.

27. Hemphill, John K., and Westie, Charles M. "The Measurement of Group Dimensions." *Journal of Psychology,* **29**, 325–342, April 1950.

28. Ruesch, Jurgan, and Prestwood, A. Rodney. "Interaction Process and Personal Codification." *Journal of Personality,* **18**, 391–430, 1950.

29. Joel, Walther, and Shapiro, David. "A Genotypical Approach to the Analysis of Personal Interaction." *Journal of Psychology,* **28**, 9–17, July 1949.

30. Thelen, Herbert, and Stock, Dorothy. *Methods for Studying Work and Emotionality in Group Operation.* Chicago: Human Dynamics Laboratory, 1954.

31. Baruch, Dorothy W. "Description of a Project in Group Therapy." *Journal of Consulting Psychology,* **9**, 271–280, November 1945.

32. Lawlor, Gerald W. "Psychodrama in Group Therapy." *Sociometry,* **9**, 275–281, November 1946.

33. Lifton, Walter M. *A Study of the Changes in Self Concept and Content Knowledge in Students Taking a Course in Counseling Techniques.* New York: New York University, August 1950. Abstract. *Microfilm Abstracts* **11**, No. 1, 55–56, 1951.

34. Metcalf, Harold H. "Group Counseling at the Eleventh Grade Level." *School Review,* **54**, 401–405, September 1946.

35. Peres, Hadassah. "An Investigation of Non-directive Group Therapy." *Journal of Consulting Psychology,* **11**, 159–172, July 1947.

36. Noble, Frank C. *A Method for the Quantification of Interaction in Psychotherapeutic Groups.* University of Illinois (Ed.D. Thesis), 1958.

37. Cohn, Benjamin, Ohlsen, Merle, and Proff, Fred. "Roles Played by Adolescents in an Unproductive Counseling Group." *Personnel and Guidance Journal,* **38**, 724–731, 1960.

38. Wigell, Wayne W., and Ohlsen, Merle. "To What Extent Is Affect a Function of Topic and Referent in Group Counseling?" *American Journal of Orthopsychiatry,* **32**, 728–735, 1962.

39. Lifton, Walter. "Group Therapy in Educational Institutions." *Review of Educational Research,* **XXIV**, No. 2, 156–163, April 1954.

40. Horwitz, Murray, and Cartwright, Dorwin. "A Project Method for the Diagnosis of Group Properties." *Human Relations,* **VI**, No. 4, 397–410, 1953.

41. Katz, Evelyn W, Ohlsen, Merle, and Proff, Fred. "An Analysis of the Interpersonal Behavior of Adolescents in Group Counseling." *Journal of College Student Personnel,* **1**, 2–10, 1959.

42. Cohn, Benjamin. *The Effects of Group Counseling on School Adjustment of Underachieving Junior High School Boys Who Demonstrate Acting-Out Behavior.* Bedford Hills, New York: Board of Cooperative Educational Services, 1963.

43. Bosdell, Betty J. "Evaluation of Counseling Treatments with Underachieving High School Students." *Cooperative Research Project #1263.* Washington, D. C.: Department of Health, Education and Welfare, 1962.

44. Baymur, Feriha, and Patterson, C. H. "Three Methods of Assisting Under-achieving High School Students." *Journal of Counseling Psychology*, 7, 83–90, 1960.

45. Clampitt, Richard R. "An Exploratory Controlled Investigation of the Effect of Group Therapy." *Dissertation Abstracts*, 15, 2292–2293, 1955.

46. Spielberger, Charles D., Weitz, Henry, and Denney, J. Peter. "Group Counseling and the Academic Performance of Anxious College Freshmen." *Journal of Counseling Psychology*, 9, 195–204, 1962.

47. Broedel, John W., Ohlsen, M., Proff, F., and Southard, C. "The Effects of Group Counseling on Gifted Underachieving Adolescents." *Journal of Counseling Psychology*, 7, 163–170, 1960.

48. Gazda, G. and Ohlsen, Merle. "The Effects of Short-Term Group Counseling on Prospective Counselors." *Personnel and Guidance Journal*, 39, 634–638, 1961.

49. Kaplan, Stanley W. "The Effect of Group Counseling on Junior High School Boys' Concept of Themselves in School." *Journal of Counseling Psychology*, 4, 124–128, 1957.

50. Davis, Donald A. "The Effect of Group Guidance and Individual Counseling on Citizenship Behavior." *Personnel and Guidance Journal*, 38, 142–145, 1959.

51. Siegal, Max. "Group Orientation and Placement Counseling. *Personnel and Guidance Journal*, 38, 659–660, 1960.

52. Wright, E. Wayne. "A Comparison of Individual and Multiple Counseling for Test Interpretation Interviews." *Journal of Counseling Psychology*, 10, 126–135, 1963.

53. Burchard, Edward M. L., Michaels, Joseph, J., and Kotkov, Benjamin. "Criteria for the Evaluation of Group Therapy." *Psychosomatic Medicine*, X, No. 5, 257–275, September-October, 1948.

54. Frank, Jerome D. "Some Problems of Research in Group Psychotherapy." *International Journal of Group Psychotherapy*, I, 78–81, 1951.

55. Heyns, Roger W., and Zander, Alvin F. "Observation of Group Behavior." *Research Methods in the Behavioral Sciences*, New York: Dryden, 1953.

56. Cohn, Benjamin (Editor). *Guidelines For Future Research on Group Counseling in the Public School Setting*, Board of Cooperative Educational Services, Bedford Hills, N. Y., 1965. Cooperative Research Project No. F-029.

57. Hare, Paul, Borgatta, Edgar F., and Bales, Robert F. *Small Groups—Studies in Social Interaction*. New York: Knopf, 1955.

58. Cartwright, Dorwin, and Zander, Alvin. *Group Dynamics: Research and Theory*. Evanston, Illinois: Row Peterson, 1956.

59. Taguiri, Renato, and Petrillo, Luigi. *Person Perception and Interpersonal Behavior*. Stanford, California: Stanford University Press, 1958.

60. _____. Chapter 16, "Interpersonal Perception and Group Effectiveness," Fred Fiedler, pp. 243–258.

61. _____. Chapter 23, "Proposals Leading to Analytic Treatment of Social Perception Scores," Lee Cronbach, pp. 353–379.

62. Polansky, Norman, Lippitt, Ronald, and Redl, Fritz. "The Use of Near-Sociometric Data in Research on Group Treatment Process." *Sociometry*, XIII, No. 1, 39–62, February 1950.

63. Stock, Dorothy. "A Survey of Research on T Groups," Ch. 15, pp. 395–441 *T-Group Theory and Laboratory Method* by Leland Bradford, Jack R. Gibb, and Kenneth D. Benne (Editors). New York: Wiley, 1964.

9

Conclusion

Terminating Groups

Groups, like all things, reach a point where they end. For continuous groups, the ending is not clearly perceived, for it may represent merely the moving out of one group of people who are immediately replaced by others. For finite groups, however, closure represents a distinctive part of the group's life. As the terminal date approaches, the discussions become more superficial as the anxiety increases.

Think of the last day before graduation and the feelings discussed in this chapter may come back to you. Remember the sense of loss of close friendships, the sudden acceptance of characteristics which symbolized a group that was formerly rejected (labels, etc.), the frantic copying of addresses to insure that the bond really wasn't being broken, and the apprehension over your capacity to face the next step alone. In a very real sense, groups go through a weaning process. Almost like an ill child, they may revert to infantile behavior as one way of saying they really are not ready to go off on their own.

The leader who anticipates the sudden upsurge of anxiety and dependency will not become anxious himself. He will be able, instead, to accept these feelings as natural. Discovering that the leader remains calm helps the group achieve perspective and enables them to go on to their next level of responsibility. If, in the end, members of a group can perceive what the group as a group achieved and if they can see what they personally have gained, the value of the group as a social force will remain in their memory for future reference.

Groups can be used in at least three ways. They can serve as a way of helping a person discover how others might help him in an individual counseling situation. For the person receiving individual counseling, it might often be helpful to relate concurrently to a group; the group might serve as a testing ground for ideas developed in the individual sessions. Lastly, the person who terminates individual counseling may wish to use a group as a weaning process. Having been secure in a two person setting, he now moves to a comfortable group situation before tackling the world at large.

The Training of the Effective Group Worker

One of the most serious weaknesses of a book of this type is that it must advocate the value of an experience that many have not shared. As we have seen, an intellectual acceptance of the rights of the individual is not enough. To live out one's beliefs, each person needs to have had the chance to experience the rewards that come from a supportive group where individual difference is truly valued.

New behaviors need to be rewarded and need to be equally effective as older modes of behavior. If, then, the approach described in this text makes sense to a reader, further implementation of the approach will require more than additional reading.

For the highly motivated person there are specific kinds of preparation that will be helpful. Included are:

1. Courses covering personality theory and the dynamics of human behavior.

2. Courses covering semantics and effective verbal communication.

3. Courses providing background of an anthropological or sociological nature which will assist the reader in recognizing the meaning or symbolic significance of various roles or acts in our culture.

4. Courses training a person in specific counseling skills.

5. Courses providing supervised practicum experiences where the student is helped to discover the way in which his needs are effecting his behavior.

6. Experiences as a group leader or member to sensitize the person to typical experiences in the life of a group.

Mahler and Caldwell* have provided one yardstick of the different levels of training helpful for different types of groups.

* Clarence Mahler and Edson Caldwell. *Group Counseling in the Secondary School.* Chicago: Science Research Associates, 1961.

COUNSELOR TRAINING REQUIREMENTS

Class	Large Group
Well-trained classroom teacher who has sufficient understanding of students to maximize the value of units with self-exploration and self-understanding potential.	Trained school counselor with good teaching skills and ability to get groups to work on their own.

Small Group	Therapy Group
Well-trained school counselor with strong psychology background for deeper understanding of behavior. Should have sufficient skill and individual counseling experience not to be threatened by an unstructured approach. If not able to do this, there is little justification for the small-group approach.	Training as a school psychologist, or equivalent, is essential. (Students in this group are difficult to help at best, and group leader must have real skill.)

Many readers would welcome the chance to secure formal training, but reality factors make the possibility remote. Although pulling oneself up by one's bootstraps is difficult, there are specific criteria one can apply as a means of gauging whether growth is taking place. After each group session it would help to ask oneself the following questions:

1. How much of the time was I concerned with the content of the group's discussion rather than on the interaction taking place or needs being covertly expressed?

2. How active was I in this session? Were my contributions a reaction to group needs, or was I meeting personal needs?

3. Did I have any trouble in communicating with the group?

4. How accepting was I of the right of each person to see things in his own way? Do I in fact accept the idea that no two people are really alike?

5. Could I really accept the fact that a group moves slowly and that it takes time to mature?

6. Was I able to experience tension in the group without getting upset?

7. How effective was I in helping the group develop leadership skills so they wouldn't need me?

Using a personal checklist can help. Having a group where others will offer their perception of your growth is even better. The really motivated lay leader will find many other people in the community eager to work with him in developing groups where human relations skills represent the purpose of the group.

There is concrete evidence[1,2] that laymen working with their peers to explore feelings and attitudes can, with minimal training, learn how to help members of a group use each other as a source of support.

Summary

This book has been focused toward helping people become more cognizant of the benefits and problems associated with the use of groups to promote affective learnings. Based upon comments of readers who reviewed this text in its early stages, there appears to be no easy way to label the procedures involved without violating the values of some readers. It is hoped that the major goal of utilizing understanding in the fields of psychotherapy, education, and social work has not created the impression that the processes being explored were suitable only for the deviant or maladjusted person. To come full circle, it is worth again repeating that it is my belief that no book can be written that will fit the personality, values, or skills of every reader. By necessity, each reader should conclude this book with a long list of points of agreement and disagreement with the author. When viewed *in toto* this list represents the operating philosophy of the reader. Each person who finds himself in a leadership role must inescapably decide how he will use this role to promote the values in which he believes.

Hopefully, this book will have demonstrated that effective group leadership is a skill that requires training and preparation. As one reviews the many techniques employed by group leaders it is easy to conceive of the role as involving only the mastery of a series of tricks of the trade. Of greater importance is an awareness that each technique's effectiveness is dependent not only on how it was employed but also on why it was used. Each technique becomes but an extension of the needs, values, and biases of the group leader. Although all of us will find ourselves involved in groups and with leadership functions, our ultimate success as a person and as a nation depends upon an increased awareness of our need to develop group process skills.

Our current preoccupation with academic achievement and conservation of manpower has had one negative result. As we become increasingly more task oriented, the value and rights of the individual are increasingly losing their position as the essential component of a democracy. Let us dedicate ourselves to the task of demonstrating to society that group techniques need not lead to mediocrity, but rather can serve as the key to unlock the potential for individual happiness and growth.

BIBLIOGRAPHY

1. Hereford, Carl F. *Changing Parental Attitudes Through Group Discussion.* Austin: University of Texas Press, 1963.
2. Lifton, Walter. *Leading Groups: A Leader's Guide for They Ask Why.* Chicago: National Dairy Council, 1963.

Appendix

A Diary Report of the Complete Life of a Group

One of the dangers in a chapter like Chapter 5, is that it tends to suggest a level of specificity that is not accurate. No group exactly duplicates another. The cross references in Chapter 5 will have demonstrated clearly to the reader the existence of numerous other interpretations of specific situations or definitions of group process.

This Appendix has as its goal the development in the reader of an awareness of the stages through which a group may pass as it progresses from its start to its termination. Since this Appendix provides a picture of the complete life of a group, it carries with it both the excitement found in group crises and the boredom that develops when the same ideas seem to be repeated over and over. This diary of a group should not be read as one would read a play or drama. Use the material instead as a vicarious training experience for yourself as a group leader or member. As you read, ask yourself what you think you might have done at each point. Consider the issues the group raises and reraises, and decide what themes seem to be dominant in the life of the group. If you find yourself bored or angry, ask yourself what needs of yours would help or hinder your activities in the group.

In order to provide the reader with this documentary report of a group, the author has secured permission from Mr. Joseph Srsnick to reproduce parts of the logs he wrote as a member of a group. To maintain the confidential nature of the group's discussion, the logs have been edited. The reader will find some of the comments repetitious, but they have been included to provide a more realistic picture of the way groups return to concepts or problems until they are worked through. The logs also provide a chronological picture of stages in a group's life and the speed with which this specific group was able to move. The material also shows the integration of thera-peutic techniques within structured university class requirements. It should be remembered that these logs reflect the perceptions of only one group member.

Log 1

Today we held our first group meeting and Dr. Lifton began by turning on the tape and mentioning its necessity. He then briefly talked about the course's limits. He mentioned the facts that we would be graded and that class members would be required to take notes, or rather, to make logs of each session.

Since G. and I were new to the group, the members introduced themselves. This seemed necessary in order to acquaint each other and to establish some feeling of solidarity. The introductions were very brief and seemed to be rattled off in a business-like fashion.

. . . E. wanted the leader's opinions on the course's content and aims. This may have expressed a need for structuring and seemed also to demonstrate a need for dependence on the leader. E. then wished that everyone mention their reasons for taking the course, in the hope that we would get a better understanding of individual goals and desires. All of this seemed like a desire to establish group unity and seemed like an attempt to get things going.

Some members seemed to think the group was heterogeneous while others seemed to think that each had some things in common. . . . The group seemed heterogeneous in that the members are of different ages, are male and female, have different positions at this time, and have had a variety of experiences and backgrounds. It was homo-generous in that we are all members of the course, all seemed reason-ably verbal, all are relatively inexperienced in group guidance, and all wanted to further their knowledge and skills in the area. . . .

Some member then wondered where we would go from here and it was pointed out that we had already made some progress and were beginning to express our views on different topics. . . .

It was mentioned that we could learn group techniques by our personal experiences in the present group. We would be living in a group for four hours a week and would gain a working knowledge of the things that could happen in such an assembly.

The group came to the realization, with the leader's help, that we had been searching for limits and for ways of feeling comfortable with one another. . . .

We also came to the realization that communication in groups is not an easy thing to accomplish and various members felt that each member should contribute something to the group—verbally. They could not accept the fact that a member could remain silent and gain from the experience.

Some members expressed the feeling that they needed some verbal contribution from every other member in order to feel secure.

Quite a few of the members seemed to revolt against G. for his statement that he may not communicate with the other members. They seemed, however, to be unaware of G.'s feelings and did not seem to be accepting him as an individual—and to me this does not show respect for him. In fact, the group as a whole had little awareness of the feelings of others and seemed to state their own views instead. . . .

On the whole the session seemed characterized by a searching for limits, for group commonness and unity, and for defining our roles and goals. . . .

Log 2

. . . He then asked the leader's impression of the article as if in an attempt to gain approval or acceptance. . . .

. . . It was agreed that we should try to be understanding of each other and have respect for each other's judgment and opinions—even though these opinions may be counter to our own.

Several group members have reached the understanding that G. has every right to remain silent since we can learn by listening. In fact, it was realized today that we, as a group, were not listening enough to each other but were more concerned with our own thinking. The group did value the perceptions of G. and one member mentioned the fact that G.'s initial silence had aroused hostility in him. . . .

The group seemed to want an authority figure present, to which they could turn in times of confusion and stress. This may be due to the fact that the group had not become entirely secure with each other and had overlooked themselves as resource people. They did seem to eventually realize that the controls and guides would have to be group created. . . .

. . . Toward the end of the session members were beginning to reveal their true feelings, which this writer feels is essential to progress. It was brought out, however, that different people react on various levels. . . .

C., who did less talking than anyone else in the group, seemed to rationalize her silence by saying that someone had always beaten her to the draw in communicating her feelings. I kept wondering why her silence wasn't questioned as G.'s was. . . .

Log 3

. . . E. brought to the group's attention the fact that we often do not give individual members enough opportunity to disclose their feelings concerning a topic that was initiated. Instead of becoming listeners we often introject [*sic*] questions and opinions that really satisfy our own needs; discounting the needs of the person who first introduces a topic. It was realized, however, that the combined perceptions of several members add to the original perceptions or understanding of the person who initiates a question or topic. We thus give mutual help in satisfying needs and enhance the security of group members. . . .

Dr. Lifton tried to point out the responsibility of group members by directing our attention to the fact that we are free to experiment in the group if we assume the responsibility for the effect our behavior has on others. . . .

. . . When E. left the room he was missed and the group felt that they had better wait until his return for continuing the discussion. . . .

. . . At this point, too, the group realized that we support each other "when the heat is on" and have gained a sharpness of perception that lets us know when someone else is reaching his "tolerance point." The group is thus realizing the value of being your real self. When we reveal ourselves to others we allow them to get closer to us. . . .

One of the last points of discussion was the problem of limits, as these relate to confidentiality and behavior toward one another outside of our sessions. . . .

Log 4

Today's session again seemed to hedge around limits, security, understanding, acceptance, and roles. . . .

Our desire to be understood, which leads to acceptance, was illustrated in W.'s, L.'s, and F.'s efforts to explain their behavior of the previous meeting. They seemed to be saying, "I'm explaining my behavior of last week so that you will understand me. I'm not changing my mind about these issues but I want to be sure you understand me; so that you will accept me." . . .

R. seemed to gain insight into the effect emotion has on objectivity and rationality. . . .

A. seemed to be saying: "If I know what hostility means to others I will know what to expect from them, when they get hostile." This again seemed to be a reaching out for understanding. Perhaps the group was wondering how a hostile person would be evaluated. Would we lose respect for one who did reveal hostility? . . . We are looking for constructive ways in which to express negative feelings. . . .

. . . Perhaps some of his trouble centered around his statement that none of us were competent enough to go around analyzing each other. . . .

. . . Others can tell us if we are being perceived as we would like to be perceived. . . .

We also seemed to realize today that we are becoming a more closely-knit body and are beginning to act as a group and are beginning to make more concrete our group characteristics. The mere fact that we stayed on the topic that G. initiated seemed to prove that we as a group can tackle a specific problem and work for the good of an individual or individuals.

The problem of behavior outside the group was again brought up. . . .

Log 5

My feelings at present are those of rebellion. . . . The group seems to want understanding but when someone tries to explain themselves, they are cut off and diagnosed. Even though my needs weren't met I tried to meet those of others. However, there did seem to be insights gained today.

I will try to list some of the positive gains—as I see them.

1. Therapy and learning take place when we put our feelings into words.

2. W. wanted to be sure that everyone understood what the limits are; especially in regard to confidentiality.

3. We should include the group in our thinking.

4. Hostility was amply displayed. This may indicate greater security to reveal our negative feelings. This will probably lead to antagonism but I have faith it will eventually lead to understanding.

5. W. felt that Dr. Lifton should be a group member. Others couldn't or wouldn't see him as such (E.). I believe he should be perceived as a member, a clarifier, and a catylizer.

6. E. noticed we are on guard—or defensive. He verbalized that we cannot be honest if we are defensive.

7. L. wanted to know what kind of a group we were. I don't think her question was answered. We are still trying to determine this.

8. E. admitted that false interpretation can be harmful but he seemed to be interpreting or judging several group members. He doesn't practice what he preaches—as I see it.

9. E. said we should be humble and not use the group solely to satisfy our own needs. I wonder if he practiced this humility?

10. The group seemed to realize we become hostile to those we like. Hostility means that we care.

11. Someone said we should accept people for what they are—even if they are confused.

12. The group realized that we are now becoming aware of what we are doing.

Now I'll list some of my own views and feelings.

1. If we are to be given a semester grade by the others we will try to find out what *they* think a good group member is and then conform to those criteria. By so doing we may not be our real selves.

2. I don't think, at this point, that the group knows what a good member is and I wonder if we can become objective enough to grade each other fairly.

3. We do not give others a fair chance to explain their views but jump in before they are finished talking and contribute our interpretation. We read *too* far beyond a person's words because we haven't given him a fair chance to clarify his views. If we listened long enough the need for interpretation or diagnosis would disappear.

4. I sense a great deal of suspiciousness among the members. We are suspicious of what the other guy *might* be thinking of us. This can be overcome if the members gain enough security to really tell each other just how they feel.

5. When I nod my head in *understanding* I am showing respect for the individual. I am not judging but am trying to demonstrate an internal frame of reference. I am not analyzing anyone—merely trying to look at the world as they do. Others have seen this as having their minds' read. I must clarify this to them if the issue presents itself or if I see the opportunity for so doing.

6. E. has accused me of offering no suggestions in the first three meetings whereas I think I did state my beliefs, goals, etc.

7. Too often we talk for others, as if we knew exactly what they

feel. We do not know exactly how they feel since we haven't given them enough time to talk.

8. After we listen to a person carefully and see his point of view, then we can add our own perceptions. In this way we will get 10 points of view on a topic—including Dr. Lifton—if he desires to contribute. This will lead to growth—I think.

9. I sensed that the group has not as yet accepted the fact that we are self-governing and must take responsibility for most of the group's behavior, direction, limits and goals. Members too often look to Dr. Lifton for direction.

10. I sense that the group does not realize that others besides Dr. Lifton are leaders. However, members do act in this capacity without realizing it. Anyone who suggests a new topic, asks a question, summarizes, or clarifies is taking the role of the leader.

11. Therapy goes on all the time. If a member leaves with a clearer perception of his self-concept, he has grown. Therapy is learning and we are learning. If a person's thinking and/or behavior changes as a result of our sessions, then therapy has taken place.

12. Members should assume responsibility for their behavior but other members can help by verbally reacting to that behavior.

13. We are not communicating enough and certainly are not effective enough. Doubt and insecurity do not lead to group unity.

14. We must learn to listen, accept, understand, contribute our own perceptions, and work for the group's welfare. If we want our own needs satisfied, we must satisfy the needs of others.

15. If each member was listened to long enough, the group could satisfy his needs. He in turn would work with the group in meeting the needs of every other individual. The group works as a group in helping each other and in working toward goals. The members add individually to this endeavor. The members get their needs satisfied in the process.

Now I have put into symbols my feelings. Now I should be able to use problem solving techniques with them. I am not so rebellious now.

Log 6

. . . group seemed more calm. . . . I find it more helpful to list things I have experienced in myself and in the group.

1. It was a good feeling to know the group is beginning to understand me. I experienced a definite sense of greater security.

2. It was disclosed that the group had suspected some sort of conspiracy between myself and Dr. Lifton during the first three or four sessions. They felt that the leader always agreed with things I had suggested. G. felt that this might be due to envy or suspiciousness.

3. A great part of the session was devoted to understanding Dr. Lifton's role. Some members definitely seem to see him as a teacher. It was noticed that A. consistently backs down when the leader appears to talk to him. This appeared as a surrender or fear reaction on A.'s part. Others have noticed this also.

4. I think Dr. Lifton should be accepted as a group member whose responsibility consists of helping the group to understand each other and become more integrated. He consistently directs the group's attention to noticing how the group is functioning. This seems to have been very helpful.

5. The members seem to be recognizing their individuality.

6. Some members seem to want Dr. Lifton to give support, structure and guidance. They still don't seem to realize that each member becomes a leader in turn. Perhaps they don't have enough faith in their own potentialities, as yet. The trend seems to be toward unity and group thinking—but we are slow in reaching this goal.

7. We definitely seemed to miss G. when he left the room and we seem to feel incomplete without him—or any other member who might be absent. The group feels that a legitimate excuse justifies an absence but we expect the absent member to listen to the tape.

8. The group realized that the leader has information on the members that is not shared with the group. This appeared to help the group see him as a teacher. The possibility of sharing the logs with the group did not seem to win favor.

9. Once we test people we get to know them. This leads to understanding and then to increased security.

10. The group sees the logs as a method of making concrete and symbolic our feelings. The logs are also used in rehearsing our behavior for future meetings. The group seemed to realize that we could test our perceptions, that are developed in the log, in the group. The group thus becomes a source of reality testing.

11. Members also realized that in writing the logs we are forced to analyze ourselves and our motives. The logs are thus a source of self-understanding—which is part of therapy.

12. Someone mentioned the fact that we must first analyze ourselves in order to do justice in understanding others. I don't think we fully realize or accept the fact that the greatest opportunity in self-analysis lies in our inter-group relations.

13. Some members seem to be afraid of self-analysis in the group, or should I say, self-analysis through the group.

14. R. pointed out that we often disregard feelings and merely focus our attention on the content of verbal interplay. I believe that focusing on feelings is much more fruitful and productive.

15. It was mentioned that it is hard to put our feelings into verbal symbols. However, until this is done our meetings will be somewhat unproductive. The logs aid this crystalization of thinking.

16. The members are beginning to realize that the ambiguity dimension of our non-directive atmosphere is sometimes uncomfortable. As a result the members strive for support, clarification, and direction. They rationalize this by pointing out that our educational system has always leaned in the "directive" direction. They are still refusing to take full responsibility for group direction and growth.

17. Our verbal content is the vehicle through which group dynamics operate.

18. We are beginning to realize that we don't have a group until we have established some common ground. We must get something from each other.

19. We benefit from others' perceptions of our problems.

20. The group seems to be the type which still does not completely solve any presented problem because we skip around too rapidly from topic to topic. Perhaps we skip in order to look at the problem from different viewpoints and in order to crystalize our thinking.

21. It was also realized that we create limits in various areas by the total import of our actions. Some limits are unverbalized.

22. It was also pointed out that we can gain nothing from an experience unless feelings are present which are experienced and perhaps verbalized.

23. W. pointed out that we can partly determine a leader's function by observing Dr. Lifton in action. We further learn the leader's role by becoming a leader in the group.

24. Some members were afraid of criticizing the leader in the log. This seemed partly due to a fear of hurting him or in losing his acceptance.

25. The secrecy of the logs seems to inhibit Dr. Lifton. However, no one definitely suggested that this confidentiality be changed.

26. It was pointed out that we force Dr. Lifton into various roles by our needs.

27. E. seemed to think that by voicing hostility in the log toward the leader would harm the teacher-friend relationship.

28. By rereading previous logs we can determine our own growth and our movement direction.

29. Dr. Lifton pointed out that it is harmful for a leader to be considered perfect. His reflection of feeling at this point would tend to prevent a real transference relationship from developing. He shows the members that it is their perceptions of him which make him appear perfect.

30. A leader is perceived as he is, due to our needs, his needs, and the environment.

31. All of the above observations seem to verify what has been written in textbooks on group guidance or therapy.

Log 7

In my impression the group seemed to move backward today. Although we have formed some group unity we seem to have drifted apart and have become nine separate individuals. . . .

Although the group decided to admit the new member it took them two hours to arrive at such a conclusion. As F. said: "Why do we fuss so much?"

. . . different individuals have verbalized some excellent insights and suggestions that would benefit the group. The group as a whole has not picked these insights up.

1. Admitting a new member would provide an interesting experiment on the effects it has on the group's unity.

2. We are concerned about an individual's absence and feel incomplete without him. An absent individual has the responsibility to let the group know the reason for his absence.

3. Group unity is disclosed by our feeling incomplete when a member is absent.

4. Dr. Lifton was right when he said that the matter of note taking would someday be a topic of discussion. Each member wants to feel that others are listening when he is talking.

5. It was mentioned that we must allow each member to help himself. We must not make the individual feel that he is helpless.

6. Movement takes place when we reveal our ugly side as well as our pretty side. However, I do not believe that progress depends solely on revealing our hates, etc.

7. Only two people in a group can relate to each other at one time. The others are involved in the meantime.

8. Verbal participation isn't mandatory as an indication of involvement. A listener has value.

9. The whole is greater than the sum of its parts. Nine cumulative perceptions gives everyone in the group a much clearer picture of a topic or problem.

10. If another member doesn't understand me or would like to know something about me, he must ask me to disclose myself.

11. I think our needs sometime blind us. As a result we hear what we want to hear when someone else is talking. We aren't really listening but are projecting our own needs into his talk and interpret.

12. The group members still seem to be analyzing and diagnosing each other.

13. Several members feel the group discussions have some therapeutic aspects.

14. Extraneous talk isn't appropriate to the group discussions; unless everyone agrees to talk on a topic.

15. When we ask someone a direct question and desire an immediate reply, we often confuse him and put that person on the defensive. Communication should be free, spontaneous and willing.

16. The total import of our actions telegraphs our feelings to others, without the necessity of verbalization—sometimes.

17. We aren't able to speak until we feel secure and have formulated our thinking. If we are too emotional we get confused.

18. Listening to group discussions stimulates our thinking and can lead to the solution of problems.

19. Some members feel that we still aren't our real selves in the group but have become an aggregate of intellectualizers.

20. L. pointed out that it might be profitable if we related in the friendly, informal manner that we use in our gatherings outside of the group. No one seemed to appreciate her efforts.

21. In a group setting it is easier to retreat in the face of threat or anxiety. This is harder to accomplish in a smaller group and so we are forced to be more sincere or revealing.

22. The matter of whether we should satisfy our own or other's needs was brought up and didn't seem to be solved. The group can help, understand, support, or assist each member in turn. That member who is being helped then willingly helps another member, in turn. The group meets the needs of the person talking. He then is stimulated to help the group meet the needs of the person who talks next.

23. We can meet our needs through others and then help them meet theirs.

24. We still seem to have a communication problem, perhaps because we focus too much on content and not enough on feeling and understanding.

25. Several members felt that the group might be temporarily slowed down upon the arrival of the new member, since it would take a while to get to know him and work out a secure, comfortable relationship with him.

Log 8

. . . No one seemed to mind the fact that the proposed new member decided not to join our group. This may be one small indication of unity. . . .

. . . This is another sign of unity. Dr. Lifton summarized and clarified the issue by saying that since we are secure we don't mind being divergent. . . .

The mechanism of displacement seems to have taken place between E. and myself. We were reacting to one another the way we would ordinarily act toward someone else. Our perceptions were thus distorted by our mental set. We saw and heard only what we wanted to hear. . . .

E. picked up the feeling which I have noticed in the last three or four sessions. It seems that the members (some of the members) have been competing with each other for some sort of recognition or status; although the purpose of this competition doesn't seem to be clear. I'm wondering whether this is good for the group or whether it is harmful. It doesn't seem to make for unity but for suspiciousness. . . .

. . . Sometimes I feel that the group is making wonderful progress and at other times I feel discouraged. I expect to be misunderstood sometimes and I guess I must try even harder to make my views much more clear.

The following is a list of some of the things I've noticed happening.

1. The group seems to realize that the majority has responsibility to and should listen to the minority. The minority also has responsibility to the majority. In other words, the group's knowledges, insights, and goal-directed behavior is improved and strengthened when everyone contributes and is concerned about everyone else's welfare.

2. W. seems to have faith in the group's capabilities to handle new problems. Other members do not hold this view. I have a great deal

of faith in the group's abilities. If we as a group develop the attitude that we are helpless—we will become helpless. Our mental set determines our thinking and behavior.

3. The group seems to be recognizing the fact that we are individualistic and are beginning to assert this uniqueness. I believe that this does not have to lead to disunity but could contribute to gains and unity. When we become secure and trusting enough to reveal our individuality, we can attack any problem more effectively because each of us will feel free to add our own perceptions to the solution of a problem.

4. The group seems to realize the importance of every member and is anxious to hear his views and opinions.

5. E. especially felt that values and attitudes could be transmitted during the meetings. I agree.

6. Our behavior reveals implicit agreement upon certain values or modes of behavior.

7. We must accept the person for his own personal worth but may disagree with what he says or thinks.

8. R. felt that first impressions aren't necessarily real. We grow to understand a person by listening to him. This is in disagreement with F.'s statement a week ago when she said that we cannot change our original impression of people.

9. B. wanted to know (sincerely) how we can get to know someone. The group sort of told him that we get to know another by employing a two-way process using the internal frame of reference. We get to know someone to the degree that we allow ourselves to look at the world as he looks at it, and we do this by listening.

10. It was noticed that by directing questions and other very direct measures against someone puts him on the defensive. A member will talk only when he feels secure and is not being pressured.

11. Silence has varied meanings to the people who are reacting to someone else's silence. Some of the members wondered how they could meet their own needs when reacting to a silent person; while at the same time respecting his right to be silent. Even though the group seems to have allowed various members to remain silent, we feel more comfortable and gain more clarity in our thinking when these people do speak.

12. We are trying harder to meet each other's needs—this may slow down decision making temporarily. It is a sign of progress in my mind.

13. The group's value system is composed of portions of the value systems of the members. We seem to surrender a little bit of our

values or needs in order to be accepted by the group—or to conform to the group. This in turn enables the group to support us and believe in us.

14. To the degree that another member seems strange, his behavior may appear hostile to us. We see only what we want to see.

15. The meaning of an action or verbalization is the thing that counts.

16. We must take greater pains to express our views and to understand those of others. Only when our own needs are understood and accepted can we more clearly see other people and their needs. We understand others to the degree that we understand ourselves.

Log 9

Meeting eight seemed to start the ball rolling in a productive direction. . . .

Following are things I have witnessed:

1. Each member seems to favor a certain role in the group. We seem to have realized, however, that each member can and should function in several different roles. We seek the most comfortable role.

2. In the "outside world" we act the roles of student, parents, wife, husband, citizen and other social roles. In the group we are not bound by such hard and fast relationships. We don't have to act in any certain way. We can be our real selves here, gain insight into our self-concept, and realize how others see us.

3. Using F. as a guinea pig we discovered that we sometimes focus only on a member's negative aspects and disregard focusing our attention on his finer qualities. We thus discovered one of the group's patterns of behavior to each other.

4. It's hard to live up to the expectations of others. We can't please all people. We sometimes set up expectations of others which may be unfair and unrealistic.

5. We should not pressure any member to speak but should allow for spontaneous verbalization. The more we pressure, question and probe an individual, the more defensive and anxious he may become. By creating a secure, non-critical atmosphere we encourage all members to participate. Respect for others leads to feelings of security.

6. Actions speak louder than words. Our actions may deliver an impression which may not coincide with our spoken words. We are thus focusing our attention on our actions as well as our verbalizations

and are able to detect any ambivalence here. We are thus learning about ourselves.

7. Our perceptions, even though unrealistic, will determine how we act, how we use the group, and how we are perceived by others as a result.

8. A person can be an active participant by listening. Many of our questions get answered by listening.

9. Even though we respect the right of a member to be silent, we cannot be positive that he is listening and gaining. We want others to tell us whether or not they are profiting from the group experience.

10. We satisfy the silent person's need to remain silent. In all fairness then, he should help others satisfy their needs—when their needs call for him to verbalize now and then. It's a give-and-take proposition between all members.

11. The way the group as a whole treat or react to a particular member will cause him to develop certain self-concepts and ideas concerning interpersonal relationships.

12. When the group expects too much of a particular member it causes that person to feel inadequate and misunderstood. We can become more realistic by allowing each member to reveal himself more fully. This can do away with misperceptions to a large extent.

13. We are all teachers in the group. We teach ourselves and others certain things. This might be a definition of therapy—therapy is a learning process.

14. Our ideas should be tested out in the group—a form of reality testing. This technique will prove whether or not our ideas are logical and sensible. The group represents a unique situation in reality testing.

15. We can crystallize our thinking better by verbalizing. When we put our thoughts into words we attempt to be logical. By verbalizing, we can determine any illogic, unreality, or conflict. We must, therefore, give each member a chance to think out loud—by listening to him.

16. Using F. as an example: she seemed to gain a great deal of security and calmness when her feelings were verbalized. The group definitely seemed to understand her better.

17. E., my former antagonist, shook my hand and told me I was conscientious. This made me very happy for I've been trying to get close to E. as a person of real value.

18. If the group as a whole doesn't know what it wants, it may gain more concrete goals as it proceeds. Our behavior, however, seems to

be goal oriented—if even at an unverbal level. All behavior is motivated.

19. The group seems to get what they want from a member. They seemed to want F. to give a talk and appeared content when she did.

20. Group pressure leads to conformity. Since we want to be accepted by the group we conform to the group's standards—at least partially. We do not necessarily have to lose our individuality by so doing.

21. We must assimilate our knowledges to the group's benefit. Each of us add our perceptions to a topic under discussion.

22. Learning results in change of behavior. We internalize our learnings.

23. R. pointed out that we can learn to accept a person for what he is and still disagree with what he says. This attitude can lead to greater understanding. What we learn in the group we carry to other situations.

24. It is hard sometimes, to put our beliefs into action.

25. I realized why the group initially disliked my reflecting and clarifying behavior. Since they did not know my motives they mistrusted me. Now the group seems to realize that more of us should act as reflectors, summarizors, and clarifiers—provided we make known our intentions.

26. Dr. Lifton noticed that some members speak for others—without really knowing how others feel. This is not showing respect for others.

27. We can be too blunt and frank. Perhaps we should be more gentle when we speak our mind. This was the reaction between E. and L.

28. The way we behave determines to a large extent how we are perceived. If we want to be perceived in a certain way, we must make our behavior conform to that picture. The group—through its reality testing ability—can tell us if we are conforming to the picture we would like others to form of us.

29. We must ask for help. If it is given without being wanted, it may be seen as hostile behavior. We must not make a member feel inferior when we offer help.

30. Dr. Lifton tried to show the group he was human when he said that he would appreciate help from the group—help in satisfying his own needs. I feel this was a wise, and humble, and sincere move on his part.

31. A silent person pays the price of being misunderstood. Verbalization seems necessary—to some degree.

32. If we are blunt in the group we may develop an accurate assessment of our actions. In other words, we should be our real selves and reveal more of our true feelings. Only when the other members realize the depth of our feelings can they understand and help us.

Log 10

This meeting continued to implement the gains that were made in the last two sessions. . . .

1. The matter of being more informal in the group was brought up and discussed. It was believed by some that this approach enables us to get to know each other better and seems to be a more comfortable method of procedure. It was pointed out that often our discussions have been intellectual, without too much regard for feeling. Other members felt that we desire something more from the group than merely informal chatting. Perhaps this informal behavior could be used initially to establish that secure atmosphere which would enable us to become more "group guidance" oriented. This seemed to be a striving for a mode of operation or a method of interpersonal relationship.

2. Although W. brought up the topic of "grading" he did not seem to feel that it was a need of his own but stated it was an attempt to present the group with a possible topic for discussion. It was realized that this issue had not been settled and was not settled today. The group seemed to realize that the responsibility is ours. It was felt that lack of decision may influence group behavior. I personally feel that the group has not yet agreed upon a method of evaluation and will arrive at one as time progresses.

3. I personally feel that the group goes about solving problems in a more objective, realistic, group method at this time which is a definite advancement over earlier sessions. We seem to allow more members to present their views while the others listen and evaluate.

4. The group was again concerned about G.'s silence and seemed to be able to pinpoint the cause of their behavior. Because G. once said that he is usually a talkative person, his silence then became object of suspicion. He has, however, clarified his point of view many times and is determined to retain his basic views. He does, however, seem to be aware of the needs of others but will not change his basic beliefs in order to conform, which seems logical. We retain our basic beliefs but conform a little to the group in order to win their approval and support. They help me solve my problems; therefore, I must help them meet their needs.

5. W. expressed a concern with the effects his behavior has on others. I think the group does let us know how our behavior affects them.

6. F. was concerned over the silence of those people who are ordinarily talkative. When members suddenly change their behavior they make us feel uneasy. Perhaps this is due to the fact that we feel more secure when we can predict, to some degree, the behavior of others. E. remained silent because he felt that his efforts in the past were not effective. Learning leads to change of behavior.

7. E.'s feeling that the group atmosphere is still strained and strange led to group investigation into the causes of this tension.

8. The group then discussed the nature and depth of personal revelation to others.

9. There are different basis for judging others. We can judge others by ourselves or by the way they perceive us.

10. If others tell me how I am seen in their eyes, I will know how I am being perceived and will be able to determine if this is the impression I want communicated. It was pointed out that this can be threatening.

11. Some people felt it may not be comfortable to be understood. I feel that a lot depends upon the person we reveal ourselves to. If the person I talk to is understanding, accepting, and non-critical, then I will have less fear of revealing myself for I will feel that he will accept me at any cost. This is the essence of client-centered therapy. However, all people will not be this accepting and understanding, probably.

12. Our false front is part of us. Our feelings, however, are not as easily covered up and become noticeable. They become a doorway to the real self.

13. I believe others become closer to us to the degree that we reveal our true feelings.

14. At various times the members expressed a desire to learn what others thought of them. The group thus seems to be moving in the direction of unity through intimacy—or revelation.

15. Some members today felt that the group as a whole has given only criticism and rejection. They have not given enough support and understanding.

16. The group also realized that we do come to the aid of a person who is being prodded and pressured. We help those who are experiencing anxiety.

17. Sometimes, when we ask a member for help, he may not be

able to give it at that moment. Therefore, we must accept his lack of assistance.

18. We yield to the needs of others somewhat in order to satisfy our own needs. In some degree we conform to group policies in order to be accepted.

19. Others' perceptions of me will determine how they will act toward me.

20. We can become able to describe our conscious self-image to others. Their perceptions of me can be a form of reality testing in that they will let me know if I am presenting the picture of myself to others that I want to present. What we think we are and what others think we are may be two different stories. Their perceptions will at least stimulate our thinking.

21. The group seemed to realize that individual members play many roles during our group sessions—although some people tend to prefer a certain role over others.

22. The group seemed to realize that we often force G. into his silent role—as a means of warding off our criticisms.

23. Our forcing people to talk often leads to defensive, silent behavior.

24. It is possible to reject a person's behavior or beliefs while still respecting him.

25. We are always being judged by others, so why not have them put their thoughts into words.

26. We give up something of ourselves to the group and are responsible for our actions.

27. E. felt that we must establish common goals. He also felt that we are competing for acceptance.

28. In order to be understood we must state specifically what we want, and not beat around the bush.

29. Some members still did not want to accept the role of the leader although each of us has assumed the leader role at some time.

30. We have faced uncomfortable issues today and have been fighting for unity. We are often impatient sometimes and expect results to occur rapidly.

31. Although we initially said that we didn't want to be analyzed or reveal our true selves, we seem to be moving in that direction gradually and consistently—as our security spreads.

32. The group also seemed to be demanding that W. realize and admit hostile feelings. Perhaps they did not want to believe that he is a perfect person without fault. In other words, if he is human, he must get mad; when he gets mad he should admit it. He should gain

an understanding of his real self. So we are, in a sense, forcing people to realize their true selves. I should say, we are forcing people to realize "more" of their true selves. We seem to be moving in that direction.

Log 11

. . . we have developed a more objective method of looking at ourselves and the things we do, as well as in realizing that we do have techniques for handling problems. . . .

1. Because E. felt that we lack free expression and a friendly atmosphere, he suggested breaking down into small groups to attain such an atmosphere and as a means of finding common topics to bring to the group as a whole. Others in the group reacted and added to his idea but seemed to feel that we should attack this problem as a group since it does concern all of us. He felt that we might be able to establish the proper rapport in the smaller groups during the first hour and then carry over this attitude to the group as a whole. This writer pointed out that we usually do get the ball rolling by the second hour and are well on our way in the solution of a common problem. The rapport, which might be gained during the first hour in the smaller groups, is usually established anyway in the large group by the time of the second hour. There would thus seem to be little gain by such a procedure—unless it would be used merely as an experimental device. There would be no guarantee of common problems at the close of the small group sessions.

2. E. pointed out that there seem to be two types of groups: one which has established definite goals and others that are attempting to determine goals. We still seem to fit into the latter category since we haven't verbally agreed upon a goal. Our behavior and attitudes, however, do seem to indicate that we are moving in a direction but this direction may not be realized or agreed upon. I believe that we will become aware of these goals as time progresses.

3. It would be unfortunate if we had to become smaller (in group size) in order to accomplish those things that should be handled as a group. Problems concerning group relationships and ways of relating should be handled as a group.

4. We still feel a necessity to let our hair down more and become personal.

5. R. felt that we still don't recognize that someone has a problem and wants help. Others feel that we still don't give each other enough opportunity to speak.

6. L. suggested we come to the group meetings with some problem we wish to have discussed. I agree that this procedure would keep the process continuing and would allow each other to know what our concerns are.

7. It was realized that someone must assume the leadership role. Some members felt that there should be more people acting in the leadership capacity. E., B. and Dr. Lifton seem to have played this role—or were allowed to play this role. The group seems to permit only certain individuals to assume the leadership role. We have practically agreed upon the qualities of a leader—at least in our behavior.

8. It was mentioned, that in listening to the tapes, we iron out things and keep the ball rolling. As was mentioned, however, we are able to become more objective concerning ourselves when we are listening to things that have already happened. While we are experiencing group interaction, it is more difficult to become objective.

9. Dr. Lifton's device of having everyone relate what he thought had happened during the first hour was a splendid technique to get the group to take a look at the things that happened. This technique is a means of obtaining objectivity, and should be developed.

10. When each member did relate his perceptions relating to the happenings of the first hour, it was realized that we each see a problem from a different standpoint. I think this is valuable for it allows us to obtain many different views of and solutions for various problems. We do seem to reach a degree of group understanding concerning various problems, which is gained after each member is allowed to wrestle with the problem and state it in his own words.

11. We noticed that certain problems keep recurring from session to session. This may indicate that problems cannot be solved immediately but require more time. I feel that understandings and insights are gained during the period of time between meetings as well as during meetings. In other words, the processes that are initiated during the meeting are carried over into daily life and aid us in the solution of our various problems. This, I firmly believe, is one of the chief values of group work.

12. We still seem to cut a person off before he has had a chance to present his views and reach a comfortable solution to an issue. We still have to learn to listen more and try to understand the other fellow's point of view. Until we understand him, we cannot meet his needs fully.

13. Problems mean different things to different people. This leads to the handling of a topic from our own point of view.

14. Some members feel that we need support when presenting a need to the group. Unless we feel that others understand and want to help us, we will probably refrain from talking.

15. We should find out what a particular topic means to each of us. We do not have to view a problem in the same way but should allow each to solve a problem in his own way. We may disagree with a person's point of view, but we should still respect him as a person.

16. There are many different methods of accomplishing a goal or in solving a problem. We are looking for a comfortable, effective method which is acceptable to the group.

17. E. felt that a learning situation must be logical. To obtain knowledge we can point out discrepancies and illogical thinking in the thinking of others, add our own perceptions, and eventually reach a solution. It is a matter of group attack on a certain problem and is a give-and-take method which necessitates some degree of objectivity.

18. It is possible to make contributions without necessarily surrendering our beliefs or points of view.

19. We seem to be looking for a common process to meet our individual needs while at the same time meeting the needs of others.

20. We are also looking for more gentle or diplomatic ways of disagreeing with someone.

21. E.'s desire for small groups has already been realized and could continue to be developed, for we do meet in small groups when we listen to the tape. While listening to the tape we do talk over common points of view more openly and aggressively. All we need do is to communicate to the group, some of the things we have picked up or agreed upon.

22. By looking back over the things we have previously done in a given session, we can find out where we are and what we are. We can then accept ourselves or take steps to change things.

23. B. and I feel that we do have a process of handling problems.

24. We are seeking a comfortable mode of operation.

25. Some members felt that we as a group should experiment with other techniques and thus develop a larger repertoire of methods.

26. It takes a long time, sometimes, to put over a point.

27. We still don't say everything we feel and we should.

28. We are searching for ways of meeting our own needs as we help others meet theirs.

29. Aggression can be more effectively handled in a large group since we come to the aid of each other.

30. If I have a technique that I want the group to use, I must show them their needs can be met while employing it. We thus have to sell

our ideas by making them clear and by pointing out their usefulness.

31. We can't evaluate a situation that seems limitless—as the small group idea. A situation without limits makes us feel anxious.

32. We are still looking for more effective ways of relating what we feel so that this might lead to unity.

33. Support may not be felt as support by the one receiving it.

34. A focus on the content of our verbalizations often leads to irrelevant talk. We must look more closely at the emotional or feeling aspects of our behavior and that of others.

35. We are still afraid that if people don't accept our ideas, they will not accept us. We are thus afraid that if we speak our mind we will not be understood and might be rejected.

36. Greater security can result if we know more clearly what is to be asked of us.

37. Preconceived expectations (set) influence our perceptions and behavior.

38. Although many varied definitions were given of therapy, we seemed to agree that it is partly the experiencing of new behavior in a secure situation.

39. Our members are anti-intellectual when we try to force our ideas upon others.

40. We must operate as a large group because we would otherwise have to relieve the experiences of the small groups in order to gain understanding.

41. We understand a problem which is before the group when we are able to put it into our own words.

42. We still seem to be competing for certain roles.

43. Means of achieving better communication still need to be worked on.

Log 12

. . . Today we accomplished in 25 minutes what it took us an hour to accomplish previously. . . .

1. Methods of handling hostility was brought up again. It seems that we are still searching for more effective means of controlling this type of reaction. As we gain in security we become more able to deal with this issue objectively.

2. Dr. Lifton gave some of the perceptions he gained from his readings in an effort to aid group progress.

3. C. mentioned reading in families, which seemed to lead the group into a consideration of the values that might be gained by having each of us bring portions of plays or selections from books to the group. This seemed to be a method of relating to the group our personal interests, attitudes and beliefs. It would be an attempt to get to know one another better—a vehicle for greater understanding. Other members seemed to imply that we might, gain this understanding by being more frank and sincere in the group—without having to use printed material to put over these points.

4. The group seemed more "ready" to accept such techniques to implement our needs and to further our growth. We thus seem verbally ready for experimentation. W. also seemed concerned about our apparent rejection of E.'s ideas of last week. Some of us are thus apparently developing more concern about other's feelings.

5. E. suggested that we look at ourselves in an attempt to determine causes of group disunity and strangeness. Although looking at ourselves realistically may be painful we would grow and gain understanding by facing such unpleasant issues. We thus seem to be getting more daring, which is probably the result of our increased feelings of security.

6. We also seem to be realizing that strength lies within the group. The group members have much potential for further growth.

7. Some members seemed to wonder whether or not we could state our philosophies and ideas after using outside writings as a vehicle. I feel that we could profit from such a technique.

8. E. tried to test out the limits of his frankness. He tried to determine how far the group would let him go by using what he called "brutal" methods. He admitted that such techniques do not make for getting ideas accepted. He said further that we cannot and should not try to cram our ideas down another person's throat.

9. It was mentioned that we too often attack another's point of view instead of looking at the possible value in the suggestions of others. To me this seemed like a statement of real gain and insight.

10. A. mentioned the fact that he felt we had built up walls between us that make gaining understanding difficult. He felt that we have been and should try harder to find ways of going around the wall. I feel that we should find out why the wall is there in the first place and tear it down.

11. L. pointed out that people often are prevented from arguing intelligently because aroused emotions interfere with logic and objectivity. She felt, and this writer supported the idea, that we could use

our group in the developing of more calm techniques of arguing. Since our group is somewhat experimental we could work out methods of conducting an intelligent, objective argument or discussion.

12. G. and I felt that a person's ideas are part of his personality. I wonder if we can really reject a person's ideas and still accept him, if we believe that his ideas are really a part of him. The validity of our ideas can be tested in the group and in the process we can learn from others. We built up our concepts concerning a topic from the concerted efforts of all group members.

13. E. felt that our personal felt inadequacies, our fear of rejection and evaluation, our discomfort with authority figures, and our ego-centered participation techniques are roadblocks to group progress. I feel that his efforts at understanding are to be praised and I feel that he has added something of value to the group.

14. We have tools among ourselves, which consist of the learnings, experiences, and ideas of the individual member.

15. Even though we are becoming more integrated we still don't give the individual member a fair chance to explain his views but immediately attack and criticize his efforts at being understood.

16. We seem to suppress the possible value of the other fellow's contribution.

17. Sometimes constructive criticism can be felt as rejection—which is threatening and anxiety provoking.

18. Repeated attacks on a person's attempting at explaining himself will lead to a stifling of verbalizing. A person does, however, owe it to the group to explain his ideas and to point out to others the value of them. If he can convince or "show" the others that their needs can be met by employing his techniques—they will probably be accepted.

19. This writer suggested that we consider the feasibility and usefulness of an idea without necessarily attaching these ideas to a person; although, the person should be rewarded for contributing something positive to the group.

20. Our perceptions of a topic add to the knowledge of the subject.

21. We should not be afraid to relate our perceptions and should be courageous enough to reveal our disagreement or misunderstanding of someone else's point of view. If we do not say that we disagree with an idea our silence may be interpreted as consent.

22. It was noticed that not all members become involved in a topic under discussion. In those instances we allow the other members to work things out for themselves.

23. We react dually to a presented topic by trying to understand its author's point of view and by reacting to the idea as such.

24. Our perceptions change from session to session, which reveals growth.

25. We aren't what we want to be but are moving toward the goals of understanding, acceptance, and sincerity.

26. We are making progress but are still too impatient. Growth takes time.

27. We are still searching for a comfortable level of communication and seem to be finding it.

28. The group members do not seem to be as afraid of Dr. Lifton as they were initially. They are beginning to assume the leadership role that Dr. Lifton tried to give them.

29. We can wrongly assume that ideas are becoming realistic to others when it is only my own perceptions that are becoming clarified.

30. We should expect everyone to see things my way but should respect the individuality of the other person.

31. A person can view a topic from several angles and doesn't have to be fully for or against it.

32. Perhaps we confuse the word "reaction" to an idea with "rejection" of it. Thus part of our problem is a semantic one.

33. At times we may not want the advice of others and openly reject it, even though we may realize it has value. We thus seem reluctant to admit that the other person may be correct in his assumptions, beliefs, or ideas.

34. We are searching for methods of rejecting the advice of others without hurting the feelings of the giver. We seem to have a need to give aid but must be more diplomatic about it.

35. We seem to be changing, are becoming more able to accept earlier ideas.

36. There is still some hesitancy to look at ourselves honestly, partly because this is a threatening experience.

37. We are reluctant to admit weaknesses in ourselves, even though this is a first step in their correction.

38. We must feel the support of others in order to gain that courage needed to try out new modes of behavior.

39. We must explain an idea more fully so that it can be understood and possibly be accepted. We must allow each other to explain things more completely. Only by listening to the other fellow can we gain a knowledge of the way he looks at the world.

40. If a member rejects someone else's idea, he should at least have one to take its place. It is thus futile to tear apart an idea without first considering its possible merits and offer remedies to it.

41. This writer is realizing more fully that Dr. Lifton is a group member with rights and privileges of his own.

42. I am happy with my own insights and with the progress of the group. They are continually verifying the faith I have in them.

Log 13

. . . I related quite a bit of the feelings I experienced while working with my groups. The discussion of group therapy seemed to give F. the courage to lay before us a problem of serious concern to her. . . .

. . . The group was calm and listening most of the time while F. spoke. We pointed out the illogicality in her thinking, showed her that the problem lies within herself, and gave her support and suggestions as to how we looked at various issues. She definitely seemed to benefit from the hour. The group has thus jumped into psychotherapy completely—perhaps without fully realizing it. The experience to me was a success and may lead to similar behavior in the future. On the other hand, some members may feel threatened by it initially.

Log 14

Today's clam chowder meal definitely seems to have brought us closer together on a friendly basis. . . .

The remainder of the session was used in an effort to help C. solve a problem she was faced with. . . . It was noticed that when we are faced with a decision we often include far too many irrelevant details for consideration. . . .

We used C. as a means and an end, for by helping her we were bringing some of our own problems into the picture. . . .

Log 15

Today was the first time that W. and B. came in late. This seemed to lead the remainder of the group to spend their time in "small talk." This small talk did have some value in that topics of concern were talked about. . . .

C. seemed more comfortable with the problem she presented last time. . . .

. . . I think both C. and R. realized, and showed the group, that there are many ways of looking at any situation and our perceptions change and become more realistic when we do more exploring or searching for answers.

The atmosphere of the group today—as a whole—was a calm, friendly one. However, this writer, who was pressed with several vital decisions in his life, felt anxious, confused and hostile. The group gave me support and provided information in an attempt to help me reach a decision. I felt a terrific sense of relief after getting my problem off my chest and presenting it to the group. I realize fully the value of sharing a problem with a group like ours. When I felt that others were on my side my problem didn't seem so large and I was actually able to look at it more logically. . . .

. . . B. told us a few of the things he had heard at a recent conference. Until he had organized the material in his mind, he was not ready to discuss it with us. This may be an expression of our desire to be logical in our thinking and talking. . . .

Log 16

. . . We definitely seemed to miss G.; especially when we discussed the topic of needs. . . .

. . . the topics, statements, and insights were so numerous that I am forced to list them in order to keep them clear.

1. It may be profitable to seek synonyms to words that are unclear.
2. Many of the words we use are ambiguous: such as need *vs.* drive.
3. A drive is the resultant reaction to a felt need. Some needs may be unconscious.
4. When we present a topic to the group, which really represents a need, we should try to state exactly what we mean or want.
5. Drive and needs are interdependent.
6. We can meet some of our own needs by helping others to meet theirs. The act of giving help is therapeutic and may meet our need of feeling important and charitable.
7. Because our needs, which are a part of us, are interdependent, we as a group are interdependent.
8. We may be able to find a mutual way of satisfying our needs.
9. We are able to meet a person's expressed needs in various ways —not necessarily in the specific manner he desires. This seems similar to sublimation or substitution.
10. There is a hierarchy of needs which is different in everyone. Some needs are definitely more important than others.

11. In defining needs we may have a small number that are so general that almost any feeling could be categorized in them. On the other hand, our list could become long if we became very specific in our definitions.

12. We may expect our personal needs to be met in quite specific ways only if this does not deprive others of their needs. This seems to be a reaction against immature, ego-centric behavior.

13. We have primary needs (inborn, biological, universal) and secondary needs (learned, social, develop from primary needs).

14. Perhaps in our search for a precise definition of need we are searching for purification where it isn't possible, because human nature is too complex and our verbal symbols are too inadequate.

15. Some of our needs appear contradictory. Example: we may fluctuate between strivings for dependency and independency—one of which may be largely unconscious.

16. Unexpressed needs may differ widely from expressed ones.

17. Perhaps we should decide which need is the most important to our happiness and survival and concentrate on its satisfaction. This again seems to indicate a way of acting mature and of doing without immediate satisfactions in some areas in order to gain greater satisfaction at some distant time.

18. The group realized at this point that our discussion had broadened considerably from the initial topic. In reality, needs are complicated.

19. We should become more intent on recognizing our own feelings as they occur and the needs of others in order to function effectively as a group.

20. We felt that a communication problem still exists, even though strides have been made.

21. Perhaps we still haven't reached a compromise between satisfying our needs and those of others.

22. We seemed to realize that an issue is not dropped until everyone has reached an understanding of it, or until all are satiated.

23. Some members felt that group silence may be a sign of defense and insecurity and not merely contemplation.

24. We seemed to come to the realization that one of our unspoken laws consists in not speaking of an absent member unless he has the chance to listen to the recording of the session. (Respect for the individual.)

25. We were concerned with methods of helping an absent member.

26. Our limits on the matter of confidentiality still are unsettled.

27. If we feel that growth has taken place in the group, we must

clarify this to others.   Unless we pinpoint our areas of advancement, they may be overlooked.

28. We must define to others what we see and feel.

29. A. felt that we have developed more affection for each other and have begun to look at Walt (Note: no longer referred to as Dr. Lifton) not as an authority figure.   We have thus developed some measure of security, closeness, interdependence and unity.

30. We still have to form a yardstick to measure ourselves and others.

31. L. felt we have become like a family.

32. Serving coffee seemed to direct our verbalization toward conversation.

33. C. gave a progress report on conditions in her dormitory.   She related that the minority group has become more integrated with the rest of the girls and have gained insight into the effects of their behavior.

34. The group's yardstick should include common perceptions.

35. Common perceptions are involved in group relationships.

36. We evaluate others in terms of what we expect from them. Therefore, we should let them know what we expect.   They will thus be more able to meet our needs.

37. We must become familiar with the yardsticks of others.

38. These yardsticks are not necessarily related to grading in the course.

39. Before we like anyone else we must first be able to like ourselves.

40. Progress will probably result when we consider the perceptions of others as well as our own.

41. Our varied yardsticks cause communication problems.

42. Although some members felt we have talked in circles, others have felt that we have progressed and that we have commonalities.

43. The suggestion came up again that we must share with others our ideas on how we feel the group has progressed.

44. E. was not sure that we have grown as a group.   He admitted being impatient with us and felt that our silences were a forced phenomena.   He felt that we haven't been willing to look at things. I feel that E. is a man of action who prefers to get down to business. However, F. and L. told us to get down to business during the second meeting.

45. A. gave E. help by showing him that he might be too impatient.

. . . We are getting to the point where we want to solve our problems and not put them off. . . .

Log 17

Today's meeting got under way. more rapidly than ever. . . .

1. Some members feel that we have become more affectionate toward one another while others feel that we are not as close as is believed. Perhaps our definitions of "closeness" differ.

2. We often hurt the ones we love but not with malice or forethought. Because we "love" someone we become interested in them and try to help them. When their behavior indicates unhappiness we become very active in our efforts at being realistic, in wanting them to achieve, and be "the best." We can become more blunt with them and often go to extremes to be kind. We are thus in a conflict state in that we try to be kind but our impatience leads us into behavior which could hurt them. A person can move forward (mature and gain insight) in personality development only at a pace in which he is comfortable.

3. Striving for 100% agreement on each topic presented to the group can hinder group progress because all members do not become equally involved in every issue.

4. We seem to want frankness. We want members to be their real selves and not wear false faces.

5. As this writer lists the events, ideas, and insights as they are presented, one gets a feeling of confusion. Many ideas are put forth but we are still working to achieve an overall integration and understanding. All the ideas seem interrelated in that they are expressions of felt needs or are suggestions toward improvement. I think we will eventually reach a stage where we will realize that this integration and harmony and understanding are realized by all.

6. We should display the standards and expectancies that we have in regard to ourselves and toward others. When others begin to understand how we think, our ability to communicate should be improved. By putting our ideals and expectancies into words they become more crystalized and thus more capable of being understood.

7. Our inability to keep our attention focused on a specific topic may be due to the fact that our needs are interrelated. A clear understanding of one issue can be attained more perfectly only when we understand the branches of this issue and its effect on others. In other words, behavior is multiple determined and can be more fully understood when viewed in totality. This is probably related to the learning principle called generalization.

8. When we put a label (a word) on a feeling or insight our thinking becomes clarified because we can handle a symbol but cannot handle feelings as easily. In our attempts to be logical our thoughts become crystalized and organized—progress then can result.

9. This writer agrees with A. in his opinion that we could almost write a textbook on our experiences. Because we have experienced so many things, their import is considerably strengthened and clarified. Our experience is more valuable than merely reading about groups in action.

10. We should be more willing to state our minds without fearing that others will be hurt in the process. Talking can lead to understanding.

11. E. feels that W. is the only one that uses an internal frame of reference in trying to understand someone. Here he is judging us without actually being aware of our own techniques. It becomes our duty, therefore, to clarify our own principles and methods to avoid being misinterpreted.

12. E. wants others to help him look at those things in himself that are not admissible to consciousness but which may be noticeable in behavior. Others thus become a means through which we can achieve greater self-knowledge. Others help us to develop a more accurate picture of our "self." Sometimes we can criticize or evaluate others but be unable to withstand a reciprocal type of behavior. This may also work the opposite way.

13. We may allow an individual member to manipulate the group by inhibiting in ourselves that behavior which he is opposed to.

14. In a sense we cannot help changing or growing because our own thinking becomes more mature, broadened, and integrated as we evaluate and consider the opinions of others. Others serve as a means through which one may gain many perceptions of a topic or problem. Others may help us fill in the gaps in our thinking and develop a broader understanding of ourselves or of an issue that is before us.

15. Perhaps too many members in our group are intent on winning others over to our way of thinking. We must respect the rights of others and not try to prove that our way of thinking or doing things is better than theirs. From the combined thinking of 10 people, we can develop better and more complete ways of looking at life and its problems.

16. We may get 100% seeming agreement on an issue due to the fact that some members may surrender their own points of view and become submissive to the wills of others. We should retain our own

individuality, develop it even further, and think collectively not competitively.

17. F. thinks that there are two major types of people in our group —those who are therapists and those who are clients. She further feels that those who do most of the talking may have revealed less of their true selves than those who talk less frequently but more honestly, or personally. She has felt unaccepted because others did not allow her to remain silent. She feels that we should be more accepting, understanding, and sincere. We should accept people as they are.

18. Acceptance and support from the majority gives the individual greater security and feelings of worthiness. This leads to more communication.

19. An individual member may have a problem that is personal in nature or may be one concerning the group and its process.

20. One of our problems may be "confusion." We may be asking for the impossible when we demand that others put a label on their felt needs. When we are confused we are unable to pinpoint the cause of the difficulty. The confused person is actually asking for assistance in pinpointing the cause of the problem. We need support in facing painful issues. E.'s shock therapy may prevent the members from exploring their problems freely and logically.

21. If we feel secure enough and know the group is on our side, we will not need to cloak ourselves or our problems but would willingly bring them out for exploration.

22. Some members feel that an individual can put before the majority a problem which he believes the group needs to face. It was argued that such a procedure would reveal that such a presentation would show that the individual must have been concerned, to some degree, with the problem or he would not have presented it in the first place—in fact, he would not even be aware of it.

23. The group seemed to disagree as to the nature of group growth. It seemed to become a matter of individual perception and expectation. Growth thus is a relative thing. L. felt that the majority should allow the minority to stay where they wished—to progress at their own rate and in the directions they desire.

24. Since groups are made of individuals, it may be possible to measure this growth as it is experienced in the individual.

25. We seemed to agree that "leaving behind" meant that everyone should feel the same way about all issues; the old idea of 100% involvement on each issue. However, it was expressed that there is no need to have 100% involvement on each issue.

26. Some members felt that we haven't decided on the limits in

which we will function. Our present limits of functioning (agreed upon by our behavior) don't permit the growth we desire. Conflict.

27. E. again persisted in asking others what they thought of him. This led to the feeling in some that we can't give help until the receiver is ready to accept it.

28. We may be able to give our opinions of other members to them but be unable to accept this type of categorizing or judging ourselves. In that event we must communicate to others (in some way) that we are not ready to accept this type of criticism.

29. We can have unity without 100% agreement. Let some members continue to think in their own way. Growth is relative since individual perceptions and expectancies differ.

30. This led to the all important insight that "we have not told each other what we do have in common." A yardstick can be created (perhaps it already exists with us) that can measure common processes. There is a distinct difference between yardsticks and processes. We do have a common process in the group through which we satisfy our needs and this process leads to security. The common process is the *group,* for our needs could not be satisfied without the group. Each of us uses the group in his own way, to satisfy his own needs.

31. What is expected of other members (their behavior) is a limit which does not have to be verbalized to be felt. We are responsible for our behavior. We are unanimous in "our lack of consensus."

32. Those limits which are not realistic can be changed, which would allow movement to take place.

33. What we say and what we do may be in direct contradiction. This makes it imperative to focus on our behavior and feelings. This would lead to insight, clarification, and understanding.

34. The strangeness and anxiety that we occasionally feel, which stifles communication, may partly result from being threatened by speaking in front of nine other people. It is easier to talk and relate to one or two others—it is harder to relate to nine others—but it can be done. Perhaps we are afraid that the others will reject us or look at us differently if we expose our true selves.

35. Until we accept ourselves, we cannot accept others. Perhaps some members are not yet ready to fully accept others. Behavior is always caused.

36. At least four people said they were ready to expose themselves. In fact, F. and others already have started this trend. Perhaps the others will gain enough courage and security to follow suit.

37. The minority has the right to try and convert others to their way of thinking. They have the right to self-expression.

38. A person will change (grow and mature, etc.) when he feels it would be worthwhile and safe to do so. He will change only when the desire to change is strong enough.

39. We can make known our need for help but others may not want to or be able to give help at that moment. This is one value of groups, in that some*one* may at least be able to provide support, when it is needed. "It is difficult to help others when some of our own needs get in the way."

40. We can accept and develop the idea that we can allow others to have different points of view while we retain our own.

41. Our thinking becomes crystalized when we put our thoughts into words. We thus become more able to tell others just how we feel so that they can understand and accept us.

42. The relationship that develops between two group members has effects on the group as a whole. The group is thus closely interrelated. We have more wholeness and unity than we realize. We have unity while retaining our individuality.

43. Accept the fact that there will never be unanimous agreement. We all cannot have the same views on various topics. Once we realize and live with this idea, growth could continue indefinitely.

44. We learn to compromise. To meet our own needs through the group, we help them meet theirs. By giving, we receive.

45. We realized that giving examples of issues clarifies them. I can meet an individual's expressed need in more than one way. A person is mature who realizes that a felt need does not have to be met in exactly the way he desires.

46. Perhaps not knowing how we will be graded threatens us in that we want to maintain a "nice" picture in the eyes of the person or persons doing the grading. We want to remain "acceptable" to the person or persons who will evaluate us.

47. Perhaps we get too emotionally involved in the group which prevents us from bringing out a problem. Strong emotional involvement may lead to disorganization in thinking.

48. Unless we let others know that some of our perceptions have changed, they will continue to react to us in the manner previously formed. They will continue to react to the "older" picture we have given them. It is again the old problem of "communication."

49. We should share with others in the growth experiences we have between meetings.

50. We seem to desire to resolve an issue before we drop it. However, those issues which are not resolved continue to crop up. We do

not resolve issues at the same speed; therefore, they are brought up again for another member to resolve in his own way.

51. G. was a great help in that he caused us to focus our attention on several pertinent areas. G. is largely very honest and sincere.

52. We haven't shown to others our acceptance by giving them support.

53. We bring to the group's attention those matters which have greatest emotional significance. This is in accord with "hierarchy of needs."

54. If we assume others are honest, we will begin to act as if they were honest and thus reveal what we feel.

55. We must be willing to look at ourselves truthfully. We practice what may be called "group confession."

56. G. pointed out that we too often are forced to defend our views.

57. It is better to air out our presently felt feelings and needs, rather than to suppress them. If we suppress them, they will demand expression at a later date anyway.

58. We must learn to use the group in the solution of our problems instead of going to smaller groups.

59. We discovered we are not the happy family we claim to be but we are on the way to doing something about it.

60. If others accept our hostility (our negative side) then we can be sure they accept us in totality.

61. We should not think for others but ask him if our perceptions of what he has said are correct. Don't put words in the mouths of others.

62. We should use the "internal frame of reference" in trying to understand others.

63. It is uncomfortable to be misperceived. It is partly our job to correct misperceptions.

64. We must place before the group those things that make us uncomfortable.

65. Others must give us credit to grow and change between meetings.

Log 18

. . . I feel that the group would grow even faster if these silent people contributed more. . . .

1. We need to become familiar with everyone's yardstick concerning group growth. When we hear the opinions of others we may

gain added insights and new ways of perceiving group relationships.

2. This writer does not feel that we need or could attain common yardsticks in regard to the things we see and feel. Since we are all unique individuals we cannot look at the world in exactly the same way as another. We could, however, understand another person better if we gained some knowledge of the way he looks at the world.

3. Our evaluation, from others, is a helpful way of discovering whether or not others see us as we think they do. This is a valuable form of reality testing. Our group has used this technique but it could be developed further.

4. Some people may not be able to take criticism or evaluation from others since this may be too threatening.

5. Until we understand ourselves, our understanding of others will be limited. Our self-understanding grows by being a group member.

6. Since a member's behavior and talk influences the group, an individual's growth would be positively correlated to group growth.

7. Although E. feels that we as a group haven't grown, others feel that we have. We allowed E. almost an hour to explain his views on groupness. He is a difficult man to follow.

8. Our common purposes and interrelationships make us a group. Added to this are: affection, communication, and interdependence. We also have the common process of satisfying our needs through the group.

9. Some of the behavior and interrelationship features that have been exhibited sort of label us a therapy group. We haven't really called ourselves as such.

10. A leader is a group member since he falls within the group's limits.

11. Some individuals in a group can grow while others may not. Unless a member tells me that he has grown and describes the nature of his growth, I will be unable to judge that he has. Part of his growth, however, will be reflected in his behavior.

12. E. doesn't trust people's politeness since he feels that politeness is merely acquired behavior and may not be a sincere effort at giving help.

13. Since all behavior is motivated, we should consider more closely the cause and effects of our behavior in the group.

14. A group has a unit regardless of purpose.

15. We should examine the latent as well as the manifest content of our speech.

16. E. wants to deal with truths and not hypotheses. This can't be

done since much of behavioral science is still in the experimental stage and human behavior is so varied.

17. Walt pointed out to E. that he has been trying to direct the group.

18. The question of "group mind" came up, but since it is such a new term to us we were unable to reach anything resembling a conclusion or consensus of opinion.

19. Individual growth is a relative thing and depends upon the individual's attitudes, needs, and expectancies.

20. We are becoming more unique individuals because others help us to determine the boundaries and completeness of our differences.

21. The growth processes that are initiated within the group are continued between meetings in other situations.

22. Our growth appears in various areas of our personalities.

23. We become part of a group by interrelating.

24. The ideas of others, when they are stated in our own words, may sound different to the originator of the ideas. No two people look at the same idea alike.

25. Understanding is best achieved if we use similar language.

26. There is a distinction between a yardstick for the group and our own yardsticks. We are still trying to construct a yardstick to evaluate the group. It must be a group enterprise.

27. We have conformity by abiding by the group's limits, and have individuality in our own ideas.

28. Group limits may be different from individual limits.

29. Our self-knowledge is increased when other members help us straighten out our thinking and logic. This is reality testing.

30. We can describe group growth by measuring the growth of each member. Then we focus our attention on interrelationships, dynamics, feelings, and procedures to evaluate ourselves as a group.

31. When people differ with our ideas, we sometimes feel they are attacking us.

32. We should share our inner security and growth by communicating it to others. They will understand us better if we do so and perhaps profit from the way we look at things.

33. When we see a particular member being pressured, we come to the rescue.

34. Some members may grow, in their own way, without being too talkative.

35. We sometimes intellectualize too much and talk around a problem.

36. One sign of growth is that we talk to the group and not to a specific individual.

37. We should let others know how they affect us and how we feel toward them. An undesirable interpersonal relationship can cause group discomfort.

38. F. sees the members as either giving or receiving help.

39. We see ourselves in another member when he presents to the group a problem that we ourselves feel.

40. We are sometimes afraid of shocking someone or of being disloyal. We do not want to become an outcast by the things we say. We want to remain an accepted member and we try to maintain equilibrium.

41. F. tried to act the therapist today. This could be a sign of increased security and self-knowledge.

42. If I say the behavior of another is unacceptable, I must tell him how to act differently. I must tell him how his behavior affects me.

43. F. says she can feel that someone else is sincere.

44. A. revealed some personal problems in order to show his sincerity to F., but she did not comprehend it as such.

45. We should look at our real selves more.

Log 19

This meeting was the first during which Walt was missing. This made us gradually assume responsibility for governing and directing ourselves. . . .

It was again felt that we should seek the causes of our misperceiving others. . . .

. . . we must not suppress feelings toward another because these ideas still strive for recognition and can cause unpleasant situations to develop. If we verbalize our feelings, we can reach a solution to any misperception we might have. It was also noticed that members cannot express their true feelings until they feel secure enough in the group atmosphere and feel that others understand and accept them. . . .

. . . He seemed to be saying that our behavior might get out of control without the limits and clarification that is set by a leader. When others told him that we are all leaders and therapists, he seemed to become more reassured. . . .

. . . We still haven't formulated the qualities of a good group member and thus are somewhat unable to evaluate each other.

. . . As I see it, one of the chief benefits of being a group member is that we can learn about group processes and functioning and then apply it to other groups of which we are either a member or a leader. . . .

Although it is not an easy or pleasant experience to evaluate ourselves, it would be a good learning experience. . . .

Log 20

Today's meeting began when Walt told us he would be out of town when two of our meetings are scheduled. After discussing possible alternative plans, we decided on either extending the time on two regular sessions or on meeting as a group without the leader. Perhaps the group is realizing its own potential and is ready to assume its own leadership.

The rest of our two-hour meeting was spent in discussing systems of grading and evaluation. . . .

We tried to decide whether or not we needed unanimous agreement before acting and this issue was not settled. . . .

It seemed that part of what we were facing today was a new situation with no apparent limits. The unknown, because it has no limits, seems threatening. We imagine that we might become too critical, hostile, or shocking. . . .

The issue was not settled today; probably because it is an important one that cannot be rushed through. We are dealing with a problem that is common to many facets of life. We have certainly initiated our thinking processes in an attempt to reach an understanding of this situation.

Log 21

. . . B. wanted help on a personal problem. This was the first time he had really asked the group for assistance, since he was usually a giver of help in previous meetings. . . .

1. In our daily lives we play many roles and fit many stereotypes.

2. Teachers and ministers are often accepted in a stereotype manner.

3. Since B. is a resource person, we discussed how such a person could be used in a group such as ours.

4. Some limits in group work are unchangeable. Others are changed as we change the criteria that were used in creating them.

5. The matter concerning majority vote on decision-making was brought up but didn't seem to be settled.

6. Group members must take responsibility for change in group procedures.

7. In a sense B. was asking to be evaluated and this seemed to be a follow-up of A.'s suggestion, last time, concerning oral evaluation of each other.

8. We can evaluate others only if we have something to contribute.

9. The problem concerning the difficulty of getting into a discussion was mentioned again. This seemed to be a rebellion against time monopolizing by a few members.

10. A. asked B. how he looked at non-Christians. This seemed to be a question concerning himself for A. has told us, in so many words, that he is anti-religious in some respects. B. had asked to be evaluated and then so did A.

11. B. felt that he did react to a stereotype of "non-Christian" but felt that people in general react to stereotypes of others. Our initial impression of a stranger is largely determined by his awakening in us, learned reactions to certain stereotypes. He becomes a cue to a past response.

12. Walt pointed out that perhaps we were really talking about interpersonal relationships and not reactions to stereotypes.

13. Our roles are determined by our behavior in interpersonal relationships.

14. When we react to a person as if he represented a stereotype, we do not really know the person. Such a reaction may prevent us from really knowing him.

15. This business is related to "labeling" in psychotherapy—which can interfere with growth and understanding.

16. In life it seems that we initially react to a person by categorizing him: is he single, married, a teacher, a father, old person, young person, and so on. Only later, by talking and relating to him, do we really get to know him.

17. In our own lives we probably hope to create certain impressions on others. We do things that help others to see us in certain ways. We try to display a self-concept in our behavior.

18. In group work we should accept another's need for reacting to us in a stereotyped manner.

19. The question was again raised as to which person's need should be met in group relationships. I think this can be answered on a democratic give-and-take principle. In order to have some of our needs satisfied—through the group—we must help others meet some of their needs: By giving we receive.

20. Our behavior doesn't always correspond to our self-concept. In

a group setting such as ours, the other members can tell us how we are being perceived. This is reality testing because we can judge whether or not our behavior is being perceived as we would like it to be perceived. If we are acting in a way not congruent with our self-concept, we are then able to change.

21. There are both verbal and visual kinds of communication. In order to really understand an individual, we must learn his language.

22. We can accept criticism from those that love us.

23. We must correct misperceptions and be frank and honest.

24. Giving help makes the other fellow feel secure—then he can help me. Our relationship thus deepens.

25. In this group we learn to make our behavior conform to the picture we hold of ourselves and wish to give others.

In summary, our meeting was a successful one in that we felt secure enough to discuss important issues. B. was secure enough to ask for evaluations from others.

Log 22

. . . E. felt that we too often criticize a person or issue without offering suggestions for a remedy in the meantime. This very issue was mentioned in previous meetings and was partly answered since we do try to figure ways out of dilemmas. . . .

L. brought up the problem of evaluation again—as it was concerned with majority *vs.* minority rule. . . . In a sense we initiated today a process of evaluation—evaluation in the group. Any group problem of importance comes up again and again until we solve it. A majority decision takes into consideration the needs of the minority. If the majority did not consider the minority, rebellion might result. We came to the realization that we are all unique individuals who cannot see eye-to-eye on all things. We become even more unique and individual as a result of group interaction. When there is unity in a group, the minority will go along with the majority decision because they will not feel left out. . . .

We came to realize that each of us has basic beliefs that are held firmly—they are part of our basic attitudes—those attitudes that help to shape our personalities. . . .

Log 23

Today A. became a leader. . . . Before we could decide upon the grade issue, we had to establish a voting procedure and it was decided that when two-thirds of our group agreed on something, it would hold. Since B., F., and G. weren't pleased with the above ideas we learned that 100% agreement is almost impossible to attain. It did not seem that we gave these three people enough support and understanding concerning their needs in this issue. By using parliamentary procedures we did settle the grade issue. . . .

. . . It was felt that the continued use of parliamentary procedure would change the nature of the group, but with further discussion we felt that we would try to keep the group as it had been. . . .

We felt that a personal, verbal evaluation would be one of the most useful things we could take away from the course. Since we will be constantly dealing with people in our lives it would be beneficial to discover those facets in our personality that may hinder interpersonal relationships. . . .

. . . this writer volunteered to be evaluated, they told me that I had good ability in putting things into short, clear sentences. I seem to possess the ability to summarize the things happening fairly accurately. This was naturally a boost to my ego and is something I've been trying to develop. The discussion then shifted to E.'s speaking ability and a few persons felt that it is difficult to follow him since he includes so many things in his verbalizations. E. seemed to gain some insight and benefited from this.

In summary, it seems that we have ironed out the grading problem and are beginning to use a method of verbal evaluation in the group.

Log 24

Today's meeting began with a discussion of Walt's job possibility overseas and his decision not to accept it. I feel it is fine when the leader shows himself to be a human being with problems of his own. It seems to have led to closer unity in our group.

B. brought up again his concern with the Christian, non-Christian statement he made two or three sessions ago. He tried to clarify his points of view and asked the group's help in order to determine whether or not there are things in his behavior, verbalizations, and mannerisms which would operate against his goals in life. . . .

The discussion of religion seemed to be related to whether or not we are self-sufficient or can we profit from sharing. . . . We don't force anyone to accept our point of view but we offer him our perceptions, in the hope that they may broaden his point of view on an issue or problem. We seemed to be looking for a common ground of communication. . . .

. . . This led A. to describe two areas in his own life in which seeming growth has taken place. It is heartening to know that people do profit from such a form of group activity.

C. got brave enough to ask A. a direct question, for which she received a reply. This may be an indication of growth on her part. . . .

Log 25

. . . This writer mentioned the fact that G. and I felt that those members that get the most from the group are those who present personal problems and those that get involved with each session. I still kind of wonder why G. is so darned silent—perhaps he is afraid or perhaps the group just doesn't measure up to his expectancies. If the group isn't going too well, he could possibly help us out with concrete suggestions. It benefits us nothing if he just sits silently. . . .

F.'s problem opened up the whole area of evaluation and we came to realize that we use our own standards and those of society. . . . I guess the final solution lies within the individual. We also seemed to uncover two other standards—one being growth up to this point, and the other being the ultimate level of attainment. It seems that in this course, we grade ourselves as to where we are now. The ultimate level will be attained in the future, with further study and experience.

So in grading ourselves we measure our growth and compare it with universal or society created standards. . . .

In the past we have revolted against using criteria, for we felt that this might destroy our uniqueness since we would try to conform to the characteristics of a good group leader, or member. . . .

Log 26

After about ten minutes of small talk on rain, hailstorms, tornadoes, popcorn, and foods, B. told us that his thinking had changed in regard to L.'s background and its similarity to American ways of life. . . .

. . . several members tried to pinpoint their hostility toward Walt. They tried to determine what aspects of his behavior made them irritated. E. felt that Walt has been too ambivalent and changes roles too often, or abruptly. He felt that needs can be ambivalent and that the group was too emotionally involved to give Walt assistance last time. It was pointed out that a person can be a leader and a client at the same time. . . . A person can be a leader nominally, by prestige, or by verbal involvement. . . .

It was mentioned that a person who brings in limits is thought of as a leader. I wonder if the group felt as I did—that we attacked Walt last week because he symbolized authority, controls, or society. . . . The group did not want to admit that the unpleasant topic of last time originated within themselves—Walt merely pointed it out more clearly, especially in showing us that it meant a lot of work. . . .

We seemed to be trying to find out who Walt is. Is he a group member or a leader? This writer thinks he has been both and at times we have made him a leader and have refused, at other times, to see him merely as a member. He has also been referred to as the expert and as the resource person. The group is saying that our roles are multiple. We also saw that the group can take over when the leader gets out of line. . . .

Someone mentioned the feeling that it can be painful to be overvalued. . . .

Log 27

Today's meeting saw the group continue to attack issues of concern and was also characterized by a deeper understanding of interpersonal relations in the group.

1. A. began by wondering whether or not drinking is a sin. This discussion was begun when F. mentioned the large amounts of liquor consumption that she had heard about. This topic was not carried long.

2. A. complimented R.'s summarizing ability. This made me become more active as I wanted to show the group that I could summarize and reflect feeling—as I've always wanted to do. I gained some feelings of success in so doing.

3. C. felt secure enough to tell B. that she was hurt by his statement of the previous meeting. B. had anticipated C.'s hurt feeling and related that he had already established good relations with her and therefore wanted to achieve the same thing with G. He realized that his behavior was probably experienced as rejection.

4. B. clarified his role with G. and stated that he wanted to establish better relations with him. He felt that reconciliation was important to him. Although some of the barriers that exist between people cannot be avoided, it is important to make restitution later. We should try to overcome these barriers and get along with others better.

5. Some people get hurt as we try to help others. We therefore searched for a process of helping all concerned at the same time—considering everyone's feelings.

6. The multiplicity of roles was again mentioned, and it was felt that society often expects us to act a certain role most of the time.

7. E. mentioned that our behavior can block communication at times. Therefore, we should try to make our behavior conform to the impression we wish to leave on others. When we forced G. into a certain role he fought back by trying to maintain his individuality. Some members felt that G. has rejected us. Today G. was more verbal than he has been in a long time.

8. When we are emotionally involved in a discussion, we do not always choose the right words, thereby allowing ourselves to be misunderstood. We should try to control our ideas more, especially as these ideas influence others.

9. Should we try to be interested in every topic of concern? It was felt that every member does not have to be interested in each topic but may be able to help others who are confused on an issue. Those things that seem important are brought before the group—the old hierarchy of needs.

10. F. questioned G.'s rejection of member interdependence since this idea tended to make the group secondary to the individual. G. felt that you cannot force interdependence on a group member since it should be a relationship that grows out of felt needs. The group is, however, composed of individuals. In considering a group, we should look at individual needs and behavior as well as group functioning and process.

11. E. seemed to tell G. that it's not as effective to operate alone as it is to receive help from others. Two or three minds are better than one. This led to the feeling that we might fear losing our individuality when we become part of a group. This group, however, has helped us become even more unique and independent. Collective thinking can be more effective than tackling a problem alone.

12. Sometimes silence can be understood as agreement. If a member disagrees with a topic or idea, he should state it or be misunderstood.

13. E. felt cheated when individual needs are placed above group needs.

14. We felt that our thinking has established our group as being therapeutic.

15. G. seemed to be afraid of seeking help in this group for he didn't know the limits of such behavior and questioned our compe-

tency. This feeling seems to have been shared by quite a few others. Unknown limits are fearful.

16. The group can't meet all needs since this is part of life.

17. We have anticipated unpleasantness in self-revelation. Fail to see possible benefits of therapy.

18. What kinds of problems can be handled in such a group? Our feelings of personal security determine the degree to which we reveal to others our personal problems.

19. To know something and understand it, we should experience it. Since we haven't experienced how it would feel to reveal our personal problems, we have left this issue alone.

20. Quite a few members felt that Walt's behavior labeled him as the leader from the beginning. R. defended Walt as a person having needs of his own. The group, however, felt insecure with a leader who had a dual role. The issue of grading and Walt's reaction to it caused him to appear as a leader or a symbol of authority.

21. We again seemed to work on the idea of the qualifications of a good group leader and have begun to spell them out.

Log 28

Very soon after our group was formed today, A. related his feelings on missing E. and he probably voiced what others also felt. Any group member is missed when he fails to attend a meeting and this seems to indicate our cohesiveness.

We determined that only three of our group will be on campus next semester while the rest will be at various jobs in the world. We seem to have begun feeling sad about breaking up and already are seeking the addresses of various members. . . .

This writer asked for the group's help in regard to his anticipated handling of classroom order and was glad to receive help from a few of the members. . . .

. . . This became related to E.'s proposed use of group guidance techniques with freshmen at . . . and then became related to C.'s use of group techniques in her apartment house for girls. . . .

In a sense we seem to be satisfying our own need to define our group more clearly with its limits. Using Walt as a resource person proved very successful. Walt told us that limits can come from the group itself or from the leader. . . .

We then turned to a discussion of therapy and its varied definitions. Part of adjusting lies in integrating what we are with what we want to be. Therapy was broadly defined as a growth process leading to a better adjustment to society and our level of aspiration. When we realize and accept our inadequacies we are in a better position to make improvements. It was pointed out that part of adjusting lies in developing more harmonious relations to society since we do not live in a vacuum. The individual can gain greater satisfaction from adjusting to society. Many of our needs can be met only through others; therefore, we must be able to get along with them.

When group members are secure enough they will correct a leader that manipulates his group too frequently. We can ignore or attack a hostile figure. We become acceptable to others by helping them meet their needs. . . .

. . . B. felt that life goals are part of the individual and should be recognized in order to understand the other person. Motivation may be attained by keeping the goals just a little higher than the achievement level. We finally agreed that "nothing succeeds like success itself." Success is the great provider of motivation. We decided that level of aspiration was a relative term and that part of adjustment lies in keeping this level in line with our capacities. . . .

Near the close, F. asked the group generally: "Have we made progress as a group?" This writer reacted by pointing out that we seem to have gotten closer together, attack problems more objectively—as a group—and certainly know each other better. Since we are now pretty secure with each other we are able to handle heretofore "touchy" subjects with sufficient objectivity and understanding. Many individual members have changed for the better. In fact, I firmly believe that each member has grown for the better—some more so than others. I know that this writer has grown quite a bit and has gained much from being a group member and leader. We felt that one measure of our growth is our ability to tolerate differences. We can become even more unique and individualistic as a group member and still contribute to group progress.

Log 29

. . . We mentioned that therapist can impose his value system on the client and that part of his job is to prevent, to some extent, this type of procedure. If the therapist is aware of his values and beliefs he is in better position to prevent this from interfering with his work. We are responsible for employing our values in therapy. . . .

We tried to determine the place of values in a therapeutic relationship. We concluded that the therapist does not try to change the client's values but helps him to look at the feelings behind the values;

feelings which may have been intentionally ignored. The feelings and abstractions behind an experience determines the kind and degree of learning taking place. . . .

There may be some degree of fear in our attempts to fully understand another, for in so doing our own viewpoint or perspective may be changed. . . .

. . . We seem to need some form of external criteria against which to compare man's behavior.

The meeting closed when this writer asked for a restatement of the grading process. I was given an answer.

The preceding log represents just one kind of group as perceived through the eyes of only one person.

Readers seeking comparable protocols describing groups conducted by other people may find the following sources helpful.

Bach, George. *Intensive Group Psychotherapy*, New York: Ronald, 1954.

Corsini, Raymond. *Methods of Group Psychotherapy*, New York: McGraw-Hill, 1957.

Driver, Helen. *Multiple Counseling*, Wisconsin Monona Publications, 1954.

Hinkley, Robert, and Lydia Hermann. *Group Treatment in Psychotherapy*, Minneapolis: University of Minnesota Press, 1951.

Slavson, Samuel. *The Practice of Group Therapy*, New York: International Universities Press, 1951.

Wilson, Gertrude, and Gladys Ryland. *Social Group Work Practice*, New York: Houghton Mifflin, 1949.

Author Index

Subject Index

Acting out, 82
Admitting new members, 134
Adult play therapy, 149
Advice giving, 56
Alleviation of feelings of guilt, 87
Ambiguity, 73
Art, 149
Authoritarian personality, 27
Automation, 154

Behavior change, 28
Blocking behavior, 107
Bull sessions, 191

Career days, 184
Case conference approach, 192
Catharsis, 141
Clarifying, an idea, 52
 by examining points of difficulty, 54
 by pointing up inconsistencies, 53
 by pointing up individual or group
  feelings, 54
 by questioning purpose, 55
 by relating feelings to behavior, 55
 by review of person's logic, 55
 by seeking origins of idea, 55
 operations, 53
 through anticipation of consequences,
  54
 through questioning assumptions, 54
 through questioning meaning, 54
 through reflection, 53
 through similarities and differences,
  54
 through use of a definition or illustration, 53

Classroom, atmosphere of, 162
 group dynamics of, 180
 social learning in, 180
 structure of, 155
 therapeutic atmosphere in, 180
Club activities, 191
College days, 184
Communication, 49
Confidentiality, 91, 112, 131
Control groups, research, 215
Counseling, definition of, 12
Crowd, definition of, 25
Cultural lag, 154
Culturally, alienated, deprived, dis-
 advantaged, 158

Data retrieval, 174
Decision making, 143
Demonstration of group counseling, 64

Education, definition of, 15
Educational media, use of varied, 171
Effects of technological change, 3
Environment, effects of, 159
Evaluation, 209
Extracurricular activities, 193

Feelings as group common denominator,
 71

Group, age level of, 132
 characteristics, 24
 cohesiveness, 98, 219
 common denominators, 25
 composition, 128
 continuous, 134
 democratic, 219
 fixed, 134